ADAM COURTENAY is a Sydney-based writer and journalist who has had a long career in the UK and Australia, writing for papers such as the *Financial Times*, the *Sydney Morning Herald*, *The Age*, the *Australian Financial Review* and the UK *Sunday Times*. The son of Bryce Courtenay, he is the author of two previous books, *Blood Rubber* and *Amazon Men*.

THE
SHIP
THAT

NEVER WAS

The greatest escape story of
Australian colonial history

ADAM COURTENAY

ABC
Books

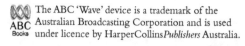 The ABC 'Wave' device is a trademark of the Australian Broadcasting Corporation and is used under licence by HarperCollins*Publishers* Australia.

First published in 2018
by HarperCollins*Publishers* Australia Pty Limited
ABN 36 009 913 517
harpercollins.com.au

HarperCollins*Publishers*
Level 13, 201 Elizabeth Street, Sydney, NSW 2000, Australia
Unit D1, 63 Apollo Drive, Rosedale, Auckland 0632, New Zealand
A 53, Sector 57, Noida, UP, India
1 London Bridge Street, London, SE1 9GF, United Kingdom
Bay Adelaide Centre, East Tower, 22 Adelaide Street West, 41st Floor,
Toronto, Ontario, M5H 4E3
195 Broadway, New York, NY 10007, USA

A catalogue record for this book is available from the National Library of Australia:

ISBN: 978 0 7333 3857 1 (paperback)
ISBN: 978 1 4607 0884 2 (ebook)

Picture credits: 29 Public Domain/State Library of Tasmania; 32 Public Domain/New York Public Library; 44 Wikimedia Commons; 60 Public Domain/State Library of New South Wales; 63 Alamy; 93 Shutterstock; 132 Wikimedia Commons/Yale Center for British Art; 217 Public Domain/Smithsonian Libraries; 260 Public Domain; 304 Public Domain/State Library of New South Wales
Maps by Clare O'Flynn/Little Moon Studio
Cover design by Peter Long
Cover images: Man courtesy The Lewis Walpole Library, Yale University; background illustration Ceyx and Alcyone (1769) courtesy National Gallery of Victoria, Melbourne
Author photo by Christian Hagward
Typeset in Minion Pro by Kelli Lonergan
Printed and bound in Australia by McPherson's Printing Group
The papers used by HarperCollins in the manufacture of this book are a natural, recyclable product made from wood grown in sustainable plantation forests. The fibre source and manufacturing processes meet recognised international environmental standards, and carry certification.

To Damon, who never had the chance.

A man who has been all his life fighting against law, who has been always controlled but never tamed by law, is interesting, though inconvenient – as is a tiger.

Anthony Trollope
Australia, 1873

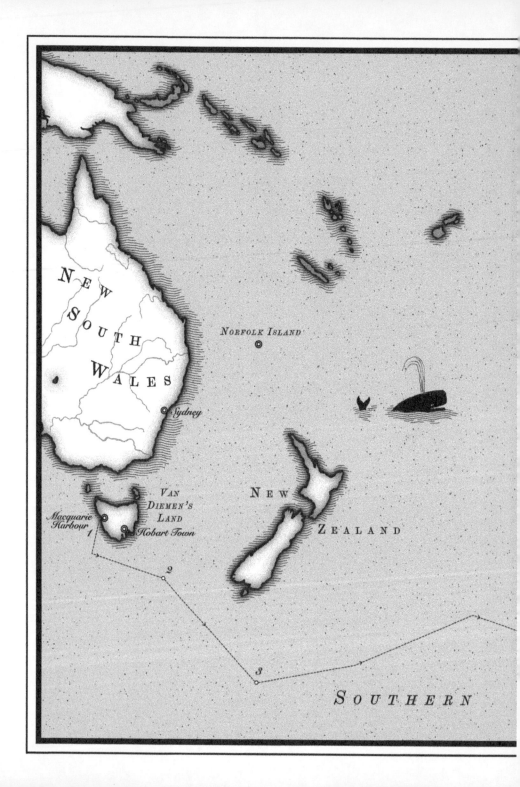

NEW SOUTH WALES

NORFOLK ISLAND

Sydney

VAN
DIEMEN'S
LAND

Macquarie
Harbour

Hobart Town

NEW

ZEALAND

SOUTHERN

THE VOYAGE
OF THE
FREDERICK
1834

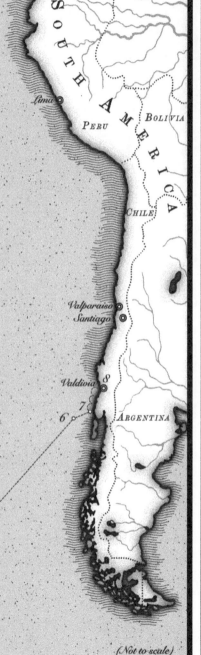

1. JANUARY 14
The *Frederick* departs Macquarie Harbour

2. JANUARY 18
Despite heavy gale, Barker takes the *Frederick*
towards Antarctic

3. JANUARY 30
Barker takes sightings; turns ship NE

4. FEBRUARY 2~11
The *Frederick* hits white squall, followed by gale

5. FEBRUARY 11
Barker takes sightings; bears further NE

6. FEBRUARY 24~25
Land sighted; the *Frederick* scuttled

7. FEBRUARY 26~MARCH 4
Convicts reconnoitre coast; meet Mapuche

8. MARCH 5
Convicts land at Valdivia

OCEAN

(Not to scale)

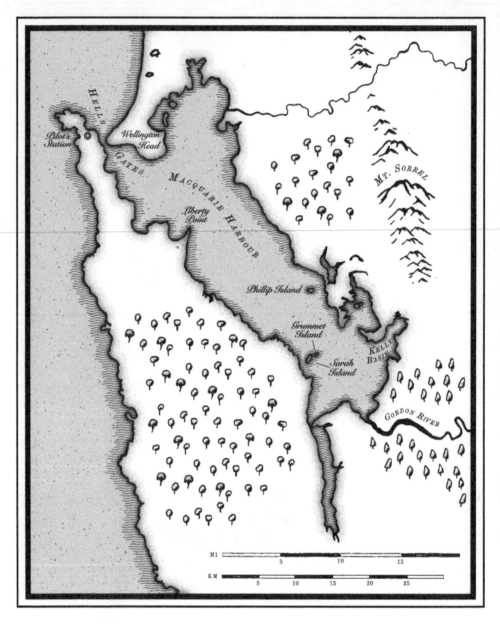

HELL'S GATES

Pilot's
Station

Wellington
Head

MACQUARIE HARBOUR

Liberty
Point

MT. SORREL

Phillip Island

Grummet
Island

KELLY
BASIN

Sarah
Island

GORDON RIVER

MI

5   10   15

KM

5   10   15   20   25

MACQUARIE HARBOUR

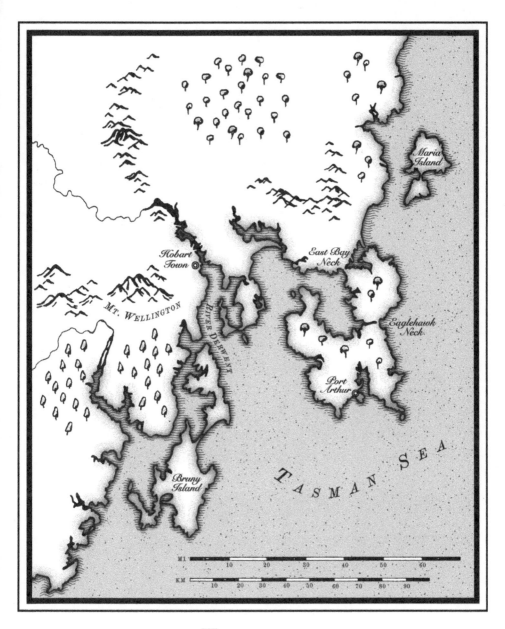

HOBART

Prologue

THEY WERE DESPERATE for land.

As he looked out on the blank blue swells of the Pacific Ocean, James Porter feared he and his makeshift crew had left too much to fate. They had trusted in a navigator who had never been to sea. They had taken a ship that had never sailed before. She'd been built to hug coastlines and harness coastal breezes, not to sail the length of the Southern Ocean. Too much had been asked of her.

Not long into their passage, the men had realised their mistake in not keeping enough rations. There was now hardly anything for themselves, each man choking down a tiny portion of hard biscuit and dried beef each night.

Porter never tired of how the ship slotted into the wind. Even now, cracked and leaking below, she made excellent progress astride a solid nor'-easter. And yet the fear remained. No matter how hard the men worked at the pumps, the green Huon pine planks might give at any moment. Their situation was both precarious and perilous. And this had been their lot for several weeks – a crew desperately looking for a hint of land on the horizon, the never-ending clank of a pump beating out a doleful time, the yearning in their stomachs growing more acute as one day melded into another.

They had a natural leader, whom Porter had always respected, but was he the right man to be their captain? He had learnt his navigation without setting foot on a boat. Did he actually know where they were, or was he bluffing while he tried to work it out?

Six of the ten-man crew grew sick every time a serious wind blew and the ship started to roll, and only four of them really knew what they were doing. Four men to sail, keep watch, work the sails and bail the water out. In truth, they needed at least a dozen men to keep the little brig going. They needed three times as much food in case the navigation went awry and they were further away from land than they'd been led to believe.

They needed rest. More than anything, Porter and his crewmates needed rest. This wasn't unusual for renegades and mutineers, but not even Porter had experienced such desperation when sailing before. He'd worked many ships but never with such a skeleton crew. Sailing wasn't a lark when you needed to do four jobs at once.

Still, they'd already survived furious ice-cold winds and mountainous waves. In their urgency to escape, they had travelled far to the south, practically into Antarctic waters. It had been almost unbearably cold, and Porter thanked the fact that at least they were sailing in summer. They wouldn't have survived the same route in winter.

But if their navigator had taken them too far south, had he adjusted the course so they were now far enough to the north? If they struck land, where would that be?

Part of Porter also silently thanked their great shipbuilder. Although he'd warned Porter that this ship couldn't make it across the Southern Ocean, Porter had heard his other boasts. He had the sight, he'd say. He knew the lines. He cut the sheer. He'd been schooled in the Boston shipyards, where the world's fastest boats scoured the seas for the great sperm whale. The Americans had taught him how to craft a line that took the boat through the water with barely a ripple. Yes, this ship was cracking up now, but Porter still counted on the shipbuilder being right about his manufacturing prowess – and wrong about their chances of survival.

Just before sunset, one of the men stared to the east, put his hands to his eyes and called for a spyglass. 'Land ho, land on the starboard bow!' he shouted.

When the crew looked eastwards, everybody saw the dark silhouette in the far distance.

'A bank of cloud – nothing more,' the navigator said. By his reckoning, they were still five hundred miles from land, at least three days' sailing.

For the first time, he was countermanded. The sails were shortened and the brig was made to hove to, coming to a halt, bobbing on the water. Had land not been sighted late in the afternoon, they could have run aground in the darkness.

The crew kept a lookout all night and by morning it was plain. After six weeks of nothing but waves, wind, squalls and driving rain, a glorious green coastline materialised.

The men jumped around, cheering and hooting – it looked like salvation was at hand. But their elation could not be sustained. The ship was mocking their joy, getting heavier in the water. A wooden coffin. They were floating on borrowed time.

Chapter 1

THE TRANSPORT SHIP *Asia* lay quietly in the D'Entrecasteaux Channel overnight, its sweltering human cargo not sure whether the following day should be celebrated or dreaded. Come the morning tide, the *Asia*'s crew would have to keep a close eye on the channel's fractious currents before making a clean run for Hobart Town.

James Porter could interpret the froth and swirl as well as any. But shackled in the hold with 149 other convicts, he'd have to wait until the morning rouse to see the lie of the water, as important to him as the lie of the land.

Like so many on this ship, Porter was a dead man walking. His sentence had been commuted to transportation for life. He had endured eight months rotting on a wretched prison hulk. By comparison, the four-month trip to Van Diemen's Land had been a release.

In the ship's indent, Porter is described as being five feet two inches in height, with a sallow complexion, brown hair and hazel eyes. He is also described as a 'boatman'. Because he'd made his background known to the sailors, somehow or other he was given leave to work and eat with them. He was still young and liked to mess about with the crew, but he had seen more of the world than many sailors twice his years.

Men like Porter rarely care for the future, just the scheme at hand. Today – his first in Hobart Town as a prisoner of His Majesty – he planned to bamboozle everybody. It would be a great lark.

At dawn, the *Asia* raised anchor and set sail. The soldiers made the usual call for the convicts to assemble, but this morning's rouse was different: the last muster before they were 'going ashore, huzza for the shore'. The first signpost that they were nearing Hobart Town was the rocky form of north Bruny Island, and as the *Asia* crept up the river, the island's forbidding cliffs remained shadowy in the weak morning sun. A foggy, leaden landscape arose on either side of the ship until around eight in the morning, when stronger summer rays parted the fog and a cobalt sky emerged. It wasn't quite the tropics but it was blue and warm enough.

As the ship approached Hobart Town, the captain ordered the ensigns to be flown: a positive flag and a negative one. The first was a red cross on a white field indicating this ship was friendly to His Majesty. The second was red, an alert to all and sundry that a new wave of His Majesty's miscreants was about to wash ashore.

By late morning the transport had moved past the green pastures of Battery Point. The cargo of men, half-stunned by the raw sunlight, were doing their best to gauge the shoreline. The government wharf could be clearly seen on the ship's port side; beyond were well-wrought buildings of stone and brick, cut through by wide and dead-straight avenues. Here and there were native blue-green eucalypts, artfully deployed to give the town the aspect of a landscape painting.

Hobart Town radiated nicely from its centre but quickly yielded to nature unbridled at its extremes. The trees had a tincture alien to British eyes. A vast clump of them ran wild to Hobart's left, and directly behind the town was a mass of rolling hills furrowed by deep gullies. Further behind stood the mountain that oversaw it all: the great rounded dome the indigenous people called 'Unghanyahletta'. The white people, however, couldn't seem to agree on a name. It was Table Hill for a while, then Mount Collins (after the colony's first lieutenant-governor, David Collins) and Table Mountain. Finally, a year before Porter's arrival they settled on a name. It would be named after the duke who vanquished Napoleon. Mount Wellington rose high into the blue sky.

On this day – Sunday, 11 January 1824 – the free and fair settlers may have been reading that week's edition of the *Hobart Town Gazette*. For them, Van Diemen's Land was meant to be a land of opportunity, and so a poem sang:

> *And may'st though on Van Diemen's Land,*
> *Possess a spot (by Nature plann'd*
> *Thy Hopes to realize);*
> *For pasture fit, and growing grain,*
> *A gently undulating plain,*
> *Is what thou most would'st prize!*

If Porter could have read such poems, he might have laughed. News travelled fast through the convict ships, and many of the crew on the *Asia* knew Van Diemen's Land well. The newspaper tended to celebrate the Empire's adopted land in glowing terms, an Antipodean version of fairest England, even if most locals knew in their hearts that order and peace hardly prevailed in Hobart Town.

7

Indeed, the colony was a battleground between corrupt law enforcement and flagrant disorder. It was still a place where thieves and bushrangers held considerable sway, and where the local gentry and merchants were small in number and vulnerable. In this society, ex-felons and former muggers rubbed shoulders with crooked soldiers. Convict escapes weren't just common, but the duty of every recalcitrant who swore the prisoner's motto: death or liberty. The worst took to bushranging, terrifying the newly landed settlers who were ripe for the taking.

Porter didn't want to terrorise anybody; he just wanted out. He would be looking to take 'French leave' as soon as humanly possible.

The *Asia* was left standing in the harbour while the colonial machinery was set in train. The prisoner protocols never varied. First came the colonial secretary, who inspected the ship and asked everyone – including the convicts – if everything was in order. After he had left, the surgeon superintendent was permitted to go ashore. He reported all the ship's news to the governor, carrying with him all the details of the convicts, including their criminal records. These were handed to the muster master, who compiled comprehensive summaries; all misdemeanours were registered in the minutest detail. By the third day after the convicts' arrival, the muster master and the prison superintendent, fully apprised of everyone on the ship and the goings-on during the voyage, would board with a number of blank-faced functionaries. Over the next two days, the convicts were questioned and assigned either to government work or to work for a settler.

The authorities were endeavouring to make Van Diemen's Land a thriving entrepôt rather than just a prison station. And the British, described by Napoleon as a nation of shopkeepers, always put profit first. The initial check served an important mercantile purpose: the cargo had to be made useful and profitable. Each convict needed to be properly assessed. *Who is he, and what can he do for the colony?*

Most convicts realised there was no point in lying as they approached the prison superintendent. The assigned clerks crosschecked the statement of each convict with the information forwarded from home. They knew what his mother and father did, where he'd been caught, where he'd been tried and anything else that distinguished him – or her. Porter either didn't know this or didn't care.

The convicts had become used to the daily muster, but not to this slow, interminable bureaucracy. Now they were in a parade on the main deck, listening to tedious and long-winded instructions, under the unwavering gaze of po-faced scribes and scrutineers. The day wore on. Men who hadn't washed in months stood in the warm sun, their sour odour at odds with the gusts of freshly heated air blowing off the shore. They were the by-products of months in a filthy hold. Their skin was milk-white and speckled with dirt and sweat. Most were little more than skin and bones wrapped in a greasy shirt and stained trousers, their boots, once brown or black, now an indeterminate colour, scuffed and wrinkled. Their faces were pinched and sallow, and whatever teeth remained were black, yellow or half-rotten.

Ill at ease, the convicts looked down on the seeming fairness of Hobart Town. This, at least, was a soothing sight for their red eyes. It seemed to promise a new start.

But the smell in the air was heavier and stronger than anything they had sensed from British soil. A wind from the shore suggested strangely scented dry leaves and wood, and the ever-present possibility of fire. Just next to Sullivans Cove was the Old Wharf, and they were close enough to pick up another smell, one Porter must have known – the unmistakable viscous, fishy rancour of whale oil.

Few moved out of the line or complained openly, even if they longed to get it over with. Porter squinted in the sun. Before him was Police No. 322, Priest, then No. 323, Pepell. The colonial chapters of their criminal biographies, which historians still draw on today, were about to begin. Finally it was Porter's turn, Police No. 324. He must have decided that regardless of how much the authorities knew about him, why not have a laugh at their expense?

'Porter, J' said he was from 'Bermondsy [sic], London' and was last living in South London, around the Elephant and Castle.

'Occupation?'

'Beer machine maker, sir!'

Porter shouted it out, as he wanted everybody to hear. There has never been such a profession and no such machine has ever existed. But Porter shared his name with the well-known North London brew.

It's easy to imagine the laughter running through the convict ranks. The little cockney sprite whom nobody could quite tame was having a laugh, but it was also a ploy. Could Porter bring it off?

Bureaucracy is humourless. The clerk didn't even look up through his pince-nez, while he duly recorded 'beer machine maker' as Porter's profession.

In his memoirs, Porter said the idea came from a Jewish convict he'd met on the *Asia*. The man had advised him to pass as a tradesman, telling him they were always given the best assignments and lodgings. And it was true that Van Diemen's Land wanted tradesmen – 'mechanics', as they were called. Blacksmiths and carpenters were most valued. Farmers were also in high demand, and anyone able to plough, harrow, sow, mow, break horses and cultivate hops would be quickly assigned to an appreciative settler. Most of the convicts on the *Asia* were none of these things; they were the urban poor, mostly shoemakers, tailors, weavers, fencers and self-taught forgers. Many were weak and debilitated. Small as he was, Porter at least appeared fit.

The rest of the interview was concerned with labelling the men should they be temporarily 'lost'. The authorities checked that every convict could be identified. Once they were properly annotated and registered, they were always retrievable. And some would look for any chance to bolt. So all convicts were stripped to the waist, their distinguishing features put on file. Escape, they were being told, was pointless.

Even though the ship's records show Porter was but five foot two inches in height, he was remeasured to confirm this. It was noted that he was blind in the left eye, and had a dimpled chin and a scarred forehead. Among his distinguishing features was a tattoo of two bare-fisted boxers on his left arm.

A man measuring over five feet seven inches in height was considered a giant among convicts. Because of their deprived backgrounds, their bodies were stunted from malnutrition. They looked like pygmies when set against the taller, better-fed soldiers guarding them. Britain's and Ireland's human detritus were scored with scars and dented by pox. Porter's blind left eye wouldn't have been deemed surprising among his fellows – convicts presenting themselves with lost digits and misshapen limbs weren't uncommon.

Many convicts had some form of tattooing, often burnt into their flesh by sailors en route with needles and gunpowder. The LD mark

('Liberty or Death') was the staple, but others were sentimental or revealed something of their bearer's temperament, like Porter's pugilists, but anything could be etched into the skin. Some happily put a bust of the reigning monarch on their arm and in one case a man had 'fool' written across his forehead. Men put flowerpots, fish, suns and moons on their bodies all of which made them more easily identifiable to the authorities. It's believed that 37 per cent of all convicts arriving in Australia had tattoos and among the convict women, around 15 per cent were marked. There were no rules, no code of decency either. One man had a sign saying 'catch me' on his left arm. On the right he kept it simple – just the words 'fuck me'.

Porter had now been assigned. Within a few more hours, the men and women were back in the hold, contemplating their first sight of land in months.

Porter might have had the smell of whale oil on his mind. It was the most putrid substance he had ever encountered. As a former whaler he could have been reminded of the 'trying out': the boiling of oil from the animal's stripped blubber. Once liberated from the body, it found its way into everything. Thick and viscous, its heavy, rank fishiness seemed not only to fill the air but also to creep into the taste of a whaler's food, onto his body, into the nooks and crannies of his ship.

Porter may have now recognised the town for what it was. The pretty streets, brick dwellings and expertly placed trees were mere camouflage. Where there was whale oil, there would be whalers. Where there were whalers, there was freedom.

Chapter 2

F ROM AN EARLY AGE, trouble had been the rule for James Porter, not the exception. James was first initiated into vice aged ten, the year after his king, George III, was declared insane. The year 1812 was possibly the worst of all Britain's *anni horribili*. The country, exhausted by conflict with the French, was in the midst of severe economic malaise. A sitting prime minister was assassinated and a poverty lay about the land that hadn't been experienced for several hundred years. There seemed no end in sight to a dozen years of war with Napoleon Bonaparte, which was hardly leavened by a trade embargo on the United States that developed into a full-blown war.

Distrust of the ruling classes and their war was pervasive. Citizens were asked to offer up their youth for a war, then to pay new taxes to fund the slaughter. A nation that seven years earlier had basked in the glory of Nelson's victory at Trafalgar now had to deal with rocketing food prices and a deepening wealth chasm. Militant textile workers, known as the Luddites, fought desperately to sabotage new technology that they believed would destroy their livelihoods. The industrial revolution was only in its earliest phases, but the ructions that came with change were already hurting the most impoverished and the most vulnerable.

As a native of Bermondsey in South-East London, Porter lived just a stone's throw from one of the most deprived areas of the country, notorious for its incubation of crime. He almost certainly would have known the byways and crannies of Jacob's Island, in the vicinity of today's Shad Thames. A few decades later, Charles Dickens would cast it as Bill Sikes' hideout in his novel *Oliver Twist*, his 1837 classic dealing with the criminal underclass of London. Dickens perceived that it was the kind of place where the fictional Sikes, a thief and cut-throat, could do the dirtiest of his work unmolested. The area fit the part. Jacob's Island smelled like an open sewer. In its time it had been labelled 'the capital of cholera', 'pest island' and the 'Venice of drains'. Residents were forced to drink water from the sewers they used for their own waste, the water also heavily polluted and stained red from tanning chemicals used by the area's leather workers.

London's poorest felt acutely that the rich were depriving them of a living. While the poor got poorer, many listened in disgust as news spread of the foppish Prince Regent, who had assumed power when his father George III was deemed unfit to rule. The Prince was known for squandering his money on pavilions and fantasy homes, but also for his refined tastes and love of art. None of these predilections kept the masses fed. In May 1812, the assassination of Prime Minister Spencer Perceval revealed the intensity of this class distrust. Perceval was shot at point-blank range by a man with a personal grievance against the government, but many saw it as an act of political rebellion against a patrician who was fervently anti-radical, anti-Catholic and opposed to any form of social change. The prime minister had been behind some of the reactionary cause célèbres of the age, and radical leaders had been imprisoned. When his murderer, John Bellingham, was hanged at Newgate Prison, thousands came out and cheered for the condemned man.

It was around this time that Porter's period of juvenile delinquency began. He was typical of the disaffected youth who held their elders and so-called superiors in contempt, and he seemed to know instinctively who the bastards were. If we need to understand the genesis of a recalcitrant 22-year-old convict, it's all there in a ten-year-old schoolboy.

We don't know why, but at six he left his parents to live with his grandmother. By the age of ten, he would skip school and play truant. The young James wasn't given to violence, and he lived by a thieves' code of honour: you never rat, you never squeal, you never tell on anyone; you look after your friends and you never give an inch to those who keep you down. His earliest act of rebellion was to sabotage the wooden cane his schoolmaster used to beat the children. He was punished severely, the first of many beatings James would bear throughout his life. He couldn't have cared less. The way he puts it in his memoir, the master could beat the hell out of him but it would make no difference.

'I was not sufficiently checked by my indulgent grandmother and my schoolmaster was too severe beating out one evil spirit and beating in two. I was at last determined to tell my grandmother that I totally disliked my schoolmaster and persuaded her to let me remain at home entirely.'

Punishment simply doubled his determination not to follow the rules, but he also possessed a natural resilience to pain that would serve him in very good stead later in life. In his writings he rarely dwells on the pain – it happens, and he moves on.

Not long afterwards he stole money from his grandmother to see the follies at Drury Lane. He sought out the theatre as the rough and tumble performances were one of the few delights a young man could indulge in that wasn't illegal.

The theatre had just been rebuilt after a fire had partially destroyed it three years earlier. The new building retained its old neoclassical features but had lost some of its former lustre – these were hard times and parts of the building had been rebuilt cheaply. A flat ceiling now replaced the once ornately crafted, lofty dome. There were two royal boxes, a huge gallery and four tiers of seating on each side. The upper and lower classes were filtered through different parts of the building so that respectable patrons were spared the likes of Porter and his crowd. The wealthy were carefully lodged in the upper wings while the poor were safely placed out of touch on terra firma in the 'pit'. Just outside the pit there were lobbies, rooms and avenues, crowded with London's most disreputable characters. As one commentator of the time noted, these lobbies were, 'subject to scenes of the most disgusting indecency'. The pit was not really a place to watch theatre but where London's lower classes carried on their own business, drank and cavorted, regardless of what was showing. For them it was closer to a football match than a piece of theatre and the proprietors understood this market. The people wanted thrills and spills.

What would Porter have seen? It's likely that he would have gone to see the 'shows' – not high theatre. There was bareback horse riding, circus-style acts and lion taming. It's also possible that he witnessed the greatest actor of his generation. A year after Drury Lane was rebuilt, Edmund Kean appeared as Shylock in Shakespeare's *The Merchant of Venice*, one of the great performances of the time. Kean's Shylock was considered a sensation. He played Shylock as a dark, twisted, evil person, rather than a comic one. It's still remembered among theatre historians as a breakthrough performance.

We don't know whether James loved the theatre for itself or just for the carnival atmosphere within it – the main attraction for him was probably the dubious goings-on in the pit, but in his memoir, it's also evident that in some form or another, James loved to play a role.

Roles may have been something he enjoyed, but role models for a young lad were few and far between in 1812. Without the guidance of a mother and father, and with only a frail grandmother to look after him, he fell in with the wrong crowd. Theatres such as Covent Garden and Drury Lane were the nineteenth century's version of the bright lights, even if he probably knew he would never be a real part of it. In another time and place, James would have been the boy who ran away to join the circus. But his peers were not performers, musicians and actors but a bunch of wastrels and tearaways, similarly dissolute and lost children from East and South London who took to the wealthy west side with light hands and nimble feet. James was well in with them, and he needed money for his beloved theatre. He would find any way he could to support his own 'villainous extravagances', as he called them.

Porter was desperate to find more money for his theatre addiction – as he says in his memoir: 'I could not get the thoughts of the theatre out of my head'. He requested money from his grandmother to buy a new whip (what he used this for, was never explained), but instead treated himself to another night on the town. On his way he fell in with two 'playfellows' and together they concocted a plan to rob a valuable timepiece from a gentleman's house. While James would do the stealing, his friends would fence the article. James was the only one caught in the act and was quickly apprehended. When the constables brought him to his grandmother, she simply 'swooned away'.

He mentions in his memoir that he regretted hurting the one person who cared for him, but he couldn't help himself: 'To this day and through all my misfortunes and rambles the same propensity for mischief haunts me.' This too, was typical of the young James Porter. He may have understood the implications of his actions, but there was an addiction to thrills. His instinct was to escape and move on from any damage he may have caused. He never looked back.

James may have been no more than twelve, and because of his age the gentleman didn't prosecute. But what was to be done with this unruly, difficult boy? In those days there was only one way to beat sense into such boys – send them to sea.

When James reached thirteen, his uncle in Gravesend sent him aboard one of his brigs. James reviled his uncle perhaps as much as his old schoolmaster: 'I do assure you, I did not like his stern features.' Here was another authority figure, and this one hardly counted as a role model. Apparently his uncle had lost numerous vessels – the implication here being that he fraudulently collected on insurance – and traded on the wrong side of the law, smuggling banned goods from the coast of France into Britain. Some British merchants of this time were experts at producing coffin ships, prettied up to appear solid and seaworthy but deliberately over-insured and thus worth more to their owners sunk than afloat.

James' uncle told him that he'd be made to pay for the pain he had caused his grandmother. He would be sent to a captain who would 'either make a sailor out of you, or an idiot'. But the young James had learnt to show neither fear nor favour to anyone. *Go ahead*, he seemed to be saying. *I simply don't care.*

The young James never really had a chance. Before he could make his escape, he was summarily packed off, boarding the brig *Sophia* 'bound for Rio de Janeira [*sic*]'. It was late in 1815. His uncle, it appears, made good on his threats, as the captain treated the youth as a semi-criminal. James 'felt the cruel hands' of the captain and was 'mastheaded' for a trifle – as he describes it, he was obliged to hold on like grim death to a topmast backstay: 'and worse of all we made very bad weather and a long passage'. All the same, he says, his mistreatment made a 'sharp lad of me'.

Porter's career as a part-sailor, part-thief had begun. Whenever those in authority were oppressive, his response was to bolt from them, steal from them or both. Porter was intelligent enough to know what he was doing – and he was well aware of the consequences of his actions, but the thrill of the game, the adventures and larks along the way, were just too attractive. Porter could not sit still. He was always about finding the next big thing. It wasn't in his character to rest, think and plan ahead. Porter only knew the here and now.

In the next two years, he absconded from a ship with the captain's money in his pocket and later slipped aboard another vessel bound for home. Bored and listless back in England, he signed on to a whaleship for Peru in early 1818 and eventually left that one as well, skipping the ship to spend time on land with a young Chilean lady named Catalina. Porter was just sixteen and living in Valparaíso, one of Chile's busiest ports, where boats docked from all over the world. Very quickly, he was learning the language of the sea and the ways of the whalers, sealers and mariners who frequented the port. He was too young for marriage so told his intended and her father that he needed more time and experience.

His next move was to take passage with an armed Chilean schooner, the *Liberta*, which deployed troops along the Peruvian coast and was also engaged in fighting the Spanish. Chile was fighting a war of independence against Spain, and Porter was in the thick of it. He felt that fighting was what finally turned him into a man and that he was now 'fit for any hardship'. A more experienced James Porter, now around the age of seventeen, returned to Catalina and they were married.

But fighting the Spanish was hardly an apprenticeship for domesticity. The Porters had a boy and a girl in the first couple of years of marriage, but it seems Porter, at least in his memoirs, was almost oblivious to his conjugal responsibilities. He mentions briefly that their daughter died soon after birth, but it seems this was relatively trivial to him, far less important than events taking over Chile at the time.

> *The patriots were contending for their independence. Lord*
> *Cochrane was very busy along the coast – scarce a man could call*
> *his life his own without being on the alert – I again (like Gulliver)*
> *felt an inclination to go to sea for a trip or two and I mentioned it*
> *to my wife which gave her great uneasiness.*

It was the lure of adventure with the greatest sea captain of the time that broke whatever family bonds Porter had fostered. Thomas Cochrane, the 10th Earl of Dundonald, was a living legend, whom Napoleon described as the *loup de mers* (sea wolf). Cochrane had never lost a battle, but had been dismissed by the Royal Navy for alleged stock market fraud. He was a double hero: a great commander who had shown the French how to fight at sea, and a maverick captain who had gone out on his own. Cochrane had literally hired himself out as a naval commander for any South American country wishing to shake off their Spanish overlords. Brazil, Chile and Peru all answered his call – which came at a very large price. Cochrane made himself rich, but the men he commanded knew nothing about that. The South Americans venerated him, and sailors of all kinds wanted a piece of the glory. James Porter wasted no time finding a berth on one of Lord Cochrane's rebel boats, leaving the burden of a wife and child behind. He would never see them again.

Soon enough Porter was on a Chilean brig heading towards Lima. He may have been a patriot to his bones and believed in the rebel cause to fight the Spanish, but even in the service of Lord Cochrane, he could not stay obedient – or at his post – at all times. He needed diversions. When he arrived in Lima, he slipped away from his boat without leave and soldiers were sent to retrieve him. He and two others were found in one of the local 'grog shops', as Porter called them, and the three men took severe umbrage at being caught. A fight ensued. Armed with a slingshot, Porter fired on the boat's chief mate and hit him in the back of the head. According to Porter, the man was about to knife him. He later discovered that his shot had been fatal. Now Porter wasn't just a thief but was also marked for the gallows.

However, the slippery James Porter found his way back to England. By 1823, he decided to carry out one last scheme that 'would make me rich or cost me my life'. In the dead of night, he and two men quietly boarded a cutter off Northfleet, close to the mouth of the River Thames. Porter and his accomplices 'secured the men on board' and 'took a great quantity of silk and beaver'. They reached London undetected, but one accomplice was caught with some of the booty, and he implicated Porter in the plot. The twenty-one year old went before the Surrey justices and was sentenced to death, which was only later commuted to transportation for life.

His beloved grandmother, whom he felt he had let down so many times before, was quite incapable of taking the news of his death sentence. 'The shock was more than she could bear – and before the news could reach her that I was reprieved she died – my name (as I was given to understand by my friends) was the last words that escaped her lips.'

Porter spent eight months on what he described as a 'wretched hulk' at Woolwich where he said he often contemplated suicide: 'Nothing but the hope of soon going to some other land, could induce me to remain in that dreadful place.'

He would get his reprieve. He was bound for Van Diemen's Land.

Chapter 3

THE LONDON BEER machine maker of no repute whatsoever was immediately taken under the wing of a blacksmith, John Pulling. Porter may not have known it but he'd been given a good start, despite his British prison reports. He had been sent to the top of the queue, starting his new career as a first-class convict assigned to a settler. Perhaps the tattooed pugilists gave him the air of a mechanic, or his joke had also been lost on his new master.

When the man he would live with and report to arrived, Porter told him he was no blacksmith. Pulling apparently said, 'Never mind I'll chance you. I can tell by your looks you are a tradesman.' On Porter's first attempt as a blacksmith he failed miserably and feared the worst: he might be put into government employ, which invariably meant breaking rocks and hauling trees. But Pulling was kindly – he would find some form of employment for Porter around the house.

It was only a few months into Porter's apprenticeship that his taste for adventure returned. The Derwent River was dotted with ships trading in whale oil, seal skins, wool, timber and flax. Business at the port was thriving. Porter says he felt compelled to steal for his master and children, who had fallen on hard times, and was determined to do the right thing by them 'by fair and foul means'. The ships were the easiest and most obvious targets for robbery, and Porter knew his way around them.

In his memoir he says that he pushed quietly off from the riverbank late at night in a small dinghy, paddling in silence towards a nearby barque. The ship was sitting still at its moorings, no light emanating from any of its quarters. With the ease of an acrobat, he shimmied up the anchor rope and slipped onto the bowsprit: the long spar protruding from the front of the boat. As quiet as a mouse, he crept past the forecastle, slinking across the upper deck and down into the cabins. He must have known where crew and passengers were likely to keep their valuables, for with no light at all he purloined a bag containing three hundred sovereigns and a 'quantity of loose silver'.

After stuffing as much as possible into his pockets, a far less agile James Porter made his way back to the upper deck. Passing the mizzen chains, he was about halfway across the boat and at the mainsail when he found himself face to face with a watchman, who was completely thrown by his appearance. Each man stood staring at the other, unable to know how to react. Porter, in the end, was the quicker: 'He was so much astonished but he gave me an opportunity of pushing him down on the deck before he could give me an alarm.'

Here was the weak point of Porter's plan. He had let the dinghy drift rather than tethering it to the ship, and before long he was plunging into the icy Derwent – replete with heavy coinage. As the alarm went out, other ships were rousing, and it was quickly telegraphed that a thief was at large somewhere in the water. Boats of all descriptions came out in search. Despite being laden with booty, Porter swam to a buoy and remained partly hidden, treading water.

If boats came too near, he submerged for long periods. After what must have felt like hours, the search for the thief was called off and the hunting craft departed.

In the water, Porter resembled a water rat: he could swim brilliantly and evade detection, drifting like a log or slicing his way silently through reeds. Icy water didn't seem to worry him; indeed, it was his natural element. Somehow he made it back to shore, still heavy with silver. He had escaped – for the moment – and reputedly handed the money to John Puller's appreciative wife. But his master turned him in because he couldn't abide the fact that another man had fed and clothed his children – or so Porter wrote.

When the case came to court, it was thrown out – nobody could identify Porter as the thief, and he claimed that the money he'd given the master's wife was his own savings.

This is all part of his memoir and worthy of inclusion as an insight into his character, although it's an unlikely story. True or not, it reveals something of the James Porter dichotomy – there was a streak of generosity mixed with a taste for recklessness and an addiction to thrills. In the end, none of it was ever added to his convict record, which was supposed to list every suspicion and infraction. But Porter was apt to paint himself as a Robin Hood, a helper to the poor and dispossessed, ever in defiance of an unjust establishment.

Pulling might have wanted him to be a man about the house, but Porter had more exciting and profitable schemes afoot. Domestic servitude, a bit like wedded bliss, wouldn't be the way of the Bermondsey boy.

Just three months after his arrival, a man of his description was seen stealing a cask of butter, and he was also pulled up for 'having no lodgings'. The butter theft was mere suspicion, but if the authorities judged that he had no fixed abode it's likely he had by now left his assigned billet. In all, it was enough to place him into government bondage. His beer-machine-making lark, his pretence to be a mechanic, was over. He had attracted the authorities' attention. On 22 April, he was placed back among the government men, returned to the main prisoners' barracks as a second-class convict. Porter skips over the entire episode, and simply says he was 'turned into the government boats crew'.

*

By THE EARLY 1820s, the governor of New South Wales, Lachlan Macquarie, believed he had solved the bushranger problem in the still fledgling colony of Van Diemen's Land. This was more than a bit of wishful thinking on his part. Just over 50 per cent of the 10,000-strong population were convicts under sentence, many of whom felt that cutting and running was part of the accepted credo. For ten years, dozens of convicts had escaped their masters, slipping away from penal gangs or even breaking out of gaol to go bush. Macquarie and his visiting judge advocate set up circuit courts with the help of the local lieutenant-governor, William Sorell, to deal with the problem of absconders who had gone rogue. The net result was the hanging of nine bushrangers in Launceston and ten in Hobart Town. 'Now that these dreadful examples have been made,' wrote Macquarie to London, 'I am enabled to report that there is every reasonable prospect of the Bush-ranging System being completely at an end, most probably for many years to come.'

Macquarie couldn't have been more wrong. The theft, cattle-rustling, sheep-stealing and general violence of the bushrangers would not abate over the next few years. Van Diemen's Land was getting beyond the control of the hapless Sorell and his hopelessly under-equipped local police force. The southernmost colony's future was at stake. It needed more free settlers, and they needed protection. If the ever-growing local economy was to be kept humming, the convicts had to be brought into line.

Back in London, Sorell was considered a lightweight. He was unable to report the exact number of convicts. He failed to deal effectively with the increasingly violent and frequent skirmishes between settlers and the Indigenous population. Settlers were making greater inroads into the country and inevitably falling foul of the local inhabitants, who resented both their presence and inclination to ring-fence traditional hunting grounds. The settlers, of course, wanted a free hand to expand and protection to go with it. As far as they were concerned, a heavier hand was needed.

Four months after Porter arrived, Sorell was replaced. In May 1824, a veteran of the Napoleonic wars arrived in Hobart Town. He had learnt his administrative craft as superintendent and commandant of the British Honduras.

Lieutenant-Governor George Arthur, thirty-nine, was always exceedingly well turned out, but so short that whenever he appeared in full vice-regal attire, his sword would drag against the ground. Arthur wasn't given to compromising on anything – not even the size of his ceremonial weapon, which remained steadfastly regulation issue. The little army officer with the very long face and weak smile had grand ideals and a passion for reform but, owing to his height, always conducted inspections on horseback.

In Van Diemen's Land, Arthur didn't waste any time getting to work. Two days after his arrival, the *Hobart Town Courier* of Friday, 14

May mentioned all the people he planned to meet. New government appointments were to be effective immediately, while the convicts would be scrutinised in ways they had never known before.

Arthur was one of those ramrod military types, straitlaced and humourless, a devout Calvinist who believed he had a divine mission. He had the look of a man mildly appalled at everything he surveyed – while he also made a note of whatever he surveyed. He was first and foremost a military man, and he always dressed the part. He would stride up and down the long room of government house with a sense of purpose, dictating letters to his lackeys while wearing a semi-military coat. His trousers had a red seam down the outside, and he always wore a high-necked stock, a formal neckerchief of the type worn by aristocratic riders when hunting.

A gifted, highly intelligent soldier, Arthur had a brilliant mind for numbers and a taste for accuracy and organisation. He would take the raw data compiled on every convict in the colony and have it updated by a legion of clerks who worked through the day and much of the night. These data would become the governor's 'black books', thick ledgers recording behaviour that determined what kind of work, treatment and forms of mercy would be bestowed upon the convict throughout his or her penal experience. It was Arthur's moral index, and it was always being edited, annotated, tabulated – and probably triplicated.

Arthur became so immersed in the details of everything and everyone that the convicts felt he knew them all. They were almost correct. Their overlord was slight in stature, but his presence was all-pervading. He cultivated an extensive network of spies and informants in all walks of life. If he couldn't oversee everything, he would pay men to watch, listen and report back. Arthur believed that wickedness resided in the hearts of every man (except, presumably, God-fearing Englishmen such as himself) and that it was his responsibility to uncover it, expose it and punish it with all the severity at his disposal.

To obtain this kind of power, he had to ensure that Van Diemen's Land was independent of New South Wales, and that the southernmost colony had its own Supreme Court and Legislative Council. Due largely to his efforts, the colony achieved a form of self-rule just a year after his arrival. Hobart Town could now make its own laws – well, more precisely, *he* could make the laws. He was now free to 'raise the moral tone' of the place he felt was his in all but name.

Lieutenant-governor George Arthur wielded more power than any other politician in Australian history. He made the laws that suited his predilections, ensured they were carried out with the utmost rigour and kept a network of spies, magistrates and police to execute them.

No other Australian political leader has ever had the powers George Arthur wielded. He would continue to hold them for another twelve years, overseeing the biggest of pictures and the tiniest of minutiae. He wasn't just chairman and chief executive but also head of homeland intelligence, moral arbiter, and chief data manager.

As an example, he ordered the weights on men's leg-irons be increased. He surmised that the heavier the 'old wives' – as the convicts used to call them – the speedier a man's path to correction and improvement. Most of the irons weighed about four and a half pounds, but Arthur had the heaviest increased to about fifty-five pounds. He also ordered that the space between leg-irons be shortened. It wasn't difficult to know who was truly out of favour with the governor; in Arthur's land, the lowest of men had the slowest of shuffles.

Convicts who were perceived to be naturally difficult or negligent were often taken directly to a magistrate, who could have them whipped or sent to a road gang. On the road, a convict guilty of a lesser misdemeanour worked without chains, while a more serious charge warranted chains. The chain gang was probably Arthur's greatest gift to the colony. They had been employed before his rule, but he brought them to the fore of the punishment system and made them widespread. As one admirer of his methods wrote at the time, 'The chain gang is one of the best things that has been projected in this reign, never were men better worked, better flogd [sic] and better managed than they are in the gang.'

All government men, as the convicts were euphemistically called, quickly came to understand what their new overlord wanted. Digging holes and filling them up again were entirely acceptable tasks if the prisoner learnt compliance. The 'immediate toil of the convicts,' Arthur wrote, 'is the only official result of the labour'.

The upper echelons of Hobart society also understood that working with the new regime – agreeing with its overlord and adhering to his way of thinking – was the only way to move even higher in their hierarchy. Arthur bestowed privileges and removed them at his own pleasure. No matter what a man or woman's station in life, he offered small carrots to the compliant and heavy sticks to the recalcitrant.

*

JAMES PORTER AND George Arthur had arrived just as renovations to Hobart Town were nearly complete. The new town had been designed by men trying to transplant the quaintest parts of Devon and Cornwall to the South Seas. Its most pleasant parts had that English countryside feel, built in order to delight and therefore lure the growing middle classes that the colony wanted to attract. It smelt like old England as well: that countrified mix of fresh horse dung, lavender, baked bread and hearth smoke, slightly leavened by the fresh winds that blew regularly off the Derwent.

When Macquarie had first toured Van Diemen's Land in 1811, he'd noted that even government house, built just six years previously, was falling to pieces. He wanted drastic urban renewal. He came, saw and divided the dusty, dirty streets with makeshift hovels into longer, broader and leafier boulevards. Out went the ramshackle assemblage of turf, log and wattle huts known as 'skillings'; in came stately roads and grand designs – government buildings made of freestone from the local quarries, expertly chiselled by skilled convict stonemasons. Macquarie's vision was for one principal square and seven major streets: Macquarie, Elizabeth, Argyle, Liverpool, Murray, Harrington and Collins. He also planned a new church and courthouse.

When Macquarie returned in 1821, the *Hobart Town Gazette* recorded that he was especially pleased to see a quay being built around Sullivans Cove, making it one of the best places on Earth to anchor ships. Soon after came a hospital, army barracks and a system of signal stations. There were longer tree-lined avenues and well over four hundred individual houses. The best of these were stone and brick structures, many of which were built around lower Macquarie and upper Davey Street, and beginning to approach Battery Point.

A view of Hobart Town circa 1833 by visiting French artist Louis Auguste de Sainson. By the time James Porter arrived in the mid 1820s, Hobart Town rivalled Nantucket Bay as the world's biggest whaling town.

Macquarie's network of streets hadn't quite gone to plan, however. Geographic reality intervened at certain points. Some streets were too steep for a horse and cart, and others ended blankly onto a cliff face above a beach. And while the inner-city grid was lined with smart timber shops, this was more about appearance than substance. Behind them were rough courtyards where tradesmen lived in far less salubrious digs. The poorer cottages, where emancipists and the poorer citizens lived, were no more than a wooden front which had been appended to an older skilling. In places like Wapping, on the low-lying waterfront, there were a number of tiny cottages, little more than two rooms looking out on the street. Any additions were made of rough-cut weatherboarding. Hobart Town, both rich and poor, was taking shape.

Three years later, Arthur had a town he could work with: a thriving commercial centre that for the most part had the kind of mathematical orderliness he loved.

Meanwhile, it was in the areas overlooked by government architects that Porter found the town he could work with. Down by the docks, a rougher part of town was being born. Wapping would eventually encompass an area east of the city, on the edge of the Derwent, that stretched from Sackville Street – behind the Theatre Royal, which opened in 1837 – down to Hunter Street, where the Old Wharf was sited just around from Sullivans Cove.

There were two putrid streams, both used by the general population for all manner of purposes, that meandered down towards this low-lying, boggy area. They both merged into the town's water supply and drainage system, the Hobart Town Rivulet. Emanating from Mount Wellington, the rivulet had been a source of fresh water for the local Aboriginal people just twenty years previously. By Porter's time it was well on its way to becoming the town's dumping ground and default sewage outlet. When flooded, the rivulet would carry human and industrial refuse from higher up, and it wasn't unknown for dogs or pigs – even sheep and horses – to be brought down dead or alive. But flooding was the real problem. With such refuse being sent down the rivulet, it silted up frequently, breaking its poorly constructed banks and inundating residents with Hobart Town's discarded filth.

Wapping was aptly named after its London equivalent. It was where boarding houses met abattoirs, shipyards sided with taverns and the town's roughest trade tangled with the women who were viewed as its most wanton. The government slaughterhouse, butcheries and tanneries were sited there from the early 1820s and even in the best weather a pall hung over the district. Wapping reeked of all the things it produced, a foul mix of whale oil, dead fish, dank wet earth and raw sewage. The dockside hovels were rat infested, their foundations resting precariously on a base of evil-smelling, muddy putrilage.

While it was a putrid area in Porter's day, Wapping would become a by-word for the wrong side of Hobart Town. A little ditty for Wapping was printed in the Hobart *Mercury* in 1838 which neatly summed up how it came to be viewed:

We used to call it Wapping
Where the rivulet's rare scent
Sent our noses at an angle
That Dame Nature never meant.

It makes sense that convicted felons, cut-throats and forgers would break bread in Wapping with the whalers and sealers who were pouring into Hobart Town at the time of Porter's arrival. The unwritten code among whalers and convicts was mutually self-serving. American whaling vessels were manned by itinerants who used the job as a means of moving around the world. They would lose men at some ports and have to take on fresh recruits at others. American whaleboat captains barely distinguished between the average tar and the average convict – they didn't care about undermining British penal policy, but of course contrived to avoid the penalties if possible.

The sealers who worked Bass Strait were also often targeted by convicts, as their smaller crews needed regular replacements too. There was plenty of work for absconders in the strait, and convicts would use it to make a little money and get closer to New Zealand, where men could easily be secreted in a thousand bays and inlets. Sealers were of a different disposition to whalers. They were less transient and better known for creating fringe communities, sometimes trading closely with the local Indigenous people, sometimes raiding them or stealing their wives.

Whaling was the bigger business. Hobart Town now rivalled Nantucket Bay as the world's biggest whaling town, and often there were as many as three or four dozen whaleboats being fitted out in the harbour while others cruised the waters, hunting the great sperm whale. It was whaling that created the early character of Hobart, centred on the Old Wharf and Wapping with its plethora of related industries: shipbuilding, chandling, sail making and merchanting.

And so it was that low and high Hobart Town were taking their separate forms in the mid-1820s, thrusting themselves onto the landscape. Officially the number of convicts was around half the population, but if any visiting traveller factored in the drifters and seamen, it would be clear to them that the free common folk – the merchant class, administrative, military and land-owning gentry – were heavily outnumbered.

Throughout the colony, a vernacular was being born. While Macquarie named the principal streets after high-ranking dignitaries (including himself), Van Diemen's Land grew infamous for demotic names that described the lived experiences of its white inhabitants. In the 1820s, Tasmania's *Colonial Times* remarked sniffily that 'the appellations given to some of the places in Van Diemen's Land are detestable and show great want of taste'. There was Dick Browns River, Kittys Rivulet, Devils Kitchen, Fat Doe River and Murderers Plain – even Hells Corners. A nineteenth-century Tasmanian writer, Edward Curr, explained that the names reflect the poorer people's experiences, and were often bestowed by bushrangers, convicts and hunters; this was, Curr said, 'their way of coming to terms with their exile in the New World'.

One of the toughest problems for much of the male population to deal with was their limited contact with women. The disproportion between the sexes was enormous. Of course, when opportunities arose, relations between convict men and women were possible. From October 1824 to August 1828, a mere eighteen women escaped from the Hobart Town Female Factory. They either pushed themselves through a hole in the wall or climbed to the top of the gaol then jumped onto the street outside. But many more women tried and failed to get out.

With convict women few and far between, and most of the free women either married or otherwise ineligible, women were badly needed in Van Diemen's Land. But the first group of single women – two hundred of them – didn't arrive in Hobart Town until 1832, under the so-called Bounty System that had been introduced the year before. On arrival they were lodged at the female orphan school, under the supervision of eminent ladies; they were to be assigned as domestic servants, and those households seeking employees had to state the wages on offer and the type of woman required. But Arthur wasn't happy with the ladies who arrived. He complained in a letter to the Colonial Office Under-Secretary, Robert Hay of this 'most injudicious measure of associating the depraved characters from the public institutions, and I believe from the streets of London also, with women of good reputation'.

In some ways, colonial norms were different from what we might expect. Neither male nor female convicts thought there was anything morally wrong with living together out of wedlock (known as 'dabbing it up' – 'dab' was a term for bed), but the language belies this apparently progressive state of affairs. A 'blowen' could mean either a prostitute or a woman who cohabits with a man. Even if cohabiting was deemed to some degree permissible, the strong prejudice against women, that pervaded the penal colonies, was hardly so. Convicts degraded women in name and in deed. They had plenty of demeaning labels, including 'crack', 'mollisher' or 'mott'. At this time the average woman was not described as the better known 'Sheila' but as a 'Judy'. If she was a 'blowen' or a 'mott' she was suspected of being a 'woman of the town', which seems to be code for an actual prostitute or a woman who might be easily compromised. Prostitutes themselves were also called 'burricks'. When a woman was seen as beautiful, she might be called a 'ewe' or a 'flash piece of mutton'. If a woman already had a man, she was his 'natural' or 'peculiar'. Women were generally seen as whores, livestock or chattel. Especially among the poor and the imprisoned classes, women in

Van Diemen's Land in the 1820s and 30s – and well beyond – had an extremely difficult and precarious existence.

How the men dealt with an absence of women has often been translated into a pandemic of sexual activity between them, the so-called 'buggery in the barracks'. Undoubtedly there were convicts who participated in this. And some men may have raped animals – 'bestiality in the bush'. But Porter doesn't mention any of this in his memoirs. For him, as for many of his time, such activities would have been kept (in the vernacular of the time) 'under the rose' – that is, only spoken of in hushed tones. Nor does he mention Wapping by name – where he may have found female sexual partners – even though he boasts in his memoir that he knew every nook and cranny of Hobart Town.

We do know that Porter, like many convicts, cultivated another type of close relationship. He was well in with his natural allies, the whalers and sealers, fellow seamen with whom he shared knowledge and experience. If Porter was to steal a boat and head downriver, he needed to know which ships were amenable to taking on new crewmen, and where and when to find them.

Governor Arthur, of course, kept a step ahead of everybody. Escape was not to be countenanced under his watch. The man who dealt in minuscule details was keen to block all attempts to get away by sea, and he introduced a number of regulations relating to ships at port almost as soon as he arrived. Arthur, as ever, was prepared to wield the stick. If a ship in the Derwent didn't maintain a 24-hour officer-watch its crew paid a severe fine. Not only were the suspect vessels searched, but they were also smoked: fumigated with sulphur to winkle out the stowaways. Arthur warned the captains that if any convict was found on a vessel, each officer and seaman would be fined the equivalent of a month's wages, which had to be paid up before the ship set sail. The crews of smaller boats were asked to remove their sails and rudders before going ashore.

Then there was Arthur's carrot: if a seaman helped the government to find a stowaway convict, then he would be allowed to divvy up the forfeited monies – taken from his fellow crewmen – with the search party. Arthur knew what would happen to an informant if his crewmates ever found out he had snitched on them, so the governor allowed informants to be discharged from the ship if necessary and granted government protection.

From the time he took over as governor, Arthur was gathering lookouts, watchers and beaks (magistrates) of all sorts in his pay. Wherever a convict might set foot beyond his legal remit, it seemed the spymaster general would always have eyes on him.

Chapter 4

O N 22 MAY 1824, the month of Arthur's arrival, Porter scaled the Hobart Public Barracks and for more than a fortnight was nowhere to be found. He almost certainly tried to make for Bruny Island, south of the main settlement, where whalers often took on escaped convicts as crew. He may also have tried to approach a ship at anchor in the Derwent, even if everyone knew these would eventually be searched.

The manner of Porter's discovery is not recorded, but in eighteen days he was back at barracks and served with a hundred lashes. It was said at the time that fifty lashes was enough to expose a man's backbone and one hundred enough to kill some men. Those ordering the punishment often made sure that it was a convict's friend who did the flogging. Porter would have been tied to a triangle set up in the prison barracks and flogged with a short whip made up of nine strands of knotted leather. Porter felt the lash three hundred times throughout his term as a convict and yet in his memoirs rarely mentions the pain. The man seemed indestructible.

With the punishment carried out he was finally placed in service as a seaman convict working on government brigs for the Hobart Town harbourmaster, Captain Welsh. Little is known about Welsh, except that he appeared to relish the help of his convict crews and used them to great effect. It was a busy time for the harbourmaster, as an increasing number of ships of all shapes and provenances were putting into port in the mid-1820s. Being under the harbourmaster's wing was something of a reprieve for the 22-year-old Porter, who was back in his native profession. In his memoir he speaks kindly of Welsh, an avuncular figure who didn't always take the authorities' side in their disputes with his convict charges.

Porter was proving that he could stay – at least temporarily – on the right side of the law. He was soon promoted to coxswain of the secretary's gig, a small to medium-sized rowing boat that probably had not more than four or six rowers and a coxswain. It was used to ferry captains and colonial officials around the harbour. For a couple of years, another kind of James Porter was in the ascendant: an industrious and loyal worker with no apparent desire to abscond. Between June 1824 and August 1826, he recorded no adverse marks at all.

At some point in 1826, Arthur approached Welsh to provide his best men for an urgent errand. The governor needed to convey an important despatch to Maria Island, a newly constructed penal station a few miles off the east coast of Van Diemen's Land. Men were often sent to Maria Island arbitrarily to make up the numbers, or on Arthur's whim. The island was small, only about twelve miles in length, but it was rugged and hilly with a thriving forest – good timber that needed to be extracted.

Porter was selected for the mission and was even able to choose his own crew. The men would have to cross East Bay Neck by foot carrying the boat, where local Aboriginal people – described loosely by Porter as 'the Stony Creek Tribe' – were still very much in control of the land. Porter was given charge of the boat, and the crew were given firearms and cutlasses to protect themselves. Captain Welsh had even lent Porter a blunderbuss.

The people who inhabited East Bay Neck were known to fight back fiercely against any incursions from white interlopers. Within a couple of years, they would prove among the sharpest thorns in Arthur's side when it was decided that they – as well as every other Indigenous group – must be removed from the rapidly expanding settled districts. There was growing hostility between whites and blacks. Even by 1825, two years before the officially recognised start of 'The Black War', the *Government Gazette*, which had at one point described Aboriginal actions as 'retaliatory' began to describe them as 'acts of atrocity'. The newspaper was the official government organ, and its most prominent propaganda sheet. By the time Porter was asked to do this crossing in 1826, the so-called Stony Creek Tribe, along with clansmen from other related tribes, were reported to be conducting a sustained campaign against settlers across the midlands of Van Diemen's Land.

It was no small errand that Porter was being asked to run. He and his crew had to navigate around 55 nautical miles (around 65 miles) of water that took them south of Hobart, past Sandy Bay to just north of Bruny Island. From there it was a circuitous route – first dead east then north, rounding Lime Bay and heading north-east through Norfolk Bay, before reaching the narrow neck – and potentially hostile Aboriginal people. When Porter and his crew finally got there, they would have to haul their boat to the other side of the isthmus. It was a non-descript piece of land, just a quarter of a mile wide and when crossed, led to Blackman Bay and finally the open sea. It was at this time the only quick route through to Maria Island.

Porter and his men reached the neck without incident. Once ashore they spotted the clan's fires at a distance and, as Porter put it in his memoir, felt that they could make the land crossing with a little subterfuge. But as they crept to the far end of the neck, they were spotted. Within moments, spears rained down on them. According to Porter, the bowman was killed: 'A spear went through his intestines and he never spoke more.' Somehow they made it to the far end of the neck and onto the beach, sailing the 17 nautical miles across Blackman Bay to Maria Island. The crew were attacked again on the return trip, which they repelled, Porter wrote, 'with a determined cutlass charge'.

Back in Hobart they were considered heroes and awarded tickets-of-leave. This was just one step away from a conditional pardon and two steps away from a full pardon. With a ticket-of-leave, Porter could have married, brought up a family, owned property and even work for wages – but he was still a prisoner. He couldn't carry firearms or board a ship. While these tickets sounded valuable, their award was considered tenuous. They could be easily suspended or withdrawn for the most trivial of reasons. Porter was placed in charge of a cutter, a small single-masted boat, rigged at the front and back. In convict terms at least, he was back in the top division.

All seemed to be going well for James Porter, but his memoir then records: 'Some scoundrels gave information that I was going to take away the Cutter. This caused the first suspicion on my Character and the Cause of my Misery. I was not looked upon as a man trustworthy – therefore I was determined to make my escape from the Colony as soon as I could get a Chance.'

Whatever these 'scoundrels' did to Porter at this juncture, it marked the beginning of a new descent in his convict career.

*

FROM AUGUST 1826 to mid-1828, Porter's ledger shows a fresh spate of minor offences and misdemeanours. There was a six-month stint in the chain gang after he was discovered stowed away on a boat. He was later restored to Welsh's government boat crew, but this didn't give rise to any sense of contrition. In July 1827 he was charged with robbing a sailor; his fellow robber was given twenty-five lashes, but Porter wriggled out of it and was found not guilty. Welsh had given him a favourable character reference, and he was let off with a warning. But within a few months he was back to his old form.

Chain gangs were made up of fifth- or sixth-class convicts. Fifth-class convicts were sentenced to hard labour in chains, a punishment which Arthur described 'as severe as could be inflicted on man'. Sixth-class convicts endured the same, but under more rigid surveillance. Seventh-class convicts were sent to Macquarie Harbour.

In one instance he was found drunk and abusive. He managed to disappear three times. In another episode, he received twenty-five lashes for 'making use of a government boat to his own advantage'.

All these infractions meant that James Porter had very little chance of being emancipated in the near future. Arthur's predecessor, William Sorell, had offered a loose system of indulgences and punishments, and Arthur elevated this into a social order. His system worked like a game of snakes and ladders, introducing new types of carrots and sticks to help elevate or lower the player. If he played the game and kept out of trouble, even the inveterate thief or notorious fencer could climb out of his misery, shirk off his chains and gain his ticket of leave. Toe Arthur's line, and a convict could even earn a wage and marry before their sentence was up; steal, drink, abscond or cause any other form of trouble, and they would slide rapidly down a snake. The first-class convict was permitted to sleep away from barracks, while the fourth-class convict was employed in chain gangs on public works. A seventh-class convict, a so-called incorrigible, would be banished to the worst place on Earth: Macquarie Harbour Penal Station situated on the cold and weather-beaten west coast.

Of all the sticks that Arthur wielded, Macquarie Harbour was the heaviest. It was a cold, dark wilderness at the end of the world, whose reputation for dread preceded it. In the mid-1820s it wasn't much more than a rough encampment peopled mostly by inveterate bolters. The commandants were given free licence to wield a painful stick of their own: the cat-o'-nine-tails specially made for the colony, the 'Macquarie Cat'. Macquarie Harbour was Arthur's Hobart Town multiplied by ten, except nobody could hear you scream and some enjoyed it when you did. Arthur was known to send men there without sentencing, if he felt the moral bearing of the unfortunate reprobate was in extreme need of elevation.

This was the last trip a man could take before becoming an eighth-class convict, the last on Arthur's scale – an unnecessary classification, as the unlucky recipients of this honour had long since perished, treading air.

But if Porter understood the calculations that would see him rise or fall, he didn't seem to care. Perhaps he saw it all as a game and was unafraid to roll the dice. Like many convicts under Arthur's system, Porter might have grown sick of its arbitrary nature, dominated as it was by masters, magistrates and other authority figures with their own agendas. Beyond this, there was the luck of the draw in the assignment system: a well-behaved convict could find himself at the whim of a tyrant who had no interest in his redemption, while a rogue convict could do anything he liked while working for a weaker master.

The system worked for many, but it was never considered fair. Arthur allowed arresting police officers to be given a percentage of any fine from a conviction. These officers, many of them convicts, were under the control of magistrates in charge of sentencing. It skewed the system towards conviction. Once judgements have a value, a fair and just system is impossible. Arthurian justice could be rorted at every turn.

Porter may have hated that small infractions, or even the whiff of suspicion, could heavily counter-weigh against years of obedience. He'd seen men benefit from a fellow prisoner's downfall. Arthur had created a convict class system whereby self-elevation depended partly on betraying others, and Porter wasn't having a bar of it. Of course, he was no angel and seemed to live for dodging, diving and larking about. He was naturally adept at seizing opportunities, particularly those of an illicit nature. And yet he was living in an informant's paradise – rewards flowed for those who did the accusing, fairly or otherwise. Porter was no snitch – and proclaimed that he abhorred others who were, but there may have been many wolves in sheep's clothing who might easily snitch on him.

Many, like Porter, would find that the snakes were many and varied and extremely slippery. Even when they went straight, the system worked against them. The rungs on the ladders, meanwhile, were heavily greased, and Porter knew it. But he could not help himself. In the end, he always seemed to infringe in some form or another. He simply could not work with this system.

That said, Porter somehow managed to avoid serious sanction in his first four years as a convict. It may have been that Captain Welsh protected him or had sway among the prosecuting magistrates. Perhaps the work Porter did was deemed important enough for some minor acts of rebellion or petty crimes to be overlooked. Through it all, he was always returned to the government boat crew.

But in 1828, he slipped again. One of his crew was caught stealing wooden boards to make a seachest; in Porter's memoir, he claims that he took the blame. The young crewman was only ten days from completing his sentence, and Porter surmised that if he said the theft was all his doing and endured the punishment, the newly freed thief might help him. As a debt of honour, the young man could arrange a whaleboat for Porter's escape. The lad apparently swore on the Bible that he would.

Of course, we'll never know if Porter was actually implicated in the robbery, but swapping a guilty plea for a chance at freedom indicates either supreme stupidity or sheer desperation. 'The ungrateful wretch whom I thus sacrificed myself for never came near me,' Porter wrote. Porter had been (in the convict parlance of the time) 'bridged' – thrown over a bridge – deceived. He was back in chains and, from the tone of his memoir, at his wit's end. He could handle pain, hardship, punishment and destitution. But not servitude. He could no longer handle the chain gangs. All he wanted was his freedom.

*

AT SOME POINT the next year, Porter made another desperate attempt at freedom. Police No. 324 was now a fifth-class convict in chains. Still obsessed with the notion of finding a whaleboat, he concocted a new scheme: this time he would orchestrate a mass breakout, not take a lonely vigil. Porter's plan wasn't particularly inventive, but he was following the only course he and others of his kind knew – to get themselves somehow or another to Bruny Island, keep as well out of sight as humanly possible, and wait for a sympathetic whaler.

On the appointed night, all seemed set. But when the time came for the breakout, James Porter's crew backed out. Porter, never afraid to try his luck, decided to go solo after all. His first move was to push the watchman off the bank and bolt as quickly as possible to the river. Men came howling after him, but Porter knew he had one advantage: most soldiers couldn't swim. Leaving them shouting at the riverbank, he jumped in, leg-irons still attached. He swam steadily out and was soon lost amid the swirl of the river. Halfway across, he thought he'd made a clean break until he saw a boat pursuing him. When the boat had passed he doubled back towards the town, crossing just behind government house, dripping and reeking of river mud.

Porter says that while he slipped through the back streets, he was recognised. He was pursued again and, with no other idea what to do, headed for the home of a fellow mariner, Mr Mansfield, a harbour pilot and one of the few who might shelter him. How Porter says he evaded pursuers seems impossible. Still in leg-irons, and chafing badly around his ankles and shins, he could only move at a fraction of his natural speed. But apparently with luck, he made it to Mansfield's door. The older man received him genially, with no hint that he knew Porter was on the run. Mariners weren't the type to ask too many questions. Fugitive or not, Porter was given supper and a bed for the night.

A surreal episode ensued. Porter was to sleep with one of Mansfield's two sons, who made room in his bed for the still-dripping convict. If Porter took his clothes off, he knew that the boy would see the irons attached to his legs. Porter elected to stay clothed, wet and dirty. Sometime during the night, the boy was scratched by the metal rings. Porter awoke to find his trousers pulled up from the ankles and two boys standing over him with a candle, staring in awe at the rings lashed to his calves.

Porter says that he told them the truth. The boys, perhaps half-afraid of the escaped convict, said they would alert nobody – not even their father. They would even let their pet mastiff keep guard of the house, so that if anybody approached, Porter would know.

By dawn, Police No. 324 was back on the run with a new plan. He would make for the signal station where he knew another likely lad who might help him out.

That was a mistake. Arthur had offered a £50 reward for bringing convicts in, and Porter's 'mate' attempted to take him prisoner. While the lad reached for his musket, Porter felled him with the pole of an axe. Porter says he had 'a great mind to settle him' but resisted finishing the job.

As a destination for escapees, there was always the lime burners' camp at Oyster Cove, a crossing point for Bruny Island, in the bush about twenty miles to the south-west of Hobart. Perhaps the men there, Porter thought, would be just like himself, and sympathetic to his plight. Porter's plan was to make it on foot, steal a boat and wait for a passing whaleship to weigh anchor at Bruny. It would be a long run through some of the heaviest and most difficult terrain around Hobart Town.

Porter may have known the sea, but on land he was at a loss. The dense, untrammelled bush south of Hobart provided good cover, but he was soon disoriented. Three days after leaving Hobart, he stumbled by chance on a dead kangaroo only recently mauled by dogs. There, he 'took a hearty meal of the raw flesh and blood of the kangaroo'. He described it as 'refreshing but insipid'.

Eventually he made it to camp where two men were burning the middens and shells left by Aboriginal people and converting it into lime. The men were sympathetic. He was finally able to strike off his irons with their help.

The next day, while he sought a dinghy, a party of soldiers fired on him. As the bullets flew, he again made for the only cover that worked for him: the water. Few were willing to follow him into the river. Halfway across, he took hold of a clump of kelp and, aided by the incoming tide, drifted slowly towards Bruny Island. Exhausted, shivering and hungry, he had made it to his destination.

Porter's luck was still holding – but only just. Again, he needed to rely on a mate. He made his way to a convict he knew on the island whose master, Richard Pybuss, happened to be away. Porter remained there for nine days before his chance came. Porter says a vessel was anchored at Blubber Bay, which was probably Esperance Point (known locally as Blubber Head) to take on whale oil and was bound for London. Porter says he tried on several occasions to swim to the vessel but was thwarted by the raging surf.

In between Porter's attempts to board the vessel, Pybuss returned and immediately recognised the runaway. Porter was back on his heels, this time to another part of the island. The next day he awoke to the sound of rowers nearby. At the front of their boat was Pybuss, on his way to notify the authorities about Porter.

Porter had to work out a new plan. Waving to Pybuss to take him on, he was 'arrested', taken on board the boat, and placed at the bow: 'all of a sudden I snatched the Boathook off the thwart and requested him in a menacing attitude to land me at the Bluff. He remonstrated with me, saying he would lose all his government men if I compelled him to land me.'

Porter then told Pybuss to hand him over to a cutter that was passing nearby. He would try to escape from that instead. Taken prisoner on board, Porter waited his chance. When the crew wasn't looking as the ship went about, he jumped over the stern. Nobody saw him bail out – James Porter had wriggled free again.

But if he had been chancing his luck, it had now run out. Not long afterwards, staying at yet another man's house, he was picked up by constables. His latest 'mate' had given him up and claimed the £50 reward.

Porter had slipped down the final snake. There were now too many black marks in Police No. 324's ledger. He was tried on 30 January 1830 for being 'illegally at large while under a second conviction' and was sentenced to be hanged.

Chapter 5

WHILE JAMES PORTER was in gaol contemplating the inevitable, the man who had looked out for him over the previous five years was arguing for the young man's life. But even Captain Welsh knew that he couldn't bring Porter back into his fold this time. The best the veteran mariner could do was attest to the lad's good character once more. What he said on Porter's behalf wasn't recorded, but it must have been creative: Porter's convict conduct record clearly shows that good behaviour hadn't come naturally to him for most of the previous four years.

The judge must have deliberated for some time, as Porter was forced to sit glumly for weeks in gaol, no doubt expecting to be taken at any moment from that place and hanged.

However, when the call finally came, it wasn't for the prison gallows but a return visit to the Supreme Court in Murray Street. The beak who had so recently pronounced Porter's death sentence now proclaimed that it had been commuted. Porter was off the hook yet again, but this time it was debatable if it was in his better interests. He was sentenced to serve seven years with the incorrigible, irredeemable and depraved: he was going to Macquarie Harbour.

Porter was immediately sent back to gaol to await the next transport ship. A week or so later, he found himself being fitted into a set of heavier chains and snatched roughly from his dark cell by two soldiers. He was now officially a seventh-class convict, and the soldiers escorting him knew it. He even looked the part. As a secondary offender, he was in the 'harlequin uniform', which consisted of alternating sections of yellow and black. Yellow was the colour of disgrace, and the men who wore it were 'canary men'. This was all part of the humiliation. As far as his guards and the rest of their world were concerned, Macquarie Harbour started now. Men like Porter could be abused with virtual impunity – under Arthur's system, they had been shorn of all rights. Frogmarched directly to the docks in his suit of shame, Porter was pushed and prodded towards an old transport ship, the *Prince Leopold*.

The smells, tastes, sights and sounds of the bustling little entrepôt town would all be left behind. Part of the torture Porter was about to experience was a sensory deprivation, designed to commence well before he arrived in western Tasmania. There would be no more beer and biscuits, pies and pork sandwiches. Tobacco was banned. He wouldn't taste a fresh cup of tea or a bracing tot of rum for seven years. There would be no women.

The man who'd once claimed to be a first-class mechanic was jerked up the gangplank like a dog, led past the boat's mizzen mast and down to the gun deck. It was dark there, but Porter would be kept deeper, down two more flights of stairs into the ship's nethermost regions. He was practically thrown in the pitch-black hold, where he was chained at the feet and tethered to the wall. He was kept alongside the food stores and stone ballast. It was an aquatic version of solitary confinement, with only brief interludes of supervised freedom to take in the ocean air.

In the lower holds of a convict transport ship, men would be forced to subsist in a swill of excrement, urine and dirty bilge water. There was often very little light, and fresh air and water were in short supply. On the *Prince Leopold*, Porter was lucky to be left to his own devices, far from the stench of fellow prisoners. But this solitude also had its drawbacks – a man can only contemplate his own existence in a perpetual dusk while soaking in his own shit and piss for so long.

The worse the weather, the more unconscionable the voyage of a convict ship. The hold was shaken about and its contents strewn everywhere. Self-protection was impossible, because convicts could barely move. The irons around their calves were heavily riveted, and a chain linked the manacle on each leg. A convict thus trussed needed a bar or stick to lift the chain and allow the slightest of forward shuffles.

One consignment of prisoners was shipped to Macquarie Harbour with a load of tin. The sheets of metal arrived in an unusable state; they'd taken up so much space that the convicts had nowhere else to urinate. On another trip to Macquarie Harbour, thirty-five convicts endured a winter voyage with the sum total of four blankets. One of the men was found to be wearing nothing but a shirt; he had been sent over semi-naked, and had somehow survived. Like the tin in the hold, the convicts were just freight.

In his memoir Porter says his journey from Hobart to Macquarie Harbour was marked by 'dreadful weather', which would have made life in the hold close to unbearable. In truth, however, he had it relatively easy. The journey took just over two weeks, whereas difficult voyages could take more than three months. Sailing west and south-west against both the wind and currents in the Southern Ocean, the ships had to cover the two hundred nautical miles from Hobart Town. Exposed to the rough Antarctic weather and enormous swells, it was a coastline where many a ship had been brought undone by hazardous reefs and unpredictable currents.

On the sixteenth day after leaving Hobart, the *Prince Leopold* rounded the rocky coast south of Macquarie Harbour and came to rest at the sandbar, where it awaited a pilot boat that would guide it to shore. Macquarie Harbour was a man-made prison encircled by a natural one, with geography that made both entry a challenge and exit as good as impossible. Ships had to be threaded through the harbour's narrow headlands: twin bluffs sardonically named Hells Gates. These span a mere seventy yards across. So the ships couldn't cross the sandbar without the help of a pilot boat, high tide and suitably calm conditions. Sometimes they would have to wait days to pass safely. At low tide, the water depth was a mere one and a half fathoms, or about nine feet; as the tide went out, a tidal current – fed by the Gordon River at the far end of the harbour – flowed strongly against all incoming vessels.

When Porter's brig finally slipped through Hells Gates, a vast harbour opened up. It wasn't quite the wilderness it had been when operations had begun eight years earlier. The pilot's house, south-west of Hell's Gates, served both as a lookout for incoming boats and a signal house to the authorities further along the harbour, where there was a military detachment and a number of small houses.

The geography of the harbour remains as it was. At the bottom of the headland still runs an abandoned beach, and beyond that the ubiquitous hinterland: a green, featureless barrier of trees. This leads to the cold, wet uplands that encircle the harbour, which in turn lead to thickly wooded mountain ranges and strong-flowing rivers. Most prominent of all features is Frenchmans Cap, a bald-headed and often snow-capped mountain standing like a beacon above the tangle of green.

The water in the harbour is the colour of black tea, brackish reddish-brown, stained by tannins flowing in from the Gordon. Some writers of the time believed the water looked as if it 'were forever stained with blood' and surmised that fish venturing into the harbour would be poisoned, but this was part of the propaganda that permeated the place. Fish of all types flourished in Macquarie Harbour as did flocks of swans. It was the men who found it difficult to thrive.

Guided by the pilot boat for the first stage up the river, the *Prince Leopold* sailed up the harbour past two small islands into calmer waters. About three nautical miles into the voyage it would then sail itself, rounding Wellington Head and, a little later, Liberty Point. Within half an hour, the ship was in view of Sarah Island, also known as Settlement Island, where there were barracks, a penitentiary, and a number of makeshift workshops and dwellings. It was a small but busy-looking island, less than two miles in length, which the convicts had completely denuded of all vegetation. It had one distinguishing feature: several heavily buttressed long boards or palisades had been erected behind the shipyards, around twenty feet in height. The palisades acted as a break on the raging westerlies that blew across the harbour, and also lent the island a military aspect, as if prisoners were about to enter a fortress of no return.

GEORGE ARTHUR NEVER visited Macquarie Harbour, but he had his own idea of the type of convicts he sent there. The law classed them all as secondary offenders, but to him they were simply 'delirious'. Those who didn't subscribe to his perfectly balanced system of social calibration were mentally sick. As he put it, they saw things 'through a false medium' that required extreme treatment. Arthur prescribed a bracing dose of *'enlightened rigour'*.

But 'rigour' isn't a strong enough word to describe what was demanded by Macquarie Harbour of its captives. And when looking at the prison's first incarnation, it's also difficult to see where the 'enlightened' part came in. It began as a sinkhole at the bottom of the Earth, where men killed each other for scraps of food and the commandant danced to the beat of desperate souls being flogged. It was, in its mid-1820s heyday, indisputably the most dreaded of Britain's penal stations. By 1830, it was still a brutal place, which demanded total obedience and afforded little comfort to its prisoners.

There was something ironic about the 'enlightened rigour' that Porter was about to experience, because it needed to be cloaked in darkness. He and his fellow convicts weren't just geographically remote, but placed in a pen ring-fenced from society. Men could be kicked, beaten, insulted and whipped with impunity because this was deemed to have a civilising effect. In Macquarie Harbour – as in other remote colonial prisons, such as the French-run Devil's Island off the coast of South America – social norms and reasonable human interactions had no meaning.

These prisons in the middle of nowhere generated their own propaganda of woe, which authorities exploited. Politics demanded that society's waste matter should be far from contact but not from control – whatever was prescribed by the authorities could avoid both public attention and legal sanction. Fifty years after Macquarie Harbour's closure, when the Australian author Marcus Clarke wrote about it in his novel *For the Term of His Natural Life*, the dark mutterings about what went on there had barely died down. For decades, that part of Tasmanian history whispered but dared not speak its name.

Arthur had once written to colonial secretary Lord Stanley that in Van Diemen's Land 'coercive measures' had to be 'bounded by humanity'. 'If they are not,' he wrote, 'the criminals are driven into a state of mind bordering upon desperation.' This did not apply to Macquarie Harbour. There Arthur threw out his own rulebook.

'You will consider that the constant, active unremitting employment of every Individual convict in hard labour is the grand and main design of the settlement,' he wrote to the incoming commandant Lieutenant Wright in 1824. '[I]t must not only be felt, but considered by the whole Class of Convicts a place of such strict discipline that they may absolutely dread the idea of being sent there.'

Wright was told never to lose sight of a 'continued, rigid, unrelaxing discipline', and even the labour of digging holes for the sake of digging holes was deemed 'civilising' by Arthur. The lieutenant-governor felt so strongly about this that he sent a follow-up letter nine days letter, just in case Wright hadn't fully grasped his message. 'Unceasing labour, total deprivation of Spirits, Tobacco and comforts of every kind, the sameness of occupation, the dreariness of situation must, if anything will, reform the vicious characters who are sent to you,' he wrote.

Macquarie Harbour was a case of cruelty as policy.

*

ON ARRIVAL PORTER was sent directly to the commandant, Captain James Briggs, who immediately had Porter's clothes burnt. He was issued with a new set, this time all in yellow. 'I found him everything but a gentleman,' reports Porter. Briggs was yet another man in the Arthur mould. He didn't care for petty pleasantries, worshipped rank, and had some of the Arthurian-approved qualities of accuracy and unbending rigidity.

Briggs possessed that military trifecta that all officers desired of their charges: a combination of orderliness, subordination and hard work. He was said to have caused upset when he mandated that all the military personnel sit ahead of any ranking civil personnel in church. That was just the natural and right order of things, according to Briggs. The civil personnel soon boycotted Sunday services.

The convicts, too, knew their precise place in life, but they weren't able to boycott anything. Briggs had his most trustworthy prisoners working as tradesmen, carpenters and gardeners; they were described as billets and enjoyed various privileges, decent food and regular work hours. Life for them on the main settlement, was reasonable. Then there were the mid-tier working gangs who had a tough life felling and sawing timber but were considered reliable enough to live in camps on the mainland and to go fishing or trap kangaroos. Last on the commandant's ladder were men like Porter, who would head immediately to the outgangs, which did all the hardest work at the fringes of the settlement. These men were considered the most dangerous and suspicious – until proven otherwise – and were the most heavily supervised. They were rowed out to the mainland under soldier escort to perform the roughest job in the settlement: felling, hauling and rafting the Huon pine, the lifeblood of the harbour's rapidly growing shipbuilding industry.

Porter may have disembarked on Sarah Island but his home for the next two years was about 160 yards to the north, on a much smaller island between the main shore and Sarah. Grummet Island, also known as Small Island, was little more than a rocky outcrop covered in scrub. A steep path led from the shore to the summit, where sat a hut with four small rooms. Here all newcomers were chained together with the hardiest of old lags, the so-called 'out and outers', those whom Porter says were always 'straining every point to get away'.

There was nothing else on Grummet Island. Water and firewood had to be supplied daily, and the wood had to be green so that it couldn't float. It also didn't light properly, making winter colder than it needed to be. The hut was badly built and draughty, and often when

Painting of Sarah Island by convict artist William Buelow Gould. This painting is not correctly proportioned, but worth noting is the convict penitentiary to the far left (part of which still stands) and on a slope nearby, the dreaded triangle, with soldiers and a victim. Just below that are the ribs of a ship – the slips used to launch boats remain visible today.

a new batch of prisoners arrived, men were forced to sleep side-on as there wasn't enough room for them to lie on their backs.

By the time Porter turned up, the shipbuilding industry in Macquarie Harbour was gathering pace. The British, as ever, had found good commercial reasons to keep the harbour running. It was a natural source of Huon pine as well as a number of other timbers suitable for constructing boats. Huon was among the world's best shipbuilding timbers; it doesn't rot at sea and is resistant to the *Teredo navalis*, a species of saltwater clam shaped like a red worm that tunnels into submerged timber hulls. It has been known to turn oak ship timbers into brittle honeycombs less than eight months after their first contact with sea water.

Macquarie Harbour was an intense microcosm of Van Diemen's Land. It had to be profitable – but, as it was also a penal colony, it had to be painful as well. The structure Briggs brought to everyday life, especially for out and outers like Porter, reflected this.

*

PORTER COULD NEVER get used to the brutal monotony of everyday life and sometimes he couldn't sleep simply for the dread of it. It wasn't just the obvious privations, but also the nature of his tasks, which seemed never to end. Each day was a replica of the last. It began with the rouse before dawn, then the insipid breakfast of gruel that he swallowed not by choice but necessity. This was followed by a walk across the beach straight into icy water – there was no landing stage at Grummet Island. Each Grummet Islander, under military supervision, waded onto a launch to the morning muster at Sarah Island. There Porter and company would be hauled into line to be searched. Wet from the waist down, they suffered the daily indignity of a full-body search, the soldiers looking for anything that might aid a convict in escape – including food.

Porter saw tiny bits of bread and biscuit confiscated. So-called sea biscuits were considered serious contraband because it was believed that they could keep a man on the run for days. Fishhooks, too, were outlawed – a man who could fish was a man who could survive. Indeed, anyone caught with a fishhook or a knife would be immediately served with fifty lashes. The gruel was designed to keep the men working, but only just; known as 'skilly', it was little more than a bland and insipid pudding of salt, flour and water. On it, the Grummet Islanders had to row ten nautical miles to the mainland and work the entire day.

By sunrise, Porter and his men were suffering from this arduous voyage, the first of the day's exertions. Sweat poured from them in the summer; their teeth chattered in the winter. The seasons didn't change their routine – only the most severe weather would ever grant them a reprieve. The winds on the harbour came straight out of the west, direct from the Southern Ocean. Even Porter, who was known to be able to survive extremely cold water, had trouble with the elements at Macquarie Harbour. So hard did the winds blow that Sarah Island had to be walled and buttressed against the elements to help men survive their exposure.

Each morning, once the men had made it to the mainland, they were expected to cut the Huon pine trees with rude axes and cross saws. The Huon pine is among the most beautiful and elderly of Tasmanian trees, some of which are more than three thousand years old, so if there was any respite for Porter and his men, it may have been in the wood itself. Huon has a pale straw-like colour when first

The Huon Pine was relentlessly logged for shipping at Macquarie Harbour and was renowned not just for its malleability but its ability to resist decay at sea. It was considered by master shipbuilder David Hoy as the world's finest wood for building ships.

cut, which deepens in time to a mixture of amber and gold. It's a soft wood known for its oiliness and perfumed sap. Its high oil content makes it one of nature's most malleable woods; it's relatively easy to bend, shape and work with.

Porter and the gang's next task was physically the most demanding. If the trees were reasonably pliant to the axe or saw, they were also extremely heavy. Those rolling the logs were armed with can hooks and handspikes, and with these crude tools they were asked to shift logs along a makeshift road. The branches were lopped off and cut into lengths that could be feasibly moved. Some of the bigger trees were sixteen feet in circumference and weighed in at twelve tons. The men levered them down to the riverbanks, where they were lashed together with chains to make rafts. Waist-deep in icy water, the men worked in body-numbing conditions. If a chain broke and a log drifted off, they had to retrieve it, haul it back and re-harness it.

And as the men sawed, hauled logs and swam, they were in chains.

Their work was tough, but their greatest misery lay in the lack of food. They were engaged for twelve hours with few breaks. By sunset they hadn't eaten since morning, but the physical demands of their day hadn't ended – they still had to row back to Grummet Island, this time against the prevailing wind.

While Arthur may have believed this kind of work was the path to sublime mental health, for outgang workers like Porter, the daily experiences were, in his own words, nothing but 'misery, flogging and starvation'. The results of constant hard labour and lack of nourishment were turning men homicidal and suicidal. In his memoir, Porter recounts the story of a man killed for saving his evening bread to enjoy with his gruel the next day: 'I knew two men to be executed for knocking a man's brains out (on this very island in question) for the sake of a bit of bread he had concealed under his head when in bed, and divided it between them with the blood of their victim on it (this my gentle reader will give you a faint idea of the acute sufferings of an unhappy captive).'

Porter was given to exaggerations – according to him there were two to three murders a month, but in its eleven-year life as a penal station, less than a dozen murders were recorded at Macquarie

Harbour. Porter also claims that six out of every ten men at the harbour had been lashed. It may be true, but can't be substantiated. It is known that the lash was being used far less by commandants from about the late 1820s onwards.

The historical record shows that men did kill as a means of removing themselves from the penal station, but many of these occurred before Porter's time. The convicts called this 'having a slant' – committing crimes in order to be removed from a situation they could not handle. Some simply gave up and took the easiest route out of the place, murdering without cause or provocation, a guaranteed ticket to the gallows in Hobart Town – a man could not be tried and hanged at Macquarie Harbour. One convict named Trennan attempted to stab a fellow inmate with a knife. It was his form of suicide. Asked why he didn't drown himself, he said the two things were completely different: 'If I kill myself I shall immediately go to hell, but if I kill another man I would be sent to Hobart Town and hanged for the offence. The parson would attend me, and I would be sure of going to heaven.'

Another convict struck an axe into the head of a fellow inmate because there was no tobacco in the harbour. He said he'd rather die than go through life without smoking. In Hobart Town, waiting to be hanged, he felt sure he would be able to have a last smoke.

Porter may not have seen these deaths, but he makes it clear that he understood why they happened. 'So bad was the treatment (that if a man was prepared for a future state) death was preferable,' he states in his memoir.

In some cases, it was food – or the enforced lack of it – that turned mild-mannered men into murderers. John Onely was killed for refusing to supply David McGee with the slush from the top of the meat boiler. McGee attacked him with a crutch, while George Driver pinned down Onely's hands. Samuel Higgins finished the job by cutting Onely's throat. One man had been set upon by three for not handing over a few ounces of gristle. In January 1828, Driver and Higgins were executed on the public scaffold in Hobart Town.

Then there was the corporal punishment, meted out for the smallest of infractions. Porter himself was treated to twenty-five lashes for a very strange offence: 'not taking care of some tobacco'. It can only be presumed that he had lost, sold or smoked it.

*

IN THE EARLY days of the penal colony, when it was opened in 1822, the lash was doled out often and in horrifying quantities. In fact, Porter was relatively lucky to have arrived when he did.

The most sadistic of the commandants who ran Macquarie Harbour was undoubtedly its first. Lieutenant John Cuthbertson was a veteran of the Iberian Peninsula War against Napoleon. His regiment, the 48th, was one of the toughest in the British Army, nicknamed the 'Steelbacks'. This wasn't a reference to their spirit or bravery but to their penchant for corporal punishment: the officers flogged their soldiers so hard and so often that their backs were a mass of scar tissue. They devised a whip heavier than that used by the army and the navy, flecked with lead. It was employed in the penal settlement and became known as the Macquarie Cat.

Cuthbertson's inimitable style was to tap out the strokes. The flagellator would watch the movement of his commandant's feet, whipping the unfortunate as the shoe stepped right and then left. Cuthbertson danced to the lash of the cat.

When the convict John Mason cut off two of his own fingers, Cuthbertson charged him with depriving the government of his labour – even self-mutilation carried a fifty-lash sentence.

Usually the prisoner was stripped to the waist and suspended by the wrists beneath a wooden tripod known as 'the triangle'. On some occasions the whipped man's feet barely touched the ground, so his skin could be made even tauter and the damage inflicted, greater. It also made the offender's weight gravitate to his shoulders, magnifying his pain.

In 1843, in memoranda addressed to the superintendent of Norfolk Island, a convict named Davis recounted the story of William Holliday, who was whipped by the Macquarie Cat. Holliday was apparently in a sickly condition when he was sent to the harbour's hospital but had somehow caused the doctor's displeasure. He was brought before the military court for 'endeavouring to impose on the Doctor'. While still unwell, he was found guilty and sentenced to fifty lashes. According to Davis he was taken to the triangle to receive them, pleading 'very hard to be forgiven on the score of illness'. Davis describes it thus:

> He was tied up and punishment whent on admist the most Heart rendering screams and cries for Mercy but his appeals was made to men that never forgave a Lash – after 30 Lashes he never spoke when he had received 5 more, the superintendant of convicts returned submisively to observe that he thought the man had fainted. The Doctor then stept of the gangway and found that he was quite dead how long he had been dead no one knew the murmers amongst the men say that he received 5 lashes after his Death but the affair ended without A question being Askd.

*

ALTHOUGH PORTER AND his fellow inmates didn't have to endure the early days of the settlement, when men like Cuthbertson held sway, their desire to escape was still overpowering. But the one subject that meant anything to them was discussed in low tones, well away from the ears of authorities.

After twelve months' hard labour on Grummet, Porter had come through and survived. He was 'promoted' to Sarah, but his spirit hadn't been broken and he didn't grow submissive. All the same, the positive change in circumstances didn't bring on a similar change in attitude. Not long afterwards, he was given three weeks on bread and water – of which nine days were remitted – for 'leaving his work contrary to orders'.

Five weeks later, he would yet again throw caution to the wind. He just couldn't take it anymore. James Porter was about to go back on the run.

Chapter 6

PORTER WOKE BEFORE DAWN, ate his gruel and joined seventeen men. They were checked for the usual contraband, then led onto the launch, escorted by two soldiers who took up their usual positions at each end of the boat. For the next two hours, they were straining at the oars, heading towards the timber camp at Kelly Basin at the eastern end of the harbour.

As they approached the shoreline at Kelly Basin, Porter's eyes moved from James Sheedy to William Holt. At fifty yards from shore, the three of them could hear the shouts of woodsmen behind a wall of trees. One of the trees cracked, tottered and hit the ground with a thump. But there were other things on Porter's mind as the launch approached land. In just a few moments, he and his mates would be causing havoc. If the job was done right and done quickly, it meant liberty. A few yards from the shoreline, he nodded almost imperceptibly to his accomplices.

The three men leapt up at lightning speed, brandishing the axes they had secreted under the boat's planks. Before the two corporals on board had clocked their movements, all three were upon them, waving weapons at two paces. The corporals sat transfixed, their mouths agape, like stunned mullets caught somewhere between surprise and dismay. Before they knew it, they were relieved of their firearms.

The other convict gang members, fast realising what was playing out, looked on with bemusement. They neither hindered nor helped. Maybe they hadn't been in on this one, but it was far more entertaining than the usual daily fare. They all knew Porter, Sheedy and Holt weren't dangerous. So they remained in their seats, watching the lark play out. You had to give Porter and his men their due: they looked desperate enough, risking death for liberty. In a very short time, these three men had wrested control of the boat and its seventeen occupants from their dumbstruck captors.

The boat was now just offshore, and Porter jumped out. Keeping a hold of it with one hand, he ordered Sheedy to pass him the two Brown Bess muskets. Sheedy grabbed them while Holt screamed at the other convicts to deliver up any remaining oars and tools. Within a few seconds, the whole collection was piled on the beach. Holt and Sheedy, their jobs done, now jumped out, joining Porter at the water's edge.

With a heavy push, they heaved the launch, still with its soldiers and crew aboard, back out into the harbour. They watched it intently until it sat there motionless, thirty yards out. Porter had at least thought this one through – water was his greatest ally. None of the soldiers or convicts could swim, and nobody on board would have any tools to row or steer the boat. The final part of the scheme had gone to plan: the boat had been successfully stranded, with its crew and soldiers drifting helplessly on the water. With a bit of luck the three men would now make good headway before anybody could signal back to the settlement for reinforcements.

Porter looked up at his next destination. As he recalls in his memoir, he would make for 'Sugarloaf Mountain' – likely to have been present-day Mount Sorell – and from there he would have a bird's-eye view of all the traffic sailing up and down the harbour. It was the best vantage point for the three men to plot their escape, or so Porter says.

Without so much as a thought, they bolted into the bush. Porter was living his dream, but he knew that facing armed troops was just the first of many risks. His plan was to find a boat, take it to the mouth of the Gordon at the south-eastern end of the harbour, and row as far upriver as possible. All the while he would have to keep out of sight of the logging gangs that dotted the riverside. When the waters were no longer navigable, he and his companions would ditch the boat, leave the river, and head east then finally south-east to the settled areas.

*

PORTER'S WAS A well-worn route for a number of escapees. Others had struck north or west of the harbour by foot, plunging into the thick mountain woodlands before eventually striking the same eastward path. There was another option: they could sail under the nose of the harbour pilot, who kept a tight watch at Hells Gates. But this required an expertise and level of planning beyond Porter, Sheedy and Holt. You needed a favourable wind and the right tide to escape, and a bevy of men, all of whom knew how to sail. In ten years only one boat had escaped that way.

Any fugitive from Macquarie Harbour, no matter how accustomed they were to the open-air prison, would be entering a new form of trial – a trial by natural ordeal. Running overland involved extreme exertion, and almost certain starvation and exposure. There were stories of barely recognisable men-skeletons emerging from months half-naked in the bush, their clothes rotted by the heavy rains, their bare feet wounded by thorns and roots. Even those few who had reached the settled east had been captured at some stage. Escape in the Van Diemen's Land hinterland reduced men to total wretchedness, but it was a gamble Porter was willing to take.

He couldn't have known that of the one hundred and fifty escape attempts from Macquarie Harbour, fewer than ten were successful in reaching settled districts. From 1822 to 1828, around one in eight men made a run for it mostly striking north overland before making their way to settled country in the east and south. Many of them were never heard of again.

There was James Woodward, once the chief baker at Sarah Island, who absconded with a load of flour. He vanished without a trace. The brothers Philip and Michael Flanagan, who were sent to Sarah for stealing canvas bags, also tried their luck. They, too, were lost to history.

Some of the escapes would be pathetic if they weren't so desperate and brave. In February 1827, three men escaped from Grummet Island on a raft made from two water casks, a night tub and a portion of a water closet. The raft broke up and all crew were drowned. Other convicts became experts at manufacturing home-made coracles, which were at least watertight. Most were made of branches lashed together with bark and covered with hide, tar or canvas. The penalties for making a coracle were extremely severe, but many were secreted all around the harbour.

Who was successful? In March 1828 James Goodwin and Thomas Connelly hollowed out a Huon pine log to make a canoe. They rowed it up the Gordon until they could go no further, abandoned the canoe, and headed inland to the central highlands. They kept Frenchmans Cap to their right, to keep away from the river systems and mountain ranges.

Goodwin and Connelly had several things going for them. They had managed to store about twenty-five pounds of salted beef and ten pounds of bread. Goodwin had a compass as well as fishhooks and a line. On one occasion they pointed sticks at natives, who believed they were aiming rifles at them and fled, dropping a freshly killed possum. Such was the luck of Goodwin and Connelly.

Once they reached the central highlands, they headed south-east. James Goodwin was eventually recaptured around Ouse, about a day's walk from Hobart – but Thomas Connelly was never caught. Goodwin was employed by the surveyor general for his unique first-hand knowledge of the western wilderness and afterwards received a pardon. It was clear from his survival that Goodwin knew something of bushcraft. James Porter, a seaman to his bones, did not.

Goodwin and Connelly's story was well known, but they weren't the most famous escapees. There was the bold and handsome Lancastrian forger Matthew Brady who escaped the penal settlement by sea, and the Irishman Alexander Pearce, who apparently took extreme measures to stay alive as he made his way to the outskirts of Hobart Town. These two men couldn't have been more different from each other.

In 1824 Brady and thirteen men stole a whaleboat from Phillip Island, where most of the farming was done in the harbour, and nonchalantly headed towards Hells Gates. When the harbour pilot,

James Lucas, became suspicious, he pursued them out through the heads and gave chase for days.

Brady was lucky: the boat slipped through the heads in the outrushing ebb tide, and was being skippered by a former navy lieutenant. It had been constructed in the convict style, using the canvas of their mattresses for sails, but it worked. Lucas hunted them relentlessly on the high seas, but Brady and his men gave him the slip.

Brady made it to the east coast, and not long afterwards began his career terrorising settlers across the hinterland. For the next two years, the bushranger became famous for exacting his own form of justice. When Brady raided a house, his first move was to ask the assigned convict if he was well treated. If so, his master was only 'lightly' robbed; if otherwise, Brady would be merciless. He was kind and generous to women, the elderly and those in need. Brady was a bushranger with standards. When his cohort James McCabe tried to assault a woman, Brady shot him in the hand, flogged him and threw him out of the gang.

When Arthur advertised a reward of twenty-five guineas for Brady's capture, the bushranger responded by sending out his own flyer, mimicking Arthur's style and use of language: 'It has caused Matthew Brady much concern that such a person known as Sir George Arthur is at large. Twenty gallons of rum will be given to any person that will deliver this person to me.'

Brady was almost a living god among the convicts, and many believed he would deliver them from their bondage. In early 1826, Brady's 'Army of Light' was rumoured to be on its way to Macquarie Harbour, his bush 'banditti' marching west over the mountains for their mates' salvation. Even the commandant believed that Brady and his men had set up a supply depot at Frenchmans Cap in preparation for an attack, such was the reputation of the gentleman bushranger. Brady had apparently talked of rescuing his comrades in Macquarie Harbour – but nothing came of it.

When later that year the news found its way to the harbour that Brady had been caught and hanged in May, an intense silence fell among the prisoners. For days they walked around with their heads bowed. Laughter was banned. Their one and only hero had been taken down. Several days later, the authorities on Sarah saw that Grummet was alight with flames. Fearing the worst, a small military detachment made its way over. They didn't find a rebellion but a bonfire: the convicts were holding a wake for the man who exemplified, more than any, the motto 'Liberty or Death'. Those responsible for this chicanery were summarily flogged the next day.

In the case of Irish convict Alexander Pearce, there would be no such reverence. In September 1822, Pearce escaped with seven men, taking the overland route – they ditched their stolen whaleboat at the last navigable part of the Gordon River and headed for the east coast.

Within two weeks, driven by hunger, they had killed the weakest member of the gang and eaten him. Within five weeks Pearce had been party to consuming all seven men. The absconders had become so desperate for food that they resorted to the seaman's tradition of casting lots to select a man to be eaten. When it came down to the last two men, it was a case of whoever fell asleep first.

Pearce survived 113 days in the bush, then was captured near Hobart and sent back to Macquarie Harbour. He admitted his crimes – but without any evidence, nobody believed him.

After bolting again, this time with just one companion in November 1823, Pearce was recaptured. This time, the evidence was clear. A lump of his companion's flesh was found in his pocket. The body was discovered nearby. The man had been gutted and dismembered, his entrails and organs hanging from a nearby tree.

Pearce was held up as living proof of Arthur's delirium thesis, and the newspapers made much of the man's vile and base character. Pearce, they said, had deliberately taken out a younger man to 'banquet on his flesh!'.

But to the convicts at Macquarie Harbour, it was probably no surprise that Pearce had resorted to such depravity. It was simply another warning about their chances of survival out there. Pearce had been compelled to eat human flesh in order to reach his destination. Such was the desire for freedom that many were at the point where death by snakes, savages or hunger – or survival by cannibalism – was better than the living death of Macquarie Harbour.

*

PORTER, AS WAS his wont, appeared to be confident, but he knew what was ahead. As he said in his memoirs, he and the two men would, 'walk over land to headquarters (Hobart Town) tho' we had two great risks to run, the one of being starved to death as many have been, and the other of being killed by the natives, the blacks, as they were very numerous about the south-west cape'.

Porter fully subscribed to the notion that anything was preferable to Macquarie Harbour. 'So strong was this feeling,' he says in his memoir, 'that I was fully determined to gain my point or perish in the attempt.'

The biggest problems for Porter weren't so much venomous snakes and hostile natives, but exposure and starvation. James Goodwin and Thomas Connelly had lived on mushrooms, grassroots and berries after their food supplies had run out. But this hadn't been enough to nourish them properly – they were capable of walking no more than two to three miles a day on this wild food. They'd also fashioned nails into hooks, hoping that they could fish from streams and rivers as they progressed.

Then there was the terrain. The best way to travel in the wilderness between Macquarie Harbour and Hobart was along the top ridges of the mountains, but this was a painstaking route. The parallel mountains run north to south, not east to west, and are separated by enormous ravines that drop steeply into thunderous torrents. It was all so different to the gentle European landscapes where convicts had been born and raised. Scottish-born playwright David Burn, who was part of an official overland trek from Hobart Town to Macquarie Harbour a decade later, found it difficult to describe the 'tenantless wilderness': 'There were no landmarks, no spot of terror or renown, not even a shepherd's cot is to be found to give an impress to the features whereby succeeding tourists may call identical localities to immediate recognition.'

Porter's plans were neither brilliant nor new. Even though he'd managed to outwit the two soldiers guarding him, he would have known that a posse of troops, almost certainly accompanied by a tracker, would be at their heels within a day. He had to find a boat – perhaps a canoe or even a coracle – then use the many coves and bays around the harbour to hide from pursuers, before he and his companions went up the Gordon.

But at that very moment, at the top of a mountain, Porter, Sheedy and Holt were looking down at the scene below with some dismay. A military detachment was already coming to the rescue of the soldiers and outgangers stranded in the harbour. Smoke was billowing from Sarah Island, the standard harbour alert that a man was on the run. The three escapees would have to move quickly. The military would be sent out from Sarah and placed in strategic positions, cutting off all possible exits. Before Porter and the others could escape the soldiers' nets, they needed food. The plan from here was to raid the sawyers' camp at nearby Phillips Creek and pilfer as much as possible for the ongoing voyage.

According to Porter, that night they crept into and out of the sawyers' tents, stealing as much food as they could. They then hid these provisions on the beach while they swam over to Phillip Island just across the water. The next part of the plan involved finding the canoe that Phillip Island convicts used for illegal fishing expeditions. Porter doesn't record how they parted the Phillip Islanders from their craft but threats of violence were almost certainly part of it; all he says is that 'we made three men get up out of their beds and shew us where their canoe was'. However they contrived it, they soon had their boat.

By the next day, everyone in Macquarie Harbour knew three men were at large. Soldiers set up a sentinel around the area where the food had been stolen, with orders to shoot the escapees on sight. Porter and his accomplices sat out the day hidden behind water rushes on Phillip Island, watching the situation as it unfolded and waiting for their chance to recover the food on the opposite shore.

As dusk fell, they made their move, stealthily uncovering their food packages under the noses of the night watch. They were soon paddling cautiously upriver. Their next obstacle would be the logging men stationed at various points along the water, who were almost always loyal to the commandant.

That night the three men slept near a creek away from the main river to avoid detection. They carried on the next day, gliding easily up the slow-moving river that rarely kept a straight line. The Gordon crawls along at its lower levels, its waters the colour of dark tea. It has a number of curved, bow-like bends, which make it difficult for travellers to detect what's around the next turn.

Porter says that he and his accomplices were spotted while 'sweeping a deep bay to keep clear of a current'. Shouts came from men in a much larger launch. In a moment, Porter, Sheedy and Holt were paddling their little canoe desperately towards the nearest shore. Their pursuers were making good headway, as they had many more hands on deck: 'They got the weather gage [sic] of us and rushed us fairly on shore.'

With the larger boat approaching fast, the three convicts jettisoned the canoe on the banks of the Gordon and fled. Their pursuers were almost upon them. Dropping everything, the escapees ran into the dense bush with nothing to eat and little clothing. Porter, Sheedy and Holt were only two days into their freedom but already Commandant Briggs's men were closing in.

Chapter 7

THE THREE MEN had been scrambling around for two days and nights, and the bush was exacting its toll. The scrub runs deep around all parts of the river, so Porter and his two accomplices found themselves fighting interlaced bushes, fallen trees and clusters of vines that hung from everything. Thin, tightly packed saplings blocked the path. It was sheer old-style bushwhacking, made worse by the fact that everything was wet. They hacked their way up the right bank of the river, slipping and sloshing through the mud. It wasn't long before severe fatigue set in, as did the rains.

As Porter put it, 'nothing on but our shirts and trousers – and nothing but small fern around us which was of no service to keep us from the inclemency of the weather. Two nights and days we remained sensible to our acute sufferings when at last overcome with fatigue, hunger and cold, we lay down on some wet ferns.'

It was mid-December, but in western Tasmania that doesn't preclude very cold and wet nights. By the third night of freezing wind and rain, the convicts were suffering from exposure. 'We were laying close to each other,' Porter recounts. 'And what with despair and misery we fell into a sleep (as it were of death).'

Early on 15 December 1832, four days into their freedom run, they were startled awake by the firing of a musket overhead.

Porter looked up to see a posse of military men standing over him, rifles cocked and ready. It wasn't the first time he'd woken up to hovering soldiers – and it wouldn't be the last.

There was another man with them whom Porter recognised: John Little. Porter and his companions had been successfully tracked by a convict who knew the Gordon extremely well. This was, after all, still Arthur's world, where convicts were given licence and reward to hunt their peers. But although Porter had been done in by one of his own kind, he was beyond complaining. Dishevelled and demoralised, he may not have survived more than a few more nights in the bush.

Porter says that he and the other two men were so tired that they couldn't walk. They were literally carried in to see Commandant Briggs.

Porter passed out and then woke up in a dank, dark cell.

His convict record says he received the usual punishment: '100 lashes, six months in irons and two months imprisonment in gaol at night.' But according to Porter, he was actually given three hundred lashes, with a hundred to be meted out each Monday for three successive weeks.

He also says that the new commandant, Pery Baylee, had just arrived and was outraged by the severity of Briggs's punishment, especially after the men's ordeal in the bush. According to Porter, Baylee tried to reduce the number of lashes but Briggs apparently overruled him – then Porter and his cohorts each received two hundred lashes *the very next day.*

Briggs was in the process of being replaced by Baylee at the time of Porter's capture, so the exact number of lashes – and who ordered them – is a little confusing. That said, Porter was almost certainly exaggerating for the shock value. One hundred lashes would create a bloody mess of a man's back and were intended to destroy all resistance; two hundred lashes would be tantamount to murder. It is inconceivable that Porter, Sheedy and Holt could have survived a flogging of this magnitude.

*

Since the late 1820s, a not-so-subtle change had descended over Macquarie Harbour. As the importance of the shipyard took over, the once woebegone penal settlement was becoming less penal and more industrial. The heart of darkness that the whip-dancing Cuthbertson had wielded over in its earliest incarnation was now just a bad memory. Briggs had been tough, as had his predecessor James Butler, but since his arrival the Macquarie Cat had played less of a part in the punishments meted out. In fact, the records show a sharp decline in flogging from the late 1820s onwards. From 1826 to 1828, an average of 188 men were being flogged each year and an average of 6,280 lashes inflicted per annum – this converted to 33 lashes per man, per year, over that three-year period. By the years 1829–31, an average of just 56 men were lashed per annum at around 973 lashes each year, which equated to about 17 lashes per man. It was clear that by the late 1820s the penal station was inflicting far fewer lashes on far fewer men.

Compare this to the much earlier period of Cuthbertson and his Steelbacks. In 1823, 9,100 lashes were inflicted on 229 prisoners, and yet there were only 228 people in the station! Many must have been flogged twice or three times – it averages out to each man receiving 40 lashes that year.

Briggs was a convert to more modern forms of treating recalcitrance. Mental rather than physical punishment was increasingly preferred, meaning that more convicts were experiencing the woes of solitary confinement. It's worth noting that in the period of 1829–31, when the lashes doled out were fewer, the number of days of solitary confinement averaged 209 per year. Before 1829, the solitary cell, which was little more than an outhouse or shed, was used only on occasion.

By the time of Baylee's arrival in late 1832, both the lash and the cell were used infrequently. Baylee was said to be quite affable and even friendly with the convicts, walking around the settlement without guards. He was hardly your standard-issue British officer; indeed, he was an Irishman born in Limerick and of quite a different stamp to his predecessors. But things had been becoming more liberal, even under Briggs. When the Quaker missionary James Backhouse visited a few months earlier, in June 1832, he was startled by the atmosphere he found at the settlement. It was buoyant, almost optimistic, Backhouse wrote in a series of published letters, a place where industry and learning thrived.

Grummet Island, once the rock of death, murder and squalid misery, had been almost completely abandoned. The convicts were eating better and housed in reasonable comfort in a new three-storey 'penitentiary' that was properly heated and spacious enough for them to lie on their back as they slept. By June 1832, there were only nine prisoners left on the rock and by the last year of the settlement, there were no more prisoners living there.

Porter puts it pretty simply: 'No more sad countenances, no more lacerations when Major Baily [sic] took charge – all was joy beaming in every countenance.'

While ships were the mainstay of the settlement's business, Macquarie Harbour was also producing furniture and house fittings, panel doors, architraves and sash windows, writing tables, and ward tables for hospitals. There were buckets, wheelbarrows and oars being produced by carpenters and blacksmiths, as well as nails and wharf piles.

The settlement wasn't just buoyant but a hive of industry replete with workshops and a school, where the majority of prisoners were involved in some form of manufacturing. One man describes it as a place where the oddments of industry and commerce were everywhere. But it wasn't just about work. The work the convicts did was connected to their ongoing education: 'heaps of shingles and staves, tables, a stack of window and door frames, mountains of wooden bowls. In every corner are stored boots, kettles and pots, like some oriental bazaar.' The shipyards were complete and in full operation. There was a sense of purpose in the air, and even the potboys (who served drinks and collected glasses) and sweepers around the yards were enjoying life. 'They were chanting as they worked, like nursery rhymes, some strange incantation till I realised they were spelling: the letters of their tools, the bricks and stones, the timber and rope and pitch were all being spelled out.'

Two main forces had been shaping the convicts' education, and one was spiritual. For four years, from 1828 to 1832, Sarah Island had boasted its very own church minister, the Wesleyan missionary William Scholfield. He was instrumental not just in Bible study but also in how the convicts were educated. School was voluntary but by

March 1830 Scholfield had fifty-two prisoners attending, assisted by twelve teachers. By April 1832, there were ninety prisoners in two classes, one of which was to teach twenty-four men how to read, write and do basic arithmetic. All reading was done from the Bible, the only printed textbook in the school.

Governor Arthur had long believed that it was impossible to reform the harbour's miscreants – in his mind, secondary offenders had long been lost to God. As the settlement transformed, the lieutenant-governor must have revisited these views, and Scholfield was sent to minister to their morals and improve their education. Porter had come to know Scholfield well – he was one of the clergyman's most valued singers in the church choir and was often asked to sing at Commandant Briggs's house.

Another reason behind the push in education was the man who ran the entire show, in all but name. During the final years of the Macquarie Harbour penal settlement, both Briggs and Baylee had less of a presence than Scotsman David Hoy, who was regarded by many as the virtual commandant.

*

Hoy was a master shipwright, without doubt one of the most gifted shipbuilders of his generation. Some have regarded him as a dreamer with lofty ideals. Others have said that he was the only official whom convicts trusted; both affectionately and respectfully, he was nicknamed 'the Admiral'. His work gangs of convicted felons seemed to fall under his spell. He seemed to have no interest in Arthur's system, with all its moral overtones and contrived incentives – Hoy appeared to offer the men a real chance to turn their lives around, with concrete, realisable job opportunities. The men appeared to enjoy being trained in the precise art of building ships. To do this successfully, they needed not only to know how to use a saw or adze, but also to possess the rudiments of a good education.

Hoy was ambitious and wanted to make a name for himself. There's no doubt his pact with the convicts was to some degree self-serving. He wanted to be known as one of the colony's – if not one of the world's – best shipbuilders. He arrived in 1828 and swiftly transformed Macquarie Harbour into the most productive shipyard not just in Van Diemen's Land but throughout the entire colony.

Hoy's style was simple but effective. He demanded exacting, hard work from his men in return for new skills that they could use for later life – and he was offering to turn a blind eye to their own, growing private enterprise. 'Work hard for me,' Hoy seemed to be saying to his convict charges, 'and whatever you can trade or make on the side is your business.'

In 1830, Colonial Secretary John Burnett wrote to Commandant Briggs seeking assurances that sugar, tea, tobacco and rum, all of which were supposedly banned to convicts on the island, weren't now freely available. Burnett had heard that convicts across Van Diemen's Land were expressing a newfound desire to be sent to Macquarie Harbour, because all these commodities were so easily bought and sold there. The colonial secretary made a pointed remark: he had already concluded that this was 'fictitious' because, as Briggs would most certainly know, the settlement was 'founded upon the strict enforcement of labour and the rigorous and severe discipline with which it is being conducted'. The letter was an implied warning to Briggs that if such substances were being traded, he would have to stamp that out immediately. By all accounts, Briggs – and everyone else – failed.

By the time Baylee was in command, he and Hoy were turning a blind eye to the amount of contraband that was finding its way into the settlement. But it wasn't just that illicit goods were flowing in: some very quirky but handy manufactured goods, sold at a profit, were flowing out. Private enterprise was becoming the norm at the penal colony, and all kinds of utensils and garments were being made and sold by the convicts. Trading was forbidden, but those in charge knew it was going on. Convicts polished walking sticks made from sapling trunks twisted by the clematis vine: waist-height, sturdy corkscrews that could bear a man's weight. Swan skins were sewn into waistcoats, and waterproof hats were woven from palm fronds. The local tannery used the bark of the celerytop pine as a tanning agent for kangaroo and wallaby skins; the only complaint was that boots coated with this natural dye stained the socks and feet a deep shade of red. In its later years, Macquarie Harbour was becoming a paradise for bush entrepreneurs and inventors.

Behind everything was the legal activity going on in the shipyard. From the late 1820s into the early 1830s, shipbuilding under Hoy's guidance was the predominant activity. In 1829 the shipyards at Sarah had produced the *Tamar* brig and that year the shipyards also produced a schooner, two sloops, two cutters, two launches and around three whaleboats – about three hundred tons of shipping in all. In total, 130 ships were made in Macquarie Harbour of which ninety-six were constructed under Hoy's direction. Every three weeks a ship was launched off the extremely well-made slip, which consisted of two double platforms of heavy blue gum with a deep keel run between them.

Hoy's specialty was constructing boats designed to lie close to the wind. On the whole, there were few long-range, ocean-going vessels being built at Macquarie Harbour, but Hoy dealt in those that could ply their trade in estuaries and navigate within striking distance of the Van Diemonian coastline.

The *Tamar* was the pride of the harbour. Hoy was said to wax lyrical about the vessel to anyone willing to listen – it was his finest creation. Its sleek design harked back to his years working in the Boston shipyards, considered the best in the world. The American merchants were demanding greater speed from their ships to quicken trade and exact profits faster. Safety was a distant second consideration for them – but not for Hoy, who claimed he could build boats with the speed of American vessels and the safe sturdiness of the traditional British design. He was also intrigued by the properties of Huon pine, which he knew was the best timber for shipbuilding. In fact, he'd come to Macquarie Harbour with the express intent of working with it.

Hoy was ahead of his time. He was achieving wonders with the convicts assigned to him. Hobart's superintendent of government vessels, William Moriarty, praised Hoy for 'making fair tradesmen out of the boys and men'. Many attributed the reformation of Macquarie Harbour's dissolute lags to him, and perhaps he achieved this simply because he was humane and respectful towards his charges. 'I treated the men as human beings, not as caged beasts,' Hoy once said. He'd helped turn a place of dread into a college of further education.

*

AT THE OTHER end of the island, something else had changed since the prison settlement's inception. The sharp-eyed pilot, James Lucas, who had skilfully navigated ships into and out of the harbour since 1822, had left the colony in 1829, the year before Porter's arrival. The man who replaced him, George Bowhill, was drowned in September 1830 attempting to bring Hoy's beloved *Tamar* through the heads. The pilot's launch, as the report said, 'had fallen prey to the waves'. Neither the launch nor any of the nine men aboard it were ever recovered. Such was the difficulty of steering vessels in and out of Hells Gates. The *Tamar* was luckier – it survived to sail another day.

The colony needed a pilot who could help navigate ships through the gates' pincers and safely across the low sandbar that ran between them. Captain Charles Taw was called up to take over these duties.

Taw was nothing like his predecessors. Lucas had famously defended the gates like a zealot; in personality too, he was said to be a hard man who would brook no dissent. While he had failed to catch Matthew Brady – the one that got away – nobody else had ever illegally entered or departed the penal station under his watch. Taw was said to be a lonely figure, softer than Lucas and Bowhill, and often inebriated. Why he was chosen to be the guardian of the gates is one of history's strange mysteries.

Commandant Baylee knew of Porter's sailing prowess and sent him up from Sarah Island, where he was given a berth in the pilot's launch. He was now away from the main settlement and nicely ensconced in the boat crew's house in Pilot's Bay, just around the corner from the southern headland. He and his crewmates were heavily guarded, but ultimately under the lax eye of Charles Taw.

By dint of luck – and others' misfortunes – Porter was now in a prime position. He had found a calling at Macquarie Harbour that didn't require the cutting and rolling of logs, or days in chains without food. He was soon promoted to the role of pilot boat's coxswain, an extremely responsible job: he sat in the bow of the pilot boat shouting directions to the crew as to the best course through the water; he also physically controlled the boat's steering, speed, timing and ease through the water. In a place of such variable weather conditions, the boat required expert handling.

It was a job almost custom-made for Porter. He and his fellow convicts could look out to sea from their vantage point in Pilot's Bay and, for the first time, not just survey the lie of the land, but also the lie of the ocean. Porter could read its froth, swirls and eddies, its winds and wave formations better than most. It was, after all, his natural element. It had always solved his problems, always taken him away from places he didn't like and people he no longer cared for. From hereon, for James Porter, there would only be one way out of Macquarie Harbour.

Chapter 8

I N LATE 1832, Governor Arthur had announced that Macquarie Harbour would be closing down. The entire operation would be moving to Port Arthur, the new penal settlement on the Tasman Peninsula, which would eventually absorb all the colony's secondary criminal offenders from both Macquarie Harbour and Maria Island. Arthur wanted a place where the worst rogues, repeat offenders and inveterate bolters were easily supervised and overseen.

Arthur hadn't witnessed Macquarie Harbour's latter-day reinvention, but he no doubt would have disapproved of the liberties being taken. Port Arthur, named after himself, was his answer to the messy, escape-prone, leaky sieve that was Macquarie Harbour. As far back as 1826, he had said as much. Macquarie Harbour had become too loose for his liking.

Arthur had other reasons to close it down. By then he believed he had rid most of Van Diemen's Land of its Indigenous people, even though a cluster of Tasmanian Aboriginal people, (who are now commonly referred to as Palawa), still held out in the west. Colonists had greater confidence in settling further into the hinterland than ever before, meaning that the harbour was becoming progressively closer to 'civilisation' and would eventually lose its remoteness.

Beyond this, the prison station had to be constantly resupplied with food, water and provisions. Macquarie Harbour was losing money. It produced a plethora of fine boats under the venerable Hoy, but this didn't pay the total bill. Port Arthur's capacity was twice that of Macquarie Harbour: around 1100 convicts could be housed there. The governor could dispense more punishment to more prisoners, more efficiently and much closer at hand.

What Arthur envisaged for Port Arthur was less a hostile wilderness and more an impregnable fortress. It would be part-industrial site, part-gulag – a penal station and a conglomerate. Shipbuilding would remain the largest enterprise, but there would also be quarrying, manufacturing, smithing and agriculture. Arthur may not have known it then, but his vision, at least in business terms, was progressive. He believed in managing profit centres and achieving key performance indicators before the terms were even invented. He was the prison's virtual chief executive.

Port Arthur is sited in the D'Entrecasteaux Channel, less than thirty-seven miles from Hobart Town and at that time was only reachable by sea. The peninsula where it lies was naturally secure. It is almost entirely surrounded by water, with only a one hundred-foot wide thread of land connecting the prison to the mainland. This thin isthmus at Eaglehawk Neck could be easily guarded and tightly secured, bolstered by guards, man traps and dogs. The penal station is sited at the western end of Maingon Bay, around forbidding cliffs and ancient stone. 'When the clouds march in from the Tasman Sea and the rainfalls lash the prismatic stone, the cliffs around Port Arthur can look like the adamantine gates of hell itself,' wrote Robert Hughes in his convict history, *The Fatal Shore*.

In its earliest phases it was just a timber station, with convict barracks, a guardhouse and a crude shipyard. By degrees it grew, with a hospital as well as a shipyard, smithies and carpenters' shops. There would eventually be a commissariat, a church, a school, hospital, a guard tower, barracks, officers' quarters and a semaphore station. It transformed into a prison complex, containing one of the most sturdily built penitentiaries in the British Empire. But from a distance, Port Arthur has never looked like a penitentiary; it has always appeared more like a wealthy English village with a few rather

Port Arthur was once the home of the Pydairrerme people. It was initially conceived as part prison camp, part commercial enterprise – Arthur knew punishment had to be made profitable. By the 1850s it had become a community in itself – a military base and industrial town complete with free townsfolk and merchants. It is now a World Heritage Site.

imposing Georgian-style buildings. By the 1850s, Port Arthur was a virtual prison town, with thirty buildings in all.

In 1855 construction finished on a building known as the Separate Prison. It was based on a new punishment theory that had become fashionable in England. Floggings were by then considered archaic, only serving to make the prisoners more recalcitrant. The panopticon, devised by English moral philosopher Jeremy Bentham, was considered to be an effective modern way of dealing with difficult prisoners. It had a central hub with radiating spokes that offered warders a view of the inmates at all times. The panopticon ushered in total silence, solitary confinement, withdrawal of food as a punishment and constant surveillance. Port Arthur's Separate Prison had a slight modification – its wings were open but its cells were enclosed, unlike other panopticon-style prisons where the prisoners could be watched around the clock. In the Separate Prison, at least the inmates had a modicum of privacy. At the end of one of the wings was the solitary cell which is bereft of any light. In the darkness, isolation and silence, many lost their minds.

*

IN 1833, THE CONVICTS at Macquarie Harbour knew – or at least thought they knew – what was coming. Anything that Arthur commanded usually spelt pain. They were being asked to trade in their college of further education, with all its rights and workers' benefits, for an institute of further punishment: a gaol with four walls, higher supervision, not infrequent use of the whip and recreation limited to the lengths of a standard prison yard. Any man could easily have felt all his efforts to reform were for nothing. The number of escape attempts from Macquarie Harbour rose again as the settlement's operations drew to a close.

The evacuation of the settlement was a long and drawn-out affair, and it happened in stages. From January 1833, convicts were being sent on to Port Arthur. By May all the sick prisoners had left the island. By August, the commissariat officer and his wife had departed. By October, two vessels, the *Charlotte* and the *Tamar*, had arrived at the harbour to evacuate the settlement of its last personnel, convicts and anything of value. Macquarie Harbour would officially shut down the next month.

But there was one ship that was still under construction, which the selected convicts had been building since the middle of 1833. The brig *Frederick* was on the slipway, about half complete, even though Arthur had wanted the harbour evacuated and asked for the timbers of the *Frederick* to be assembled at Port Arthur. One story has it that the order to finish the boat at Port Arthur was misplaced; another that Hoy strongly resisted moving until the *Frederick* was seaworthy. The truth may be somewhere in between: perhaps Hoy 'never received the message' or simply feigned ignorance of it. He wasn't a man to half-finish work, and he wanted the 120-ton brig completed in situ.

The authorities had decided that a mix of sailors and mechanics, guarded by four soldiers and directed by Taw and Hoy, would be left to finish the job and bring her to Port Arthur. James Porter, deckhand and coxswain, was among the chosen few. Porter seems to have undergone a change of feeling about Macquarie Harbour. He says in his memoir that he was pleased to stay in a place – the one he had been so determined to escape from in late 1832. He was presumably happier to be there than his next destination – Port Arthur. He wrote:

Knowing for certain that Macquarie Harbour was to be
abolished, I was determined if good conduct would do it to
remain behind to assist in working up the brig. I was one of the
ten selected by the major and I was very pleased with the news –
all hands were busy that were going to Port Arthur packing up
their things – all was noise and confusion – and in a fortnight –
all the prisoners were on board that were going away.

He and two of his pilot crewmates, Charles Lyon and James Leslie,
were selected by Taw as the best of his men to help sail the *Frederick*
to Port Arthur. Taw would captain the boat, with a free man who
lived in Macquarie Harbour, James Tate, as his first mate. Two more
sailors would join them from Hobart Town to take the *Frederick*
directly to the new penal station; the rest would be chosen from
among the Sarah Island convicts.

*

AFTER NEARLY A decade of attempting to escape his penal misery,
Porter had shown himself plainly incapable of doing it solo. Simply
bolting, or 'taking French leave' as Porter called it, was not going
to be good enough. He needed to join a team, whose various parts
would enable the whole to execute a well-wrought plan.

In late 1833, Porter started working with the settlement's best
mechanics and sailors, handpicked by Taw and Hoy, to finish
and deliver the *Frederick*. These men also happened to be some of
Macquarie Harbour's meanest felons and best escape artists, men
whom Porter would have described as 'straining every point to get
away'. In his later writings, Porter gave the impression that he was

the master of escape logistics, but this was little more than his usual braggadocio. Of the ten men, Porter was by no means the smartest, craftiest or best-suited for an escape attempt: there were others with a similar desire to gain freedom who could weave a smarter plot.

John Barker, thirty-seven, a Lancastrian, was the 'head convict' during the construction of the *Frederick*. If there was a ringleader or mastermind, it was most likely to have been him. He was an expert gunsmith and watchmaker, and at Sarah Island he was given charge of the forge. He even had his own manservant. If Hoy was the designer and overseer of the *Frederick* project, then Barker was the foreman and master of tools. He soon became indispensable to Hoy, and he was even given the task of ensuring soldiers' firearms were in good working order, handling guns daily.

In the mid-1820s, Barker's home city of Lancaster was experiencing a steady decline. Its port, which had once been at the centre of a thriving trade with the West Indies, was rapidly losing trade to the more prosperous Liverpool. In the same period, two local banks failed.

What drove Barker to steal cloth from a ship is not known, but there is no doubt Lancaster offered few opportunities even for a man of Barker's talents. Sadly, he left behind a wife and two children. For his petty theft he was first sent to Bermuda, where all convicts were housed in wretched and decaying hulks. The main task for convicts in Bermuda was to break up the very coarse local marine limestone and create a breakwater. It would have been back-breaking work.

Barker was described as 'a well behaved, clever man, particularly recommended by the surgeon' while being transported to Van Diemen's Land, but his colonial record after his arrival in May

1829 was chequered. He was recorded as absent without leave the next year and given ten days on the treadmill. A few months later he was charged with receiving a stolen watch, valued at £18, and his sentence increased from seven years to fourteen. By April 1831, he was on the chain gang and from there he absconded. After being captured, he was sentenced to life imprisonment at Macquarie Harbour.

However, it seems clear that whatever past convictions Barker and others had, at the harbour these were quickly overlooked because of the economic imperative of the shipyards. As convicts gained greater freedom under Hoy and Baylee, technicians like Barker were too valuable to ignore, so their pasts were effectively erased.

Barker may have appeared to be taking his newfound responsibilities seriously, but he was secretly concentrating on more important things. He was spending copious amounts of time with another convict, William Philips, a Cornish fisherman who had taught him the basics of nautical navigation. Unbeknownst to the men in charge – but seemingly well known to Porter, who mentions it in his memoir – Barker was learning how to steer a craft by the art of deduced reckoning.

Deduced or 'ded. reckoning' was the original term but it later became known (rightly or wrongly) as 'dead' reckoning – a method of establishing one's position using the distance and direction travelled rather than astronomical observations. The boat's longitude is reckoned based on compass readings, speed, and the distance from a known point, making allowances for drift from wind and currents. There's another, much shorter definition of deduced reckoning: intelligent guesswork. Dead reckoning is more a skill than a science. Without astronomical instruments or knowledge of the stars, it's notoriously difficult to chart one's position across the width of the Earth.

Porter's pilot crewmates, Charles Lyon, twenty-eight, and James Leslie, twenty-nine, were selected to sail the *Frederick* for their skills not their behaviour. Porter had probably come into contact with both men before their assignment on the pilot boat, as their convict careers had intertwined at several points.

Lyon, a Scot from Dundee, had arrived in Van Diemen's Land on the *Asia*, on the very same voyage as Porter, back in 1824. Like Porter, he had been sent to sea at a very early age: he worked for his uncle who commanded the *Union*, a smack (ship) from the River Tay. At eighteen Lyon was caught breaking and entering in Perth, then transported.

Lyon was perhaps the least understood of the ten convicts. He seemed to progress from a rather passive convict in his early years into a man filled with malicious intent. As we will see, certainly Porter thought so and other descriptions confirm this. His first few years as a prisoner were fairly quiet, although he was given fifty lashes and time in gaol after being caught in flagrante with a married woman. Porter would have known him in the mid-1820s, when they both worked on the government boats in Hobart Town. By the late 1820s, Lyon's crimes and misdemeanours accelerated: drunkenness, on several occasions; beating and assaulting a servant (case dismissed); idleness and neglect of duty; and fighting. He was found not guilty of highway robbery in 1828, but in 1831 was found guilty of raping another man's wife and sentenced to death – which was commuted to life at Macquarie Harbour.

An interesting description of Lyon was made by George Augustus Robinson, the man charged by Governor Arthur to find the colony's

Indigenous people and 'resettle' them – as in, coerce them into government reserves. When Robinson visited Macquarie Harbour, Lyon served as the coxswain on his boat. On one occasion Lyon nearly lost the boat through neglect, which would have killed all eighteen aboard. 'A most evil-looking character,' Robinson wrote curtly. 'I was obliged to dismiss him.'

Porter, in his memoir, says of Lyon: 'He belongs to the race of Judas, of whom I shall have much to speak about in the sequel.'

James Leslie was not malicious but was an incurable absconder in the James Porter mould – he could never quite stay out of trouble from an early age. He'd been chosen to remain at the harbour because he was a shipwright, although he couldn't have been more than an apprentice on his arrival in Van Diemen's Land.

Leslie had been in and out of trouble since he was a boy. He was also transported in 1824, for 'stealing a reticule containing a silver scent box and other articles by force from a lady in the park'. He had form prior to this and had been acquitted in two other trials for housebreaking before he was eighteen. His crimes while in the colony weren't serious, but were committed regularly throughout his convict tenure: neglect of duty; theft of government goods; absence without leave, on several occasions; being drunk and absent from his vessel; and, of all things, 'representing himself to be a free man'. He had arrived in Macquarie Harbour in 1830 but was also a veteran on the government ships, and it's likely that Porter and Lyon would have known him from Hobart Town.

Out of the ten men were two more sailors: John Jones, the oldest of the convicts at forty-two, and John Fare, twenty-seven. They'd been sent to the harbour over the winter, specifically to bring the *Frederick* back. Fare and Jones were hardly Macquarie Harbour types – indeed, both had only just begun their convict careers. Fare had been convicted of housebreaking in Southampton and had arrived in Van Diemen's Land in July 1833. Other than a reprimand for drunkenness, he had yet to make any mark on the black books. Jones had arrived on the same ship as Fare, transported for larceny. Jones, however, was hardly green. Like Barker, he was a Bermuda veteran from 1826 to 1831, and had reoffended back in London in 1832, having been caught with the proceeds of a night's takings from a ship.

Both men were staring down long sentences: Fare had been convicted for life and Jones for fourteen years.

There was also the carpenter contingent under Barker's command, needed to complete the *Frederick*'s construction and fit-out. John Dady, twenty-three, had originally told the authorities he was a bricklayer but had learnt the carpentry trade while a convict. Dady may have felt that he had been badly done by in life. He'd been sent to Van Diemen's Land in 1826 for pickpocketing a handkerchief and spent most of his convict career either in chains or on the treadmill. Stealing clothes seems to have been Dady's speciality – at one point he was found unable to explain his possession of a 'frock and pair of stockings' and a year later was discovered in possession of two pairs of 'Duck Trowsers [*sic*]'.

Another tradesman was William 'Billy' Shires, thirty-nine, who appears to have had the cleanest convict sheet of any of the men. This was astounding given that Shires had been a convict for nearly thirteen years, having been transported back in 1820 for highway robbery. He was the longest serving of the ten. Originally cited as a farm labourer, like Dady he'd gained skills as a carpenter under penal duress. Since his original conviction in England, there wasn't a single black mark against him. He was described by Robinson as 'Bill the lugger': this may have described the way he did his work – a lugger carries heavy objects – or it could have been a slight against him, a reference to a lugger boat, which is a slow and ponderous vessel.

Rounding out the clique of carpenters was Benjamin Russen, thirty, a native of Norwich who had arrived in 1822 convicted of burglary. How this weaver became a carpenter isn't recorded, but in terms of prison form he was another bolter, a little like Porter and Leslie, for which he received scores of lashes over the course of his convict tenure. He, too, may have felt aggrieved at his circumstances: he was also lashed for the pettiest of infractions – twenty-five lashes for 'repairing a box' (presumably considered a means of escape) and, on another occasion, twenty-five for 'disrespect and inattention'.

The tenth man wasn't required for either construction or sailing. William Cheshire, twenty-four, was John Barker's servant and by all accounts a sad figure. He was just four feet eleven inches tall, a runt even by convict standards. Cheshire was from Birmingham and had originally worked as a butcher. Like Fare, he'd been transported for housebreaking.

Cheshire had only known one form of service in the penal colony – as a household servant. Perhaps, because of his size, he'd been deemed unsuitable for government employ or to survive the rigours of outdoor convict life. His career infractions reflect this: insolence, disobedience of orders, 'household drunkenness' and 'household insolence'. He'd received lashes and the treadmill as punishments.

*

WHAT ELSE CAN be said of the band of merry men assigned to fit out and sail the *Frederick*, the last of Hoy's ninety-six vessels and the last to set sail from Macquarie Harbour?

If you were to look at them from Governor Arthur's point of view, you might shudder at the calibre of men being left to hold the fort. Collectively they had committed eight burglaries and tried to escape Macquarie Harbour nine times. They'd been whipped more than eight hundred times (Porter was the chief victim – he had three hundred all on his own). Between them they had a rape, three assaults, a capital conviction, and periods in the chain gang and on the treadmill since their arrival.

Major Baylee had left the selection to Captain Taw, believing that Taw was closer to the men on a daily basis and would be a better judge of their characters. But it was plain from their records that the ten convicts were – with two exceptions – a bunch of miscreants and serial bolters. It soon became clear that short cuts were made in the rush to evacuate Macquarie Harbour. Prior form was given short shrift.

When later questioned by Arthur, Captain Taw protested that he had regarded them all as 'recommended men'.

Chapter 9

Around the same time that convicts, soldiers and freemen were being sent up the coast to Port Arthur, the region's Palawa inhabitants weren't so much being evacuated as evicted.

George Augustus Robinson was in the last stages of removing the people known as the Macquarie Harbour Aborigines. Robinson, a former bricklayer and lay preacher who'd volunteered for the job, had been instructed by Arthur to bring in any remaining 'wild Aborigines' – those who had survived the war and disease that had ravaged their population for the past decade. Further away than most and difficult to entrap, the west coast Aboriginal people would be among the last to maintain an active resistance against the loss of their lands in the face of European encroachment.

Robinson's job was clearly a 'mopping up' exercise. His method was to use his group of 'friendly Aborigines' – those who had been coerced and pressured into the cause – to bring in the 'wild' ones. Robinson's entourage would go into the bush and entreat the Palawa to return with them, making all sorts of promises for their security. Once people had been taken in, they would be sent out of sight and mind – as peaceably as possible – to a new settlement on the west coast of Flinders Island. It was named Wybalenna, literally 'black man's house'.

This was all part of Arthur's greater plan. Throughout the mid- to late 1820s, he had increased punitive measures against the Palawa in an attempt to solve a problem that, from the viewpoint of the settlers, seemed intractable: either these people had to be exterminated or removed from lands that the settlers wanted to possess.

In early 1830, the Executive Council (virtually run by Arthur) made it policy to reward five pounds for every adult Aboriginal person trapped and two pounds for every child. This was a signal to all vagrants, itinerants and convicts in the outer reaches of the land to earn a quick quid. This wasn't about ridding the settled areas of Indigenous people where they might be a threat, it was about ridding the land entirely of their presence.

Arthur, with his willing faction, even defied London on this. Whitehall often transmitted its views by vice-regal proclamations, to the effect that the native people had to be treated with humanity. Arthur, for all intents and purposes, simply ignored this advice. He was using his reward system to capture people who posed no possible threat to the land-hungry sheep barons. It was a policy of pre-cleansing – clearing out the territory to make it suitable for future habitation and use, while making sure there was nothing to allay profit-making. The territory included the wildest and least-settled part of the island, the west coast.

In September 1830, Arthur issued a government order calling for 'a general and simultaneous effort' from willing settlers under the direction of the police and military. This so-called 'Black Line' was implemented a month later – in reality, it wasn't a single line but makeshift groups that tried to force the Palawa into two peninsulas. The Palawa saw it coming and were able to evade the settlers' nets. It cost the government around thirty thousand pounds and resulted in just two captures.

When this plan patently failed, Arthur raised the stakes. He offered rewards, pardons and tickets of leave to convicts prepared to do the 'cleansing' for the government. This was reminiscent of his methods to flush out bushrangers a few years earlier, except the bandits were to be committed to trial and hanged: the native people were to be shot on sight. The newly formed bands of roaming killers were not official government policy but had – for want of a better expression – been tacitly hired by Arthur. This way the government wouldn't have to mount any more expensive mobilisations – and he would not be culpable for what followed.

But Arthur's killing fields weren't as effective as he would have liked. The governor was left with the one means of drawing out the Palawa that, for most people on the island, seemed eminently reasonable – he sent Robinson out there to coax them in. By mid-1833, when Macquarie Harbour was in the throes of evacuation, Robinson had been travelling for three years with his bush troop, among them the famous Truganini – who would be known as Tasmania's last-surviving full-blooded Aboriginal person, although this is disputed – and her husband, Woorady.

Truganini was a Nuenone woman whose country was Bruny Island, opposite Oyster Cove. She and her family suffered terribly at the hands of white people: her mother was killed by sailors, her uncle shot by a soldier, and her three sisters were kidnapped and sold to sealers – one was later killed by a sealer. Truganini's one-time fiancé was murdered by timber men, who drowned him in the D'Entrecasteaux Channel. She came to know Robinson in 1829 when he set up his first 'friendly mission' on Bruny Island. In 1830 she married Woorady at the mission, and for the next five years they accompanied Robinson on his 'mopping up' exercise.

Robinson needed interpreters and guides who understood the land. Truganini and her companions could protect him in areas that white men would usually never dare to enter. These 'friendly natives' were the lure, token showpieces that supposedly proved white man's humanity to the Aboriginal people. They had to do much of the persuading to make sure the remaining tribes came in. In return, Robinson promised Truganini and her companions shelter, food and housing. He also promised to respect their customs and their desire to return to their homelands – occasionally.

Truganini helped him track the most remote areas of the colony. It seems she had come to believe that his missions were the only way for her people to survive. But she did not remain 'friendly' forever – a few years later, she became involved in guerrilla warfare around Port Phillip in Victoria.

By 1833, Robinson was becoming less patient and more aggressive in his treatment of Indigenous people. Back in 1830, he had twice tried to remove the remaining groups on the west coast, coaxing them with promises and favours, but this had failed. He was determined to finish the job. Three years later, he wasn't so much luring as trapping them: 'I ordered the two white men and my sons to uncover their fusées [flares] and to file off on each side. The friendly natives did the same with their spears so that the strangers were in our centre. The wild aborigines now gave up all further thought of going away.'

While everyone else at Sarah Island was in the throes of packing up, members of the Peternidic and Ninene people were arriving. The

Palawa were first kept at Grummet Island, which for the previous year had been uninhabited. When an epidemic broke out, fourteen of them died. They were moved to the lower floor of the penitentiary on Sarah Island where, Robinson wrote, the prisoners above them 'took every occasion to annoy and would not think it a crime to murder them'. The convicts showed no empathy: 'They harassed the Aborigines, pouring down water through the boards, urinating upon them and hammering on the floor.'

The Palawa were again moved: this time to the cramped prison hospital, where a further five died within twenty-four hours. It wasn't until Baylee stepped in that the survivors were brought to the harbour entrance, as far from the main settlement as possible, where they awaited transportation. Robinson and thirty natives left the island in early October. Soon there would be no human presence in Macquarie Harbour.

*

In the latter stages of Macquarie Harbour's evacuation, large quantities of materials were shipped to Port Arthur, but the buildings – other than reusable window frames, and furniture of any use and value – were left to decay. In the midst of all this, the construction of the *Frederick* continued.

Porter, the man who hated Macquarie Harbour more than most, sat watching with some sadness as each of the two government vessels, one with the last of the commissariat's stores and the other carrying Major Pery Baylee, cast off separately from the wharf on Sarah Island.

The boats swung around gracefully in the perfect morning

sunlight, seagulls busying themselves around them as the wind caught their sails. Once full of air, the steerage kicked in and the boats found their line, heading north-westwards up the harbour to wait for the ebb tide. It was 25 November 1833 and Porter recalled in his memoir that Baylee had been one of the few men to show him respect. Indeed, in the eleven months in which Baylee had been in charge, he had managed to stay out of any serious trouble. Porter must have felt that another of those rare gentlemen, the sort he always felt he could work with, had gone.

Baylee and his soldiers, a detachment of the 63rd regiment of Foot, would be returning to Hobart Town, where they would be embarking for India and a return to active service. The other convicts, save the twelve kept to finish off and sail the *Frederick* to Port Arthur, had now all gone. Among the convicts, there was a sense of loss. 'I felt as much parting with him as with a parent and I cannot help saying God prosper him wherever he is!' Porter wrote in his memoir. Baylee had apparently told Taw to make sure that the convicts were put on marine rations; according to Porter, they would all be given 'a gill of rum per diem'. Porter wrote, 'When we got to Head Quarters he would intercede for a ticket of leave for the whole of us, if we behaved ourselves on the way to Hobart Town.'

Macquarie Harbour had become, paradoxically, a place where they wanted to stay, not flee. The alternative, Port Arthur, wasn't worth thinking about. As the ship carrying the amiable Irish commandant slipped from its moorings, Porter and the rest sent out three cheers. 'God Bless Major Baylee,' Porter sang out and the rest of the men followed him with the same words. Porter and his mates watched quietly as the two ships grew smaller, gleamed in the sunlight and finally passed out of sight.

There were now just nineteen men left in the harbour. Hoy, Taw, Tate and four soldiers made up the contingent of free men. There were twelve convicts in all, including Hoy's servant William Nicholls and Taw's servant James Macfarlane. These men had one last request: to retain a ship's cat. For their voyage of hundreds of miles, they would be graced by the feline affections of a tomcat. The nineteen men and their cat had some dry stores, a goat, a few pigs and some potatoes to live on.

*

AT THE SOUTH-WESTERN end of Sarah Island were a series of slipways, jetties and docks. The *Frederick* had begun life on a slip, where the hull was initially fashioned. The men positioned blocks along the slip, then placed the keel on these blocks. In Macquarie Harbour, shipbuilders used blue gum for keels: eucalypts grew so straight in the region that a keel could be fashioned from just one tree.

The men added the stern, apron, sternpost, inner sternpost and curved transoms to the keel's backbone. Then came the rising floors, which were fitted on either side of the keel before the floor timbers were attached. The outer frame was composed of curved pieces known as futtocks and butt chocks, which the men slotted into position; it was for these pieces that the Huon pine came into its own, as it was very malleable. To ensure the growing skeleton didn't fall over, the frame was held in place by legs staked along the sides of the slip. Wooden pins, which swelled and tightened over time, were used for joinery, but the longer pieces were joined end on end with a slotting 'scarf joint' cut into each piece, interlocking them. From there, the men laid a keelson or inner keel along the length of the keel, and strengthened the bow and stern.

By this stage, the framework was self-supporting. The most important crafting tool was the adze, which had a curved chipping blade perfect for shaping wood. The best shipwrights could use them for a variety of purposes, such as to help construct a mast or ensure the evenness of a plank.

On 16 December, the men sent the *Frederick* down the slips and floated her. For three weeks they had prepared her with the best waterproofing methods available in her time. Her hull was caulked, which first involved scraping a hook between the wooden seams. Oakum, a tarred hemp cordage material, was beaten and compressed into the seams with a caulking iron or mallet. To prevent the oakum from rotting, the men covered her with a hot pitch below the waterline, and painted above it. Hoy, though unwell at the time, gave her the all-clear. Every sailor knew these methods weren't flawless – despite the best efforts of men, ships still leaked. They took on water particularly under duress: after being twisted or 'worked' by rough weather.

The *Frederick* was floating but incomplete. There was still much work to be done with the sails, rigging, galleys, masts and rudders. The finished ship would have eighty feet of deck and from stern to bowsprit, was roughly 110 feet in length. As was customary with brigs, there were only two main masts, each of which had topmasts reaching high above the deck. The brigs were built for speed. The foremast was completely square-rigged as on larger brigantines and barques. The foremast might also have an extra sail known as a trysail, which could be used in place of a larger sail in very high winds. Both the foremast and the main mast might also have scudding sails – these were placed on spars which could be extended outwards to lengthen the yards – they were like additional sailing wings. Set forward from the foremast was the jib, a small triangular sheet of sail attached to the bowsprit.

The main mast was also square-rigged and behind it was a large triangular sail (the spanker or driver mainsail) with its own boom attached to the lower end of the mast.

Brigs tended to have more sails than other boats, so no matter which direction the wind was blowing, the crew of the *Frederick* would have to work harder than most, as there were more sails to adjust.

In those days, as now, speed was defined by the length of the boat as well as wind power to weight. Longer boats than the *Frederick* tended to be faster, but the more important factor for speed was the amount of sail area to the weight of the ship. The *Frederick* had plenty of sail and was built by Hoy to be as light as possible.

The *Frederick* would probably outrace most other vessels but this was hardly an advantage in heavy seas and high winds. Too much sail on too light a boat could be a dangerous combination.

One of the most important aspects of the build was Hoy's creation. He was experimenting with new designs that involved the line of the boat, known as the 'sheer'. Hoy had to determine the sheer at regular intervals, while the skin of the boat was being laid on; determining the sheer was a continuous process, and it had to be judged from various distances and positions. On Hoy's instructions, the men adjusted and readjusted the frames so that the line of the boat stayed true on both sides.

*

THE TWELVE CONVICTS were under the charge of four soldiers who were usually unarmed and who spent much of their time drinking and playing cards. Then there was a master shipwright who treated the convicts almost as equals, and a pilot based at the heads who was either drunk or not overly concerned for their supervision. Added to this, Hoy had contracted an unspecified illness in the latter stages of the ship's construction and was rarely on site. It seems the atmosphere was unusually free and relaxed.

The men worked hard in an spirit of bonhomie, perfect conditions for the final seed of escape to be sown: method.

There was, quite clearly, only one way to escape the island successfully: steal the *Frederick* and take her into waters where British ships neither ruled nor had jurisdiction. Here the convicts had the benefit of one very famous precedent and possibly an unrivalled source of knowledge.

In 1832, a famous convict escapee had languished at Macquarie Harbour. He was William Swallow, one of the men behind the capture of the government brig *Cyprus* in 1829 – one of the most daring convict escapes ever attempted. Another *Cyprus* old hand at Macquarie Harbour was John Denner.

When Swallow and Denner had been sent back to the harbour in 1832, aboard the boat that transported them, the *Tamar*, were two of the *Frederick* contingent, Charles Lyon and William Cheshire.

Like the bushranger Matthew Brady, Swallow had become a living legend among the Macquarie lags and an expensive and difficult pest to the colonial authorities. He went by a number of aliases, but was originally a sailor from Tyneside. When he was first sent to Sydney, he managed to steal a boat – but this wasn't his greatest feat. He reserved that for a few years later, when he was among eighteen convicts who seized control of a brig called the *Cyprus*.

The ship had been en route to Macquarie Harbour with a load of convicts, stores and civilians. It was under the command of Lieutenant Carew, who had been lulled by the convicts into a false sense of security. When the *Cyprus* was forced by heavy weather to shelter at Recherche Bay on the south coast of Van Diemen's Land in August 1829, Carew allowed a few of them to exercise on deck without irons while he went fishing.

The convicts belted two armed guards with rope pins, overcoming them before releasing all the prisoners below. Other soldiers, blocked from exit, eventually gave up their firearms. The mutiny was complete.

All those who didn't want to join the mutiny, as well as civilians, soldiers and sailors, were dumped ashore and given minimal food and clothing. In all, forty-four people were marooned on the west coast of Tasmania with virtually nothing. It was practically a death sentence.

Swallow navigated the *Cyprus* across the Pacific, crewed by eighteen convicts with barely adequate sailing skills. They stopped for short periods on the New Zealand coast and at the Chatham Islands, and were heading for Tahiti. Unfavourable winds prevented them from docking there but they spent more than a month at Niuatoputapu, one of the northernmost Tongan islands, where seven of the seventeen convicts decided to stay. The remaining ten convict crew (one had been lost overboard) sailed on. They were trying to find the remotest areas they could and, in a mighty feat of sailing across the Pacific, reached Shikoku Island in Japan in mid-January. A local man sketched their brig and wrote an account of his encounter with them.

By February 1830, the *Cyprus* was sailing just off the coast of China. It was decided to scuttle her in Canton, around the Pearl

River and the crew took on aliases. Most of them were recaptured, but the *Cyprus* swiftly became a legend, and its story was turned into a song by convict poet Frank MacNamara:

> *For Navigating smartly Bill Swallow was the man,*
> *Who laid a course out neatly to take us to Japan.*
> *Then sound your golden trumpets, play on your tuneful notes,*
> *The CYPRUS BRIG is sailing, how proudly now she floats.*

Swallow ingeniously wheedled his way out of a death sentence but was ordered back to Macquarie Harbour in 1832. By the next year he was reported by Robinson to be 'in a poorly state'. He died at Port Arthur two years later.

Whether Swallow had any influence on Lyon and Cheshire, or any of the ten who were left behind, can never be substantiated. But it seems likely that the convicts would have spoken to Swallow and listened to his experiences. Like Brady, he was a famous escapee and even three years after the taking of the *Cyprus*, the tale was fresh in convict minds.

*

THE *FREDERICK* WAS due to set sail in January 1834. Nine of the twelve convicts may have been plotting to take the brig by late 1833, and in early 1834 the circumstances weren't dissimilar to those that precipitated the escape of the *Cyprus*. Hoy and Taw clearly believed they were among friendly, hard-working convicts who would be granted tickets of leave if they did the right thing. Porter says that 'we commenced our work with good heart'. The convicts, according to Porter, could communicate secretly among themselves without too much difficulty. Groups of men would meet at opportune times in order to discuss strategies. There was no need to be especially clandestine: nobody was expecting trouble, so nobody was eavesdropping.

Porter says this subterfuge worked well – until two of the conspirators slipped.

The convicts were adamant that the runt of the pack, William Cheshire, wasn't worth taking. But on one occasion, as Leslie and Russen discussed some part of the plan, Cheshire was listening intently from a cabin nearby. He ran from the room and without any reservation told Barker, his master.

At a later meeting, Barker informed the other conspirators about this. It put the nine men on notice that Cheshire couldn't be trusted. 'There were only nine of us determined to take the brig,' says Porter. 'Cheshire (the traitor) did not know of it at first but merely found it out by accident.' Porter was particularly upset at the news of this leak. He refers to Cheshire as being weak, lily-livered and a traitor – he wasn't one of the lads and was being 'carried'. In the world of James Porter, it didn't matter to whom Cheshire had snitched: what mattered was that he had snitched in the first place. What else would he tell others in authority, particularly when under duress? Porter decided to keep a close watch on him. 'We did not know what to do, knowing he had proved a perjured villain on two or three occasions while on the island. We at last came to the conclusion to tell him he should go and to keep all a secret – he assured us he would.'

Now Cheshire was in on the scheme, he had to be part of it. The diminutive man from Birmingham, whom Porter disdainfully says brought nothing of value, was apparently never among the real players in the plot.

Despite this hitch, the convicts were ready for their escape. They even had a template, the *Cyprus*, to work from. But the last element necessary for freedom was beyond their control: liberty or death had to wait on the weather.

Chapter 10

THE *FREDERICK* LEFT an already decaying Macquarie Harbour on the morning of 12 January 1834 on the back of a light south-westerly breeze, making its way slowly to Hells Gates.

Sarah Island was a ghost town. There was no flag flying from the staff at its northern end. The convicts had spent years laying roads, erecting buildings and tilling the earth. Now there would be no more garden plots, no more acrid, metallic smell from Barker's forge, no more toothsome scent wafting from the bakery. The natural flora was moving into areas it had long been banished from. All that was left of human life in Macquarie Harbour floated on its waters, accompanied by a tomcat and one constantly braying goat.

Taw was trying out the *Frederick* as she ran up the harbour, watching the ease with which it took the air and conveyed the brig. This was a beautiful ship that embraced light breezes with gusto and returned the compliment with speed and lightness across the water.

While all was well nautically, the convicts were giving each other some worried looks. The time to strike was soon. But Charles Lyon had just come out of solitary confinement and was livid, inveighing against the tyranny of Captain Taw, who had put him deep in the hold as a punishment for insubordination. Lyon needed to be calmed. The next few days would be crucial.

By mid-afternoon the ship had made its way to the gates. The jolly-boat, which is used to ferry people on and off ships, was lowered so a few could disembark to pick the last of the potatoes at the pilot's heads. It had been hoped that the ship could make it past the gates that evening and turn directly south-east for Port Arthur.

By late afternoon a north-west wind was blowing heavily onshore and the swell at the gates was mounting. The ship retreated to the lee at Wellington Head and weighed anchor about three hundred yards from the shore. The water had turned dark grey and even beyond the force of the wind there were flecks and chop everywhere. They would have to wait out the weather. If the wind turned offshore the next day, the boat would be able to sail. They would then have to wait for the right ebb tide to head out towards the gates and into the ocean.

The bad weather was working in the conspirators' favour. They had a little more time to plan. But the brig would have to be taken that night or the following day.

The soldiers had their normal munitions but Barker, expert gunsmith, had been busy at the forge and lathe making a few of his own. Concealed on the ship were his caches. He'd sawn off the long barrels of a few old, discarded muskets and converted them into serviceable pistols. The rest of the convicts would have tomahawks, also made by Barker; he had forged their flared axe heads using steel rasps that he fired, bent, fired again and smoothed. The ten convicts had access to serious weaponry.

*

THE NEXT DAY, sailing conditions hadn't improved. The first part of the plan came into being. Porter approached two of the soldiers and pointed to the shore. Why not a little fishing that day to while away the time? They agreed. Why not indeed?

Later in the afternoon, the two soldiers picked up their hooks and tackle and waited for Porter to come. Taw's servant, James Macfarlane had also decided to go fishing. Porter offered them a look of distress, moving his hand across his stomach – he was unwell. The two soldiers and Macfarlane stepped into the jolly-boat and made for the nearest shore. The soldiers took their muskets with them.

The convicts now had just two soldiers to distract.

James Porter was the best singer in the entire settlement. Shires asked one of the soldiers if he was in the mood for a singalong – Porter would do the singing, and the soldier could join in if he wished. The three men went below, slapping each other on the back. It was, after all, their last day in Macquarie Harbour.

But the second soldier wasn't in the slightest interested in the quality of Porter's – or anyone's – voice. He would remain vigilant on deck. He sat at the windlass.

Russen and Leslie moved into position. Russen placed himself about ten feet in front of the soldier at the windlass, while Leslie nonchalantly appeared to be working at the soldier's rear.

The other six conspirators clambered below decks, ostensibly to listen to the song. Taw and Hoy were sitting in the aft cabin well away from the party, apparently drinking while they waited for the convict servant William Nicholls to make their supper. While Porter was singing, Fare and Barker returned to the deck.

Porter recalled later that he was so scared, he could barely get through the song. 'I could not get on,' he wrote, 'my mind was in such a state.'

> *As Mars and Minerva were viewing some implements,*
> *Bellona stepped forward and asked the news;*
> *Or were they repairing those warlike instruments,*
> *That are now growing rusty for want to be used?*
> *The money is withdrawn and our trade is diminishing,*
> *For mechanics are wandering without shoes or hose,*
> *Come stir up the wars and our trade will be flourishing*
> *This grand conversation was under the rose.*

At the word 'rose', Russen and Leslie darted at the soldier on the windlass from two sides. In another few seconds Barker and Fare, coming up from the cabin, were also upon him. All the soldier saw were three sharp axes looming a few inches from his face. He didn't bother to struggle. After gagging him, Barker stamped his foot on the deck – the signal for the next phase.

Shires had been spoiling for a fight for ages, and when the heavy thud came from above, there was no holding him back. The second soldier, halfway through enjoying his rum, never had more than a few seconds to react. Shires came at him fists first. Before the hapless corporal knew what was happening, the other convicts had pinned him down.

'Any move now, boy, and you won't see the next day break,' Shires told him, his axe hovering just above the soldier's face.

The young corporal opened his mouth but nothing came out.

The convicts now had two soldiers under their control and two extra muskets at their disposal. The soldiers were now placed in the forecastle at the front of the ship, where there were a few spare cabins. They bound and gagged them, and threw them into a small hatch.

Now it was the turn of the first mate, James Tate, who was in his cabin. Russen called him to come up. When he reached the deck, Russen moved quickly, pinning him against a mast with a tomahawk in hand. Up jumped Jones and Lyon, who gagged Tate and pulled him to the ship's forecastle. Down into the scuttle went Tate, who had barely resisted.

Taw, Hoy and the convict servant Nicholls were still on board. The conspirators weren't worried about the manservants, who hadn't shown any signs of pluck. But the two soldiers who had gone fishing would be a different story. The ten convicts needed to secure Hoy and Taw before they could deal with them.

All the men knew that serious violence towards those in charge was out of the question. It would play bitterly on them if they were caught. Avoiding violence was part of their insurance policy should they fail. Shires was the man who'd pushed hardest for this: 'There will be no violence on them,' he had said repeatedly.

He and Porter now crept aft, edging towards the captain's cabin where Taw and Hoy were dining, oblivious to the trouble at the other end of the ship. Porter took a quick detour down to the steerage deck, close to the captain's quarters, to collect the soldiers' remaining arms and ammunition.

Shires, seemingly unable to wait for any support, opened the hatch to the captain's cabin and without waiting for Porter, took the ladder with a single jump. The man who'd supposedly requested no violence burst in on Hoy, Taw and the servant Nicholls. To their shock, they saw a usually quiet and compliant Billy Shires leering at them with a sharp axe in his hand. 'You had better give yourselves up,' he told them. 'We have the boat.'

As Porter came up from the steerage, he failed to see that Shires had started the mutiny early. But it was soon clear. Shouts and bangs were coming from the captain's cabin. Porter lifted the cabin hatch to see two men struggling with Shires – and a very scared Nicholls cowering against the bulkhead, dinner plates still in hand. The tomcat danced from one side of the room to the other, wailing at this interruption.

Taw tried to grab Shires, but Shires rebuffed him with the head of his axe. Hoy was still fighting, pushing Shires away with whatever strength he had. Shires looked determined, but then so did Hoy. If the convict had an advantage, it was that Hoy was already injured, suffering severe back pain, and Taw was hardly the fittest of men and may have been quite tipsy. Nicholls, just a slip of a boy, remained aghast. The cat was jumping everywhere, dodging men and objects as they came his way.

In the melee, Taw had his head split by Shires' tomahawk. Porter adds in his writings that Hoy and Taw had been 'drinking our rum' – the very rum that the commandant had promised the convicts. Shires was in a serious tangle, and Porter says they were endeavouring to take his life – 'they being very nearly drunk'.

Realising he had taken on more than he could handle, Shires pulled out of Taw's clutches and ran back up the ladder and through the hatch to where his mates were looking on from above.

'Come on deck, we will not injure you,' Barker bellowed to the men below.

There was no response. Porter seems to have believed they were too drunk to give a measured response, but most likely they were too stunned at the turn of events.

Eventually Taw replied, 'We shall not yield!'

Hoy and Taw had pistols and muskets in the cabin. With the extra time they had, they could now take possession of them. Hoy, in particular, was determined not to sell his life cheaply, according to Porter's writings. He would put up a fight, he told the convicts. Knowing this kept the mutineers at bay – nobody wanted to injure Hoy and Taw, nor did they wish to be shot, but time was critical. They needed to wrest control before the fishermen returned.

For the next two hours, Hoy and Taw would not come up, and the men would not go down. It was a stalemate.

*

WHEN THE CONVICTS eventually tired of asking for Taw and Hoy's surrender, the word was given: 'Fire down upon them.' Two muskets were poked through the hatch – but as Porter explains, it was more bluff than action, a way of frightening the two men into submission.

By some strange twist of fate, a latch bumped against one of the muskets that was poking into the cabin. A ball shot down at a ring of keys dangling from Taw's hand – he'd been trying to unlock a chest. The ball was followed by a plume of acrid smoke. Taw's keys clattered to the floor and, as Porter says, 'it had the desired effect'. Hoy and Taw 'cried out for quarters'.

There was a moment of stunned silence as the convicts realised someone might have been shot. Shires, fearing the worst, peered in. He couldn't make out much, as the cabin was still filled with smoke.

'Are you about to commit murder?' Hoy asked him.

'It can be done without,' Shires replied. 'Will you deliver yourselves up?'

'Yes,' said Hoy. 'If you are not disposed to injure us.'

'My life will be forfeit if we do,' replied Shires. 'We only want our liberty.'

Hoy came up first, looking shaken and forlorn. Two convicts had their muskets levelled at him, and another had a knife at his back. His hands were soon bound. When Taw was asked to come up, he mounted the stairs slowly, the gash over his left eye still red and raw. Nicholls followed meekly. There was no further resistance.

There remained only the last two soldiers and Macfarlane. With a musket shot from the ship, they were signalled to stop fishing in the jolly-boat and come alongside.

Just as they reached the *Frederick*, Porter jumped on their boat. Before they knew it, the boy from Bermondsey was pointing a cocked Brown Bess at them. Within seconds, the two bewildered soldiers were relieved of their guns and placed with the other captives. The jolly-boat was then put under convict guard.

The *Frederick* had changed hands in less than a few hours. And it had been done without serious violence and without injuries, aside from the minor gash on Taw's head.

Hoy asked who was to run things from now on, but he must have known that his own foreman, John Barker, was the man he had to deal with.

Barker told Hoy, 'I am now the captain of this brig, and with the assistance of my men, I can navigate her around the world.'

'You are deluded,' Hoy told Barker. 'I promise before God and with a Bible in my hand that if you give us back the brig, nobody will mention what happened today when we reach Port Arthur.'

They all knew the risks they were taking and the penalty for piracy, but the shipwright's pleas fell on deaf ears. 'We will not yield this ship. All we want is our liberty,' Barker repeated.

Neither Barker, nor any of the men, could stomach the idea of Port Arthur. Real liberty, the kind they had just fought for, was beginning to taste very sweet.

Under guard, Hoy and Taw were taken down to their cabins and allowed to pack anything they needed – especially clothes to keep them warm. It was clear what was to happen next: they and the soldiers would be marooned and forced to find their way back to the colony. Hoy apparently asked for a small gun to defend against any threats from Aboriginal people, but this was denied by all the convicts in the politest way. 'We begged to be excused,' is how Porter puts it.

Once they'd fetched their belongings, Taw's hands were tied, but not Hoy's as he complained of his bad back. At some point, Shires offered Hoy a bottle of alcohol and a pocket compass, and told him to stay quiet about it. Then Hoy and Taw, the first mate and the four soldiers, as well as the two non-complicit convicts, were lowered down to the jolly-boat. Six armed convicts would trail them in the whaleboat, which was attached in those days to most of the ships as a lifeboat or as a utility boat.

'When you reach the shore,' Barker told Hoy, 'push the boat back into the water. We don't want you rushing our boat late at night.'

The convicts kept a strict watch that night. 'It's death for any man found asleep on their watch,' Barker warned. The convicts were taking no chances. They were scared that somehow the marooned men would return to take control.

Around daybreak, a group of convicts, including Porter, returned to the men, who were huddled in the scrub just above the sandy beach, laden with some of their requests. Hoy wanted bandages and plaster for his back, and he was also supplied with two bottles of wine to soothe his pain. The soldiers were given their watch coats.

Then the entire provisions from the *Frederick* were divided between the victors and the defeated – apparently with slightly more given to the captured men.

'Do not let our affair be like that of the *Cyprus* to leave them to starve,' Shires said. 'My proposal is to share the provisions with them as nearly as possible for there are nine of them and ten of us, and let us trust to Providence, and it will also be the means of preventing them from saying when they reach headquarters that we used them cruelly or in a dishonourable manner.'

Despite his rash actions the day before, Shires was the one convict who had the *Cyprus* affair – and its failures – firmly lodged in his head.

Flour, oatmeal and salted beef were handed over, as well as tea, biscuits and sugar. The live goat was presented to the marooned men as well as cooking utensils.

But the tomcat would remain onboard. Seafaring superstition had it that cats brought good luck – they supposedly had special powers to protect ships from dangerous weather. Beyond any of that, they helped rid a ship of its rats.

This exchange was made in an atmosphere of total conviviality. Hoy then made one final plea to the convicts not to make this mistake, but again he was rebuffed. He then offered them what amounted to a blessing and his best wishes:

'Since I find you will not give her up – I thank you all for your kindness to the whole of us, myself in particular. I know you have but little provisions to cross the expanding ocean and likewise a brig that is not seaworthy for such a voyage and may God prosper you in all your perilous undertaking.'

Porter said the convicts that were present, all thanked him.

'Three cheers for the Admiral!' they shouted at Hoy.

The stranded men, including the soldiers, gave three cheers back. 'We wish you a prosperous voyage,' called Taw. He was taking it well, but he must have known the ramifications of all this. He would never have a government job again. He was, after all, meant to be in charge. Arthur would need a scapegoat, and there was no doubt who that would have to be.

Never before had a boat been seized from British authorities with such bonhomie, and this had much to do with the convicts' largesse. They must have all feared they had sacrificed their chances of success for the good of the men they were leaving behind. But this was where the story of the *Frederick* differed so crucially from that of the *Cyprus*. The roles of captor and captured had changed, but their camaraderie had endured.

On the morning of 14 January 1834, Porter's last glimpse of the marooned men was an emotional Taw wiping tears from his eyes.

*

PORTER, LESLIE, RUSSEN and Lyon had been in custody for more than ten years. Shires had been in Van Diemen's Land for close to fourteen, and a convict for fifteen. Perhaps the two luckiest of the ten were Jones and Fare – both of whom had arrived in Van Diemen's Land on the *Enchantress* in July 1833. They had barely experienced convict life in Hobart Town before they were packed off to Macquarie Harbour. By then the penal station was hardly the place of misery it once was. Now all of these men could make their own decisions and control their own destinies. They had the taste of real freedom.

The authorities would call the acts described above as 'piratically seizing the *Frederick*' – and this meant, of course, that the convicts were wanted men. But for once, time was on their side. They knew that it would take several weeks before the port officer at Hobart Town would be notified that the *Frederick* was late to arrive at Port Arthur. It would take a few days longer for the authorities to organise and equip a search party, and a few days more before that party departed. The *Frederick* ten could be at sea a month before anyone attempted to pursue them. By then, the convicts hoped to be very far away.

But as they were preparing to leave the harbour, the winds died. The ship stopped moving. It would have to be 'warped' or kedged through Hells Gates.

This was an extremely difficult exercise. The kedge anchor, a smaller anchor than the main, is set ahead of the ship; then using a cable, the boat is slowly winched towards the anchor in the desired direction. Four men took the kedge out in the whaleboat and let it go overboard. Other men had to man the capstan, winding the anchor's cable and painstakingly pulling the *Frederick* forward. The whole process was repeated for three miles, says Porter.

While they were inching the *Frederick* towards the gates, a small boat was spied on a strip of beach. They decided 'to stove it in', destroying it so that Captain Taw and the soldiers couldn't use it to retake the *Frederick*.

None of this activity was necessary. They could have waited a day or so for a better breeze, and the abandoned boat was surely too small to pose a threat. But the men, so long confined in the harbour, were showing early signs of paranoia. There was an air of impatience and disbelief, understandable given their predicament. They may have felt that at any moment their luck would run out and a government boat would appear. And nobody trusted Taw – they believed he was capable of anything.

According to Porter, 'We succeeded in getting her abreast of two islands known as Cap and Bonnet – the boat we hung astern and in another hour the tide was running at the rate of seven knots an hour in our favour.'

As the *Frederick* was being winched through the gates, she heeled round. Would she strike the northern spit?

At the very last moment, a light wind came to her rescue – the sails filled, the steerage system kicked in, and she found her line. The last boat to leave Macquarie Harbour Penal Station had been squeezed through the dreaded Hells Gates, where so many other ships had foundered. The *Frederick*'s maiden voyage had begun.

'I cannot express my feelings at that moment,' says Porter. 'My heart expanded within me and I believe it was the happiest moment of my life.'

Chapter 11

THE FREDERICK TEN enjoyed their first day of freedom moving smartly on a west-north-west wind. To keep speed, the crew broke up the whaleboat and cast its pieces into the sea, thereby losing seven tons of weight. They had now destroyed both the jolly-boat and the whaleboat, leaving only the long boat, which was attached to the deck. By the next morning, the breeze had stiffened, with the ship moving at the very brisk rate of twelve knots per hour, under a single-reefed main topsail and foresail. This was an intelligent setting for the fairly strong weather conditions they were facing. Reefing in the top sails and foresails reduced the amount of canvas exposed to the wind and made the boat manageable for the small crew.

Barker was making a west-south-west course, veering away from Van Diemen's Land to ensure they were out of sight of any inquisitive vessels.

To have the *Frederick* under their command was like a dream for the men. But despite her size and potential, they couldn't afford to ignore certain realities. Half the men were untrained. Even though they'd all experienced the sea during their transportation, the average convict had spent more time in the hold than on deck.

The *Frederick* may have been an amazing prize, in the same calibre as the *Cyprus*, but she wasn't free of liabilities. She was made to hug coasts and cruise estuaries, not to cross the Southern and Pacific oceans consecutively. In heavy seas, the *Frederick* wasn't the kind of boat they should be sailing – as a brig she had more sails than most other ships, which usually required a big crew to manage the extra canvas. It was always going to be a difficult balancing act that seemed to require a full crew of seamen, not a handful of sailors and landlubbers.

The Frederick *probably looked similar to the two-masted brig* Norval *depicted in this painting from 1833. The* Frederick *was as light as a butterfly, made to American standards of speed and British requirements for sturdiness, but her planks were green which made her susceptible to leaks.*

And the big question was, where on earth could they go that would be far enough from the long arm of the British Navy?

Of course, they could look to the voyage of the *Cyprus*, which must have loomed large in everybody's minds. Three of the eighteen mutineers had slipped away to America, but the rest were eventually rounded up. Depending on their individual circumstances, they were either hanged or returned to Macquarie Harbour.

It was reputedly John Barker who persuaded his nine companions that South America would be the most intelligent destination. Chile was the country chosen and Valdivia, the seaport they would be heading for. Why Valdivia? It's not really known, but the best guess is that arriving there would probably draw less attention from the authorities than would be the case at a bigger port such as Valparaíso, which lay several hundred miles north. Perhaps Porter had a say in this, as he knew the Chilean coastline well, and had a wife and son in Valparaíso whom he hadn't seen for more than fifteen years.

There were advantages in taking this route. They would be running with the prevailing winds and could navigate well south of the busiest shipping lanes. The other attraction was Chile's recent independence. Over the previous two decades the Chileans had unshackled themselves from Spain, and after a bloody revolution had no allegiance to any of the European powers. Porter and Barker might have surmised that most Chileans would view a group of runaway British convicts more as compadres than criminals. It was also a country with strong maritime links. Why wouldn't they welcome a group of well-trained shipbuilders?

What the convicts were attempting to do was unheard of. The brig was a tiny 130-ton vessel, nothing like the ships that plied their trade between Australia and Chile in the early nineteenth century.

Vessels at that time were 'built by the mile and served out by the yard' and tended to be deep, flat-bottomed, slab-sided and sluggish. The vessels used for this kind of distance were much heavier than the *Frederick* – at least two hundred tons and preferably three hundred.

Within an hour or two of departing Hells Gates, the crew discovered a slow but consistent leak. It dawned on James Porter that Hoy's words about the brig might be true: perhaps they were deluded to think they could take the *Frederick* far from Van Diemen's Land. The ship's planking was too young and hadn't settled. The outside seams of the bottom planks had been forced open. A second caulking, after a short initial voyage, would have sealed her up tight. What were they thinking, taking this improperly sealed boat six thousand nautical miles to Chile?

Then they found that only one of their two pumps worked: the portside pump was blocked, and only the starboard pump was clanking into action. Because the ship had been launched in haste, neither pumps had been tested.

The ships of that time used chain pumps, which generally needed the strength of two men to function effectively. It was laborious work. The men would rotate a handle that turned a chain, which in turn lifted small buckets of water up from down below and tipped them onto the deck. With just one pump working, the brig could never be emptied of water at the rate they needed.

The voyage would take around six weeks if the winds were favourable, and already they had to keep up a near-constant use of the pumps. They would have to literally bail themselves out of trouble.

*

THE WIND WAS still gaining strength. By late afternoon on the first day, it had turned into a gale. This was something the tradesmen on board had never experienced, not even on their voyage out from England. The little *Frederick* somehow forged through it all, rising and falling thirty feet at a time as she fought the waves, yet still holding her line. Lyon was at the tiller, valiantly keeping the boat on an even keel, but as time wore on, and the wind showed no signs of blowing out, he was visibly straining.

By early evening the *Frederick* was plunging into seas that burst heavily on impact, clouds of icy foam spraying across her bows. Lyon was having the worst of it, suffering the full force of the spray as the ship bucked the waves and slapped the ocean. He looked like a thin, drenched scarecrow who might be blown away at any moment. He needed an extra hand, but there was none. Other tasks were more pressing. As the wind blew harder, the sails were so full they looked like they were about to jump clean from the masts – they had to be shortened.

Fare, a former foremastman, was the first mate and in charge of making the pure sailing decisions. With the boat alternately plunging and lurching, and with virtually no visibility, he directed six men to bring in as many sails as they could muster. With too much canvas, the ship could heel dangerously and the masts could split. The seas began to break over her, and every man was soon wet through. The decks were flooded with heavy seas, which poured white-capped over the sides. Even the topsail yards were being drenched with spray. The men clambered up the main and foremast yards to reel back the topgallant square sails.

Just moving around on the deck, with the wash and pitch of the boat, was difficult enough. How the landlubbers, in particular, were able to find their way across the deck and up the masts is a mystery. Men were having to grab ropes and deck fittings wherever possible as their legs were swept out from under them. Some were wrenched onto the boiling surface of the flooded deck. It was chaos.

As night came on, they managed by degrees to reef the topgallants while the masts were swaying heavily – this was about ensuring less topsail, which could easily be blown out in such winds. It was all achieved in a wild spray of icy wind and surging saltwater. Somehow, despite the weather conditions and the utter darkness, they managed to clamber to the highest sails and reef them in.

Close to midnight, the gale was reaching such a strength that to keep her on some kind of track, Lyon desperately needed another man at the helm. The boat was becoming too heavy to steer. The two men who had been pumping out the water from the hold had been ordered aloft. The pump had to be abandoned.

But the early hours on the second day, men were down. Barker's seasickness had come on early and he was confined to bed. After being placed so high in such a turbulent sea, and without time to acquire their sea legs, Shires, Russen and Cheshire were all retching violently. This left the boat under the control of four seamen: Lyon, Porter, Fare and Jones – as well as the bricklayer John Dady. They were the only men fit enough to work in the storm.

There was nobody to keep watch, make meals or navigate. They were, as Porter put it bluntly, 'very short-handed'. The ship was under the kind of pressure that might have broken her up. So well had she been crafted by Hoy, though, that despite the constant rise and fall of the bowsprit, plunging heavily into the troughs, she stayed whole and kept aright. Hoy's boast that he could make ships with both American speed and British sturdiness was proving to be correct, even if he had warned the convicts that the *Frederick* wouldn't last the distance. The ship creaked and sighed as she climbed the mountains of waves and cut into the valleys, a tiny speck holding its own in a wide waste of water.

*

For two days the heavy weather persisted. Eventually clear patches of sky opened up around them, but four men were still out of action. Somehow discipline was achieved, and everyone ate and slept where and when they could.

In a gale the topgallants had to be furled, and afterwards this was reversed, with canvas spread as wide as possible to take advantage of a lighter breeze. This time they'd been lucky to have just enough fit men to climb the rigging and perform this difficult work, forty feet above the deck in shrieking winds. The convicts knew they might not have the same luck throughout the voyage.

Leslie, recovered from his seasickness, was the first to check the hold after the storm. It was leaking heavily. He cried out in alarm: the water was already above waist-height in parts. The *Frederick* would stay afloat, but with water constantly entering, the pump had to be manned at all hours – and steering her would be heavy.

Now that the weather had settled, the men had a chance to contemplate their circumstances. Despite their troubles, they'd made excellent progress. In just two days they had left Macquarie Harbour some three hundred nautical miles behind. But speed had its consequences. In Porter's words, 'the sea was being given greater power on the brig' than it should have.

Even during the gale, despite furling the very top sails, more should have been done to slow the ship. She was carrying 'such a heavy piece of canvass [sic] during the gale,' he said, '...we being afraid of some vessel being in pursuit of us'. Common sense would have been to take the ship at a slower pace, easing the pressure on the hull and reducing the rate of water intake. Porter, while not directly casting blame at Barker, makes it clear in his memoir that fear was pushing the ship faster than it needed to go. It was as if they expected a phantom pursuer, perhaps captained by Governor Arthur himself, to suddenly lurch into view and catch them unawares. 'We knew if we were brought back, governor Arthur would hang us to a dead certainty,' Porter wrote. It seems Arthur was the bogeyman that kept the *Frederick* moving at an unsustainable pace.

Under Barker's command, the ship was being driven, not sailed. When Barker took a meridian observation of the sun's position on 16 January, he altered the course to east by south. He wanted them to be travelling through no man's waters, as far from Van Diemen's Land as nautically possible.

Between forty and fifty degrees latitude, the strong westerly winds known as the roaring forties prevail; move further south, and your ship might have to deal with even stronger winds, the furious fifties or the shrieking sixties. The brig needed to be sailed well south of New Zealand, but not so far south as to be caught amid the worst tempests and floating white mountains of the frigid Southern Ocean.

*

BY 18 JANUARY, the wind had died down, and the ship and its crew were in better shape. The heavy laden sky broke into patches of blue, with light cirrus clouds scattered about. But the men didn't have much time to enjoy the respite. The ship was being driven into turbulent seas – it was now bearing directly towards the Antarctic Circle. Fare, the most senior sailor on board, must have been worried: their leaky brig was heading for one of the coldest and windiest parts of the Earth. They could see it all before them: the Southern Ocean, darker and more moody than even the North Atlantic, and forever whitened by the unrelenting icy winds.

There was no doubt Barker wanted to hitch a ride on stronger winds, but how far south was he prepared to go? Past sixty degrees? Most likely he was attempting to sail below the 'Clipper Route', where bigger vessels than the *Frederick* used the strong prevailing westerlies to improve their speed across the Southern Ocean. But the bigger ships would only dare to dip lower into the furious fifties as they moved south to round Cape Horn – and only because geography demanded it – a ship on the return trip to Europe had to dip into latitude fifty-five degrees south to round the Horn. A brig such as the *Frederick* was too light and small to deal with these extreme conditions. It would be tossed about like a cork – and yet there it was, heading into ever lower latitudes.

Fare ordered the topgallants, the very highest of the square sails, to be reduced – he felt they might be carrying too much sail as the brig neared the dangerous southern waters. The crew set a watch on the pump, and two men manned it for two hours at a time. The landlubbers were still intermittently sick, and the navigator was spending most of his time in bed.

More questions were being raised. Were they moving in the right direction? They soon came across a vast quantity of seaweed, which made the men very nervous. Where exactly were they? Were they close to land? They weren't expected to make landfall for weeks.

Barker hadn't made an observation since day two. A week after leaving Macquarie Harbour, the men pulled him out of bed. Just before midday, two men on either side propped him up on deck while he checked his position with the sun. Barker looked at the seaweed, then looked at the sun and told the men they had nothing to worry about. According to Porter, he said, 'Do not be in the least afraid as to my knowledge or capability of performing what I have taken in hand – for if I can take you safe to South America, although [even if] I had not a quadrant on board, for I could do it by keeping a dead reckoning, it being a straight course.'

Porter says that although the men seemed assured by Barker's statement, their murmurings persisted. In all likelihood, his calculations were faulty. A somewhat overconfident landlubber was giving the orders from his sickbed, but still nobody countermanded him. Successful dead reckoning requires regular noon sightings, with the course tweaked and the ship's position plotted on a map; whether or not Barker even had a map is unknown. But he must have known that Valdivia was on the 40th parallel, as their ship was being directed in a relationship with this line of latitude. If they veered away from it, he could check their angle from the sun and know along what latitude he was progressing – but there was always the question of longitude, or how far along they were.

Valdivia is roughly on the same parallel as Macquarie Harbour, but the ship had dropped much further south, perhaps to around fifty-five to fifty-seven degrees latitude. The greatest fears regarding longitude were that without correct speed readings, they would reach destinations before they were expected, or they would simply not come into view at all. Thousands of mariners had lost their lives when reefs and coastlines suddenly loomed out of the sea on a dark night.

The convicts would have used a logline for calculating speed and Barker had a quadrant for measuring angles to establish latitude and a compass for direction. But he wouldn't have had a reliable chronometer, which in the 1830s was vital for determining longitude – a ship's east–west position. To determine longitude, one had to know the time aboard the ship (the highest point of the sun denoted midday) and the time of another place of known longitude – at the same moment. Each hour's time difference between the ship and the known point of longitude marks a progress of fifteen degrees. It's easy enough to do this today with two wristwatches, but back in Porter's time, a reliable chronometer, unaffected by the heat or the cold or the movement of the ship, was not so easy to obtain. If they had had one, they could have plotted their course exactly.

This is why dead reckoning is considered little more than guesswork. You could determine approximate position if you were regularly recording the speeds and the exact course the ship was taking, but while Porter did mention speed from time to time, it appears to have been recorded haphazardly. There was neither enough time nor enough manpower to do this regularly.

The fear of pursuit was omnipresent but so was the feeling that they were way out of their depth. They had never been this far south. Keep to this line and they'd miss the coast of South America entirely. They needed to take a northerly direction sooner or later, which meant entering shipping lanes. They couldn't delay this forever: they had to come into the purview of other ships at some point.

spread among the men. Barker had not made an observation for many days. His calculations had taken them well to the south of New Zealand, but according to Porter there was growing discontent.

Barker, 'hearing of this discontent', made an effort to rise on 30 January, but the weather wasn't clear enough to reveal the sun. When Barker returned on deck the next day, he made a reading. To the relief of his crew, he announced they would alter their course sharply, heading north-east. They were finally turning towards South America.

142

Chapter 12

For ten days, Taw, Hoy and the assorted soldiers and servants shuffled towards Woolnorth in the north-west of the colony, crossing beaches, rivers and thick bushland.

Their initial problem had been logistical. They'd been left by the mutineers on the southern side of the harbour and needed to find their way to the north in order to begin any journey. As could be expected, Hoy came to the rescue, fashioning a raft that allowed them to cross the estuary to the northern side. The raft had been a makeshift affair by Hoy's standards. It was leaky and allowed only three men to cross at a time, but over the first day they managed to move all the men and supplies.

From there, they took the coastal route north and for the first three days trudged along lonely beaches, first sighted by Abel Tasman two hundred years earlier but almost forgotten by white men ever since. When the beaches became too precipitous, they crossed inland. After wading across the rock-strewn Pieman River at low tide, they eventually made it to the Arthur River.

Then came arguably the hardest part: they had to hack their way precariously through the dense bush of the north-western side of the island, all the while keeping a careful account of their supplies.

On 24 January 1834, around the time that the *Frederick* was rounding New Zealand's south island, the Taw and Hoy party reached their objective – the Van Diemen's Land Company, a farming concern and the only European presence in that part of the island. They were sunburnt, blistered and tired, but they were all in one piece. They owed their survival to the supplies they'd been given and another small detail: Hoy and Taw had a compass, handed over surreptitiously by Shires.

Three days later Hoy was in Launceston, detailing the party's experiences to a magistrate in a sworn statement. The following week Taw was giving his own version of events in Hobart Town. The next day, 4 February 1834, the news broke.

The *Colonial Times* reported:

> News has reached the town this morning, that the new schooner
> [sic], The Frederick, built at Macquarie Harbour, and which
> had been expected to arrive in Hobart Town for the last three
> weeks, has been piratically seized by the prisoners, left at that
> abandoned settlement, for the purpose of bringing the vessel to
> this port. Captain Taw has arrived by mail this morning from
> Launceston, bringing the above intelligence. It appears that
> the prisoners took advantage of some of the soldiers being on a
> fishing expedition, when they overpowered the remainder, and
> took forcible possession of the vessel. The Frederick is spoken of
> as being a fast vessel, and as the pirates have had three weeks
> start, there is little chance of their capture – perhaps, however,

a government brig, with half a dozen soldiers on board, will be sent to New Zealand in pursuit.

On the same day, the *Colonist* reported that Taw and his party 'underwent great hardships' where they received 'every possible kindness from the Van Diemen's Land Company, and a passage on the *Tamar*'. The *Hobart Town Courier* proclaimed that this 'daring act of piracy' should be listed among those which 'from time to time have disgraced the annals of these colonies': 'They are not more to be regretted on account of the loss they bring upon public property than for the misery they invariably entail upon the wretched offenders themselves.'

Governor George Arthur showed no interest in the ordeal of Taw and Hoy's party across the west and north-west of Van Diemen's Land. To him, this was never a case of misfortune. There were no mishaps and tragedies in his world, just breaches of military discipline. Mistakes had to be punished and offenders court-martialled. Arthur's reputation for military rigour and his standing among his superiors were now in question. There were, however, facts that could not be erased. Arthur had overseen the conditions that had enabled the fiasco to occur. The military protocols once set in stone at Macquarie Harbour had been virtually abandoned, and Arthur was no less to blame than Hoy or Captain Taw.

According to Arthur's rigorous *Standing Orders for the Masters of Colonial Vessels*, no convict was allowed to handle any form of offensive weapon. If Arthur had made inquiries, he would have known that Barker was the penal settlement's gunsmith, working with soldiers' weapons at all times. The shipbuilders, too, had to handle what could be described as 'offensive weapons', such as axes and adzes. Article 4 of the *Standing Orders* states that convict workers should be kept in heavy double irons at all times. How the men could have crewed a ship and taken it back to Port Arthur shackled in double irons was never quite explained. Arthur's seventh article states that prisoners must never assist as crew – but the convicts were the crew, and Arthur knew this. In other words, he had flouted his own procedures. His own lax oversight had allowed this to happen. In fairness to Arthur, he had wanted Macquarie Harbour abandoned immediately and the *Frederick* completed at Port Arthur, but given Commandant Baylee's (and most likely Hoy's) remonstrations that this was impracticable, Arthur had relented.

Not only was he embarrassed by his own inaction, but he was also faced with a troubling reaction from the common people: barely suppressed admiration for the escaped convicts. The *Frederick* ten weren't exactly heroes but they were anti-heroes at the very least. There were shades of Matthew Brady in all this. Many of the newspapers simply trotted out the government line that these men had recklessly and mutinously stolen a boat. That they were pirates, thieves and mutineers. But the people saw things differently. By now it was well known that these men had acted more like Robin Hoods of the high seas than Blackbeard the pirate. They'd given the nine marooned men more food than they had kept. They had even saved the tomcat! The tale had all the most daring elements of the taking of the *Cyprus* and none of its less savoury aspects. The *Frederick* men had carried off a bloodless coup, and shown enormous largesse into the bargain.

Arthur, of course, knew that this general goodwill towards the escapees was an indictment not just on his rule, but on all the principles he believed in as well. This so-called act of piracy had made the governor look weak, incompetent and fallible. It was a black mark against his governance. He had been a fool to trust in Hoy and Baylee. His superiors in London would not be amused.

The government, or at least its officials, had formed their opinion of what had happened well before there was any official inquiry into the matter. Someone's head had to roll. On 2 February 1834, Chief Police Magistrate Forster wrote to Colonial Secretary Burnett of the 'Piratical Capture of His Majesty's Colonial Brig, *Frederick*', stating that in his opinion 'the capture of the brig has been principally owing to the total neglect of any military guard being kept, or of the most common precautions having been taken for her safety'. Forster added, 'The master [Taw] appears to me to have conducted himself personally well, after the attack was made, but to have been very blameable, in not having taken the slightest precaution to prevent what has unfortunately happened.' Taw surely realised that he would be blamed for the *Frederick* debacle.

But before Arthur began to assign official blame, he wasted no time in mounting a search for the escapees. On the day that the news broke in the local press, he requested that the police characters of all ten men be sent to Captain Lambert of HMS *Alligator*, then at anchor in Hobart Town. Arthur demanded that the captain begin an immediate pursuit of the *Frederick*, which he believed would be hiding somewhere in New Zealand. He also asked the chief police magistrate to obtain all information and to draw up a statement of the circumstances around the seizure of the *Frederick* to be sent to the *Alligator*. Copies would be sent to officials in New Zealand and to the colonial secretary in New South Wales, so police in both jurisdictions would be apprised of all details.

On 7 February, Arthur wrote an obsequious letter to Lord Stanley, Secretary of State for the Colonies in London, saying that he 'had the honour' to report the abandonment of Macquarie Harbour but that it had 'not been effected without loss'. Arthur briefly outlined the circumstances that led to the taking of the *Frederick* and made it clear, twice, whom he wished to blame: Captain Taw. The man was, he wrote, the master 'entrusted with the most dangerous and responsible appointment as pilot, [who] from that degree of culpable security which is always the parent of danger, took no precautions'. Arthur hastened to add that a copy of his standing orders on the security of vessels had been reissued to the masters of government ships 'which were utterly neglected by Mr Taw or the occurrence would have never happened'.

Meanwhile, Captain Lambert decided not to pursue the convicts. Who knew if they had really headed to New Zealand? To go after them, nearly a month after the *Frederick* had departed, would be little more than a wild goose chase. The Macquarie Harbour pirates had fallen off the face of the Earth.

For the first time in years, the man who'd had a say in everything could do nothing. The *Frederick* ten had achieved their greatest triumph. Their great nemesis, the governor of Van Diemen's Land, was helpless.

*

PURSUING THE *FREDERICK* would certainly have been a hopeless exercise. By the time Captain Lambert and Arthur were discussing the possibility, the men on the *Frederick* were at least a thousand miles beyond the eastern shores of New Zealand. The *Frederick* was now moving purposefully into the southern Pacific on the back of lighter, calmer winds. They could now use more canvas, which must have improved morale even if it meant greater speed and still more pumping. They would sight South America, by Barker's reckoning, in about four weeks' time.

The *Frederick* was fast and light, but when you're so far away from anything familiar, and with no landmarks, a small boat begins to feel lost. While Porter was an experienced seaman, in his memoir he reveals no love for any ship other than the *Frederick*. His relationship with this brig was unique. He had helped create her – at least in its latter stages – and she was taking him and his mates to freedom. In so many other ships he had been a prisoner; in the *Frederick*, neat and small as she was, he was free – but somehow the faster she flew across the waves, the more vulnerable and open to danger he felt.

The *Frederick* was like a young butterfly that skipped to every beat of the wind. She was healthy aside from a tiny wound to her abdomen. But her vitality felt tenuous, as if she might weaken before her time was up. The little brig would enjoy a fast and furious life, but not a full one.

By early February there was less seasickness and more hands to do the heavy work. As the *Frederick* flew along, the waters were warming by the day. Then one afternoon, Porter noticed a few white clouds coming into view. As they grew closer, he saw that they weren't clouds but a white wall of spume – a mix of turbulent air and water, heading in the brig's direction.

It came on so quickly that Porter was never sure if the boat moved into the wall or the wall moved in on the boat. Within seconds the wind whipped up and the water began to chop and boil around them.

It started as a whistle through the rigging but within less than a minute it had become an audible shriek. Before anyone knew it, a wall of water hit the port side of the ship. The *Frederick* had been literally knocked off balance and was listing heavily to the starboard. All around them the sea was whipping and swirling, and the *Frederick* was continuing to lurch. It wasn't just the pitch of the boat that scared the men: this strange piece of devilry had other characteristics. Everything – wind, water and air – was being churned up and spat in all directions. They had entered an aquatic ambush, as if a hundred whales were blasting saltwater at them from all sides.

The waters kept battering, and the ship kept listing. The *Frederick* seemed to have lost its traction on the water. If nothing was done, the vessel could be thrown on its beam ends – the deck and mast would cartwheel into the churning sea. The shouting and screaming increased as the brig kept listing to starboard, pulled over by the sudden and furious assault on the sails. Men who had been standing on the deck found themselves scrabbling for something to hold on to. The ship was visibly tilting, and the weight shifted from their legs to their arms as they lunged for whatever piece of the ship was close enough to grasp. The deck was slipping as the *Frederick* shuddered and groaned from one end to the other. Something crashed above. The main boom, a large wooden spar connecting mast to sail, broke from the main mast and smashed into the sea. A mass of ropes and shattered timber trailed from the ship.

The *Frederick* men didn't know it but they were in the midst of a white squall, one of the least-understood of weather phenomena. In essence, it is a storm of wind and water that emerges from nowhere, without the associated black clouds that signal a normal sea squall. The white squall is still not completely understood – and was a complete mystery then. Nineteenth-century meteorologists were at a loss to explain it – they were clear about a normal black squall but when it came to the cloudless 'white' version, all they could do was describe it.

'The sudden falling of a vessel into such a stream, or the being overtaken of it, is more difficult to account for, on any definite principle, than in the other case,' wrote meteorologist Luke Howard in 1833. A white squall arrives with no warning and sweeps up anything caught in its path. As the turbulent clouds flash into view the wind speed can soar from ten miles an hour to more than seventy miles an hour in a few moments.

In Porter's version of events, Fare was able to keep his head while the squall was passing through the boat, reducing the weight of sail and managing to bring the ship upright. But a white squall comes with such speed and ferocity, it is impossible to do any work on the boat while it occurs.

What is more likely to have happened was that the squall passed, allowing Fare to react. The broken spar, still attached to the boat through the rigging, could wait. Fare called in as many sails as he could. He ordered the men to put a reef in the main topsail, furl the fore topsail and clear the yards on the masts. Some of the men clambered up the masts and, as quickly as possible, shortened some sails while others were set clear, dropping with a thud onto the deck.

Slowly but surely, they released the boat from the phantom grip of the squall's trailing winds. Setting the *Frederick* aright had seemed to take an eternity.

Fare realised he now had longer-term problems. The boat may have been sitting upright, but they had shorn it of its sails. It was a sitting duck, bobbing precariously with nothing to pull it forward.

Fare now reversed the order, realising that he had to keep moving at a speed that could outrun the flurry of wind and water that might follow the squall. If they did not, there was a strong chance that the ship could be 'pooped' – that large waves, coming up from behind, could swamp the boat.

The new call was to increase the number of sails, and it wasn't a popular one. The men were now forced to reclimb the masts and somehow a new set of sails was added and hoisted. Porter seemed to feel the weight of Fare's order because it had so many repercussions. Speed meant the men in the hold would be waist-deep in water for days, mast-climbing for hours on end and grappling at the wheel all night. Speed meant pain not just for them, but also for the little brig on which their lives depended.

Two things were now happening in tandem: Fare was attempting to sail the boat ahead of waves, while others were desperately trying to haul in the two halves of the broken spar, which were attached to a mass of ropes. The spar pieces had to be retrieved and patched up quickly. Using two spare lengths of wood like splints, the crew bound them around the broken boom. It did the trick.

The little *Frederick* was fast enough to skip free of the onrushing waves, but as soon as the mayhem abated, a gale took its place. The men who had climbed the masts and fixed the broken boom were close to physical exhaustion. As the winds began to swirl and gain strength, the mechanics dropped off one by one. They were yet again falling prey to seasickness, just as they had in the South Seas. The swell was now breaking over the deck and coming down the hatches, but the boat, as ever, kept its line.

According to Porter, the heavy weather continued for another nine days and nights, putting enormous strain on both bodies and brig. Two men were at the helm to stop her being pooped or broached by the menacing seas. And, as ever, the pumps had to be kept going at their fullest capacity.

Mast, hull, lookout and wheel – it was an endless merry-go-round of exertion, and Porter admits he was at his wit's end. Every time the winds became more violent and the seas more turbulent, the number of hands willing or able to work the boat diminished. 'With so many hands being sick, the remainder of us were nearly exhausted unto death,' he wrote.

When the winds finally relented, the landlubbers came up from their sickbeds, blinking into the sunlight, wondering what had been done to keep the ship on course and upright. The seamen were on deck, looking hollowed out, their faces scoured by salt and wind, and their eyes staring into the distance. They had executed their duties automatically, in a half daze, and somehow the *Frederick* had come through.

*

IN THE FIRST week of February, Barker announced that they were around five hundred miles south of the parallel he wanted to take which would bring the ship in line with the point where they would reach the Chilean coast. They would need to bear even further north. The ship had survived two gales and a white squall, and on 11 February, a threat of an entirely different kind loomed. They caught sight of another vessel. With paranoia running high on the *Frederick*, there was an instinctive fear that this was a British ship.

When two ships pass each other, marine protocol demands that when one ship hoists its ensign, the other is bound to do the same.

Of course, they had no such ensign. A British ship, on observing that no ensign was flown, would almost certainly perceive the *Frederick* as a hostile or rogue ship – and possibly engage. The last thing the men needed was an interrogation from a suspicious captain. Even being reported was a risk.

They soon saw that it was a whaleship. This was a relief to some, but a source of anxiety to those who knew the sea better. Whaleships tended to do their own thing – most sea protocols were usually anathema to them, but they could be jealous of other ships in their waters. The captain might surmise that the *Frederick* was an unwanted presence in his hunting territory. Or he may just want to exchange civilities.

Barker called out for arms and ammunition. 'We had not a flag or a bit of bunting on board and had they come alongside and made themselves inquisitive, we were determined to run on board of them, capture them or die in the attempt,' Porter says.

Fortunately for the tense crew, the whaleship simply ignored them. Neither vessel desired to follow protocol. And there was an upside: the sighting of a boat was a sign that land may not be too far distant. As the whaler passed, the men on board must have felt that the most difficult leg of the voyage was over.

Supplies, however, were growing scarce. The largesse of the *Frederick* ten was beginning to undermine them.

Around 25 February, land finally came into view, but not everybody believed what they were seeing. Barker thought it was a bank of cloud and that they were still five hundred miles – or three days' sailing – from landfall. Fare begged to differ; he shortened the sails and brought the brig to a halt. They were lucky. Had the men not sighted land before dusk, they could have sailed right into it.

By morning the coast of Chile had officially been sighted. Barker's reckonings had failed him by three days, but as he had directed them to land, everything else was forgiven. He took a sighting at noon and announced they were indeed off the coast of Chile, but still a hundred miles south of Valdivia.

They had wrestled with nature and, through sheer grit and determination, they'd survived. But too much had been asked of the little *Frederick*. The butterfly brig had done her duty, taking them to freedom across two oceans in six weeks and a day. The crew knew instinctively that this was the *Frederick*'s last stand.

Chapter 13

THE CONVICTS HAD performed a miracle of seamanship. They had travelled six thousand nautical miles in a leaky boat on some of the most turbulent seas on Earth. They had covered a vast portion of the southern hemisphere with just ten men, only five of whom were bona fide sailors. It's worth remembering that Matthew Flinders who had circumnavigated Australia in his similar-sized *Investigator*, crewed by thirty-five seamen, seven times the *Frederick*'s number. Even the *Cyprus*, so often compared to the *Frederick*, started with *eighteen* working convicts on board.

The diligence of the *Frederick* crew, the intelligent sailing of John Fare, the motivating fear of being caught and the visceral desire for freedom had combined into a potent fuel to propel the little brig. Now, just off the coast of South America, the *Frederick* was spent. 'Proud we were of it,' Porter says in his memoir, but 'the brig was getting the best of us in the leakage'.

The amount of water she was taking in was now too great. The men were hungry and tired but exhilarated, but there was still so much more to do. They had only one way off the brig: the far less majestic seven-ton longboat, a small vessel that had to be rigged with its own set of sails and rebuilt to allow more space for the men. They had no choice but to make this their coastal cruiser until they discovered Valdivia.

The prospect of leaving their home of six weeks was an unhappy one and there were still plenty of fears. Not everybody was confident that Barker's geographical guesswork was solid. How far exactly were they from the promised port? They needed new identities, and they needed an air-tight alibi that would thwart any Spanish inquisitions.

Porter felt that it was his personal duty to test the resolve of the men to keep to their story, but Cheshire – who would increasingly incur Porter's wrath – was being recalcitrant. Porter warned his companions that if Cheshire was 'pinched' he would 'come to'. In other words, it wouldn't take much pressure on the diminutive Cheshire from an inquisitive third party to extract a confession. The man who knew nothing but servitude simply did not have the wherewithal to go through with the deception. In Porter's eyes, he wasn't hard enough, nor could he be trusted. There was even a story that Cheshire had once been kicked in the head and had not been mentally stable since. Whatever had happened, Porter says in his memoir, 'We knew him to be a determined villain previous to him coming to us.'

Porter, impetuous as ever, declared that it would be best to finish off Cheshire now. Standing at the top of a ladder, Porter snatched a pistol, cocked it and declared he would save their lives by taking Cheshire's. Barker, still the man in charge, quickly pulled him down. Barker told Porter he would put Cheshire on shore at the first land they came to. 'I was vexed and threw the pistol on the floor with such violence that it went off,' Porter recounts.

The Cheshire problem would have to be settled later. The *Frederick*'s timbers were sounding the stresses and groans of death by slow immersion. The men rigged the longboat for sailing and added two extra planks to the side of the hull in order to increase the freeboard, its clearance above the waterline.

The time had nearly come for them to leave the *Frederick*. She was half-drowned, her galley half-filled with water. There were sucking and gurgling sounds as various parts of the ship were slowly claimed by the rising waters. The cat prowled around the deck looking skittish, waiting his turn to leave. Into the longboat went the two remaining pounds of biscuit and beef, as well as the arms and munitions.

By late in the day, the water had reached the bulkhead and a slow list to the side began. Ten men and one cat boarded the longboat. In his memoir, Porter says that leaving the *Frederick* was one of the most difficult moves he'd ever had to make – worse even than his first trip to sea. 'I never left my parents with more regret nor was my feelings more harrowed up to such a pitch as when I took a last farewell of the smart little *Frederick*.' In only a matter of hours Hoy's beautiful square-sailed brig would go down. She'd brought them further than they should have asked of her.

As they set off from the brig, the upper portion of the ship's outer planking, was nearly submerged. The men had left all the hatches open, so that when the water finally reached the deck, she would drop quickly to the bottom. They couldn't stand the *Frederick* suffering a slow death. Nobody looked back.

*

IF THE FREDERICK ten felt they were owed calm seas close to the shore, they were mistaken. Almost as soon as they launched the longboat, two enormous waves broke over them, dousing them in cold saltwater. It was a sharp reminder that the pain of this voyage had not yet ended. Their only defence against the rough first night on the longboat was a wet and wretched one – four of them sat with their backs to the waves, a human dyke.

They hung on until dawn and immediately headed for land. The long-term plan was to run the longboat north along the coast in their quest for Valdivia, but first they needed food and water. As day broke, the seas subsided and they approached the beautiful green coastline, untouched by anything man-made. They were moving steadily, all the while hoping that over the next headland, after the next bay, they would view the promised port. At 3 p.m., they turned around one headland to find a perfect little bay that could shelter the longboat; by 4.30 p.m., they had anchored under the lee of a reef of rocks. They would finally set foot on South American soil.

Porter, three others and the tomcat went ashore with high hopes of finding some form of civilisation. They landed on a stretch of beach separating the sea from the luxuriant growth of forest that smelled distinctly of pines and fresh soil. They soon reported back to the boat and the rest of the men followed. After six weeks at sea, they found it hard to remember what land was like, and they scampered around the trees and flowers, excited by the prospect of fresh running water. But after a few hours the untouched forest lost a bit of its appeal – they saw nothing that suggested human activity. But they were fortunate to spot some shellfish, which made an interesting change of diet. A luxury to Porter, who'd been used to little more than salted beef and almost indigestible sea biscuits for as long as he could remember.

The tomcat, too, had decided that the lush forests of Chile were preferable to the constant sailing. One morning, without so much as a by-your-leave, he left, never to return.

In their longboat the men explored the coastline: mile after mile of low cliffs, empty rocky beaches and a thickly wooded forest that came down to the sea's edge. At one bay the men killed a seal, the first fresh meat any of them had eaten for months. In another they found fresh water.

On the fifth day since leaving the *Frederick* they rounded another point only to be stunned by a familiar noise emanating from the shore. It was a cow. 'All was silent on the boat,' says Porter. 'Not an individual could be heard to breathe as we intently listened that we might again hear the welcome sound, afraid that our ears had deceived us.' Just after the cow bellowed again, they heard the unmistakable sound of a human voice. The first sign of civilisation. 'Satisfaction was beaming on every countenance.'

A little later in the day the men saw fires onshore. They couldn't contain themselves and hollered loudly. The Chileans shouted back, but Porter thought their responses were more akin to alarm than a greeting: 'They gave a kind of yell.'

The men held back from the shore that night, and on the next day rowed to where they had seen the fires. Not far out, they spied their first South Americans. Just past the shoreline men were half-hidden behind boulders, all armed with long knives. Five men stayed on the longboat while the others, including Porter, went ashore.

They had come upon the Mapuche people, one of the few indigenous peoples of Chile and Argentina who had fended off repeated incursions from both the Incas and the Spanish. The

Frederick men could now be pinpoint exactly where they were. They were on the shores of Chile's Araucanía Region. The Mapuche lived in small, isolated pockets. They were hardy warriors, skilled artisans and brilliant backwoodsmen. At the time of the crew's arrival, they had largely maintained their culture and way of life. The men of the *Frederick* were about to meet a very proud and independent people.

*

EACH PARTY CAUTIOUSLY approached the other, leaving a gap of a dozen yards. Communication was by gesticulation. What would the Mapuche have made of a bunch of skinny, dirty white men, their beards streaked with salt, who looked more like wind-beaten scarecrows than tough mariners?

To the convicts, the Mapuche appeared to be asking a series of questions in their language, known in those times as Araucanian but now known as Mapudungun. The *Frederick* men understood nothing, but still tried to respond. They pointed to their mouths and rubbed their stomachs in an effort to communicate their hunger. This had little effect, so the crew began imitating livestock – mooing like cows, baaing like sheep and grunting like pigs. The Mapuche looked on, dumbfounded.

The conversation was going nowhere when a very tall man, wearing a poncho and an old pair of trousers dyed blue and indigo, stepped into the gathering and breached the gap between the two groups. He had a large knife hanging at his side, which he gripped at all times. To Porter, he was obviously the chief. Porter wrote that the crewmen walked up and offered him an axe, which he brandished above his head. Satisfied with this gift, he gestured for them to follow him.

The Mapuche men were dressed in the South American *chiripá*, a rectangular woollen garment that is freely wrapped around the hips and thighs. Over this they wore a classic poncho and on their feet Spanish-style leather boots. The women wore their hair in two long plaits and covered themselves with blankets that they tied to their waists with bright sashes.

The weapons of the Mapuche included the *boleadoras*, heavy weights attached to cords that they tied around their waists. South American gauchos used similar weapons (also known as *bolas*) to trap animals. In both cases, when thrown they wrap themselves around an animal's legs and torso. But the Mapuche also used the *boleadoras* against their enemies – some cords had eight weights attached, which were capable of breaking bones. And the weapons could be ornamental as well: these people took pride in their workmanship. The most luxurious *boleadoras* are made of ivory and covered in precious metals. Some *boleadoras* are considered works of art.

Porter was seeing an adaptable people who lived in comfort. At that time the Mapuche were nomadic, moving not just across regions but over thousands of miles, which made them an elusive foe, capable of ambush and surprise. They slept on sheepskins in homes that could be packed up and carried from one place to another. For three hundred years the Spanish tried to conquer the Mapuche and failed, for the most part. They could never be pinned down to any one place. Just when the colonists thought they had conquered an area, they would be confronted by another assault from another clan.

Porter was impressed by the Mapuche, who seemed well organised and meticulous in everything they did: 'I observed a man and a boy ploughing with some bullocks … they appeared to be a very industrious people.' He and his crewmates followed the chief up the beach and through a cluster of trees until they found themselves in a large clearing with a beautiful stream running through it. In the middle of the clearing were well-ordered huts, which Porter describes as being constructed in 'strong workman-like manner' and 'of remarkable cleanliness'. These were surely *ruca*: traditional circular Mapuche homes, made of wood and straw.

In the interests of obtaining food, Porter offered the people a piece of gold. Where he had this secreted, is never mentioned. Still, there was no food forthcoming. In common with most South American tribes, they had no interest in the metal – they were more interested in the buttons, pins and needles the men offered.

Crucially, Porter gained one important piece of information, just as he and the men were leaving. When Valdivia was mentioned, an elderly woman raised three fingers and uttered, '*Leghos.*' Valdivia was three leagues – around nine miles – distant. Barker's most recent reckonings had been broadly correct.

Around midday, the crewmen took their leave of the Mapuche, who had been cordial with everything except foodstuffs. The men now knew the distance left to travel and had a renewed hope in their mission. They pressed on.

*

By mid-afternoon the longboat rounded yet another nondescript point and there it was, the port they'd been searching for for seven weeks. Porter must have recognised Valdivia – he'd been there with his wife at the tender age of eighteen – but he does not mention this in his memoir. It was a large, well-sheltered harbour, not so different in appearance to Macquarie Harbour and on roughly the same latitude, but far more industrious and with a greater sense of connectedness to the world. The water was clear blue and the men were surrounded by green pine trees, not grey-green eucalypts.

The water was as smooth and unruffled as a millpond and studded with small islands. The low hills at the back of the town fell away in favour of a large mountain range. The fort on the largest island had a twelve-gun battery, and on another was a flagstaff bearing the red, white and blue of the newly independent republic of Chile.

To the convicts' astonishment, they weren't looked upon with suspicion – they were welcomed. Boats of all descriptions approached them, pointing to the best landing areas ashore. At around 4 p.m., with the shore just yards away, soldiers in bright blue uniforms were gesturing them in. The convicts must have been delighted by the friendly, grinning soldiers, who helped them haul the longboat as far as possible up the beach.

Barker seemed less interested in his new surroundings than in parcelling out to the men all the remaining possessions, his gift to everyone for making it this far. It was a trifle, but in the spirit of fairness that had always prevailed under his leadership, each was given clothes, blankets and a half-sovereign coin.

It was 5 March 1834. The men of the *Frederick* had changed the background of their lives from a remote penal settlement, which few ever entered, to a newly free, industrious, cosmopolitan port. Death, pain and isolation were gone, replaced with hopes for joy, friendship and hospitable society. No doubt, as Porter might have put it, they were beaming from one countenance to the other. Their scarcely credible journey from western Van Diemen's Land to the Chilean coast was over.

Chapter 14

THE MOMENT THE men of the *Frederick* stepped ashore in Valdivia's port, they became the men of the *Mary*, who had left Liverpool and been shipwrecked en route to Valparaíso. Unsavoury pasts were erased and they were suddenly ten gentlemen, down on their luck, washed ashore on the wrong side of the world. John Barker became Benjamin Smith, William Cheshire was William Williams, William Shires was now William Jones.

James Porter, ever the man to shift identities, changed nationalities. The one-time Bermondsey 'beer machine maker' was now an Irishman named James O'Connor. Why Porter chose to be an Irishman is a mystery. He may have known that the liberator of Chile, Bernardo O'Higgins, had an Irish father. Throughout Porter's writings, he describes himself as a 'patriot'. Those who fought the Spanish to gain independence were patriots; those who supported Spanish rule were royalists. O'Higgins was considered Chile's greatest patriot, and Porter was always at pains to reveal his pro-patriot sympathies.

Porter says that he planned to find his wife and son, but this was more a statement than an expression of intent, and neither was ever mentioned again in his writings.

The story concocted by the *Frederick* ten went broadly like this. The *Mary* had left Liverpool on 6 December. On 24 February, at around eight o'clock at night, she had struck a bank. The ten men had managed to set up the longboat in haste and left the vessel as she was sinking. The captain had perished with the boat, refusing to leave his *Mary*, but had – a little miraculously, given the ship was going down – told them how to navigate to the coast. The rest of the sham story would have been simple to remember – all they had to do was repeat the turn of events after the *Frederick* was abandoned.

The Chileans soon learnt that some of the men were carpenters and told them they could be useful. Roughly ten miles upriver from the port was the town centre, where there was plenty of work for carpenters. Indeed, a large vessel was sitting on the stocks in mid-construction. The crew decided to split up, with the carpenters seeking work upriver and the seamen heading for Valparaíso, an abrupt change of plan. It was a smart idea, or so it seemed. If one group found themselves in a difficult position, the others might not be compromised.

The four carpenters and Cheshire hired a canoe and paddled up the Río Valdivia, but somewhere during their journey they were stopped. One of them had apparently revealed something of their true story when out drinking with a man named Cockney Tom, an English-speaking 'spy' who was employed by the locals as an interpreter. This Cockney Tom appears from time to time in Porter's writings as part of the Valdivian governor's team, but may have been an invention of Porter's.

The carpenters were sent for interrogation, while the five seamen were enjoying the life of the port, carousing on the beach. 'We enjoyed ourselves very much with the patriots, dancing and singing to the guitar,' recounts Porter. They planned to enjoy the beach life at least until the next day, when a suitable tide arrived for them to relaunch the longboat.

Porter already had his doubts about some of the locals, but this was probably just his natural suspicion of anything foreign. Seemingly without any sense of irony, he wrote that the 'lower orders' couldn't be trusted and 'shewed a great disposition towards thievery'. Perhaps he had momentarily forgotten his own origins and track record.

It was a brilliant night on the beach for Porter and his mates, with plenty of local red wine and fresh fish. Freedom tasted good – but it didn't last for long. After falling asleep where they'd been eating and drinking, Porter was woken sometime the next morning by the butt of a rifle on his shoulder.

Two soldiers had their muskets cocked and aimed at Porter and the others. Waving their guns menacingly, the soldiers ordered them to rise. Five bedraggled convicts, wiping the sand from their clothes and the sleep from their eyes, staggered to their feet half-slipping and groping in the sand. The glare of the sun, the pain behind their eyes and the incomprehensible shouts of the soldiers added to the confusion of waking in a strange land. They were still half-drunk, but the soldiers didn't care.

Porter, Jones, Fare, Leslie and Lyon were marched off in a line along the foreshore of the Valdivian River, past the remains of old Dutch settlements that had once graced the shoreline, across a wooden bridge and onto the Isla Teja where two fortified towers, El Barro and Los Canelos, stood as beacons of defence.

It was a ten-mile march to the centre of the town, where they came face to face with a rather large and imposing fortification: the military headquarters known locally as the *cuartel*, which covered an entire side of the Plaza de la República. On the other side stood the main town cathedral and Bishop's palace; on the third side the governor's residence and offices; and on the fourth side the law courts and some of the largest houses belonging to the most prominent Valdivians.

The five men were marched to the barracks and politely ushered into their cells. The carpenters were being kept apart from them so that they could be questioned separately. Porter's fear, that someone would spill the beans, was playing on his mind. Seeking information, he paid the guard a dollar to send a note to the other prisoners. Porter admitted to a weak knowledge of Spanish despite his previous time in Chile, but understood enough of the guard's talk to work out that one of the carpenters had revealed something of their true story and their real personae to Cockney Tom. Porter immediately pinpointed Cheshire as the culprit, but there is no evidence that the man was responsible. With the guard's help, Porter placed a note in a piece of bread and had it sent to where Barker was confined, expressing his suspicions. Barker did not confirm them, but replied that he couldn't believe anyone could have been so stupid to have admitted the true story.

Only two days in as South American 'liberty men' and they were back to experiencing the sort of subterfuge and conditions they'd known so well in Macquarie Harbour. Gaining their freedom would not be so easy. Initially, the men were kept in prison, awaiting the summons and even given money, an offer, apparently, from the governor. They used it to buy food and other paraphernalia. They were treated particularly well – almost guests of the state – but were told nothing.

Porter overheard that the crew of the whaleship that had sailed past them had also been held in the *cuartel*. They had also been shipwrecked on the Araucanian coast. It was a French whaleship, but the Frenchmen's stay under guard was far shorter. Their captain had retained all his papers, while the *Frederick* had none – Barker had made sure that all papers identifying the *Frederick* went down with the ship. In Chilean eyes, the British were still unaccountable for themselves, while the French were set free.

*

A WEEK INTO their detention, the men were sent to the governor for questioning. It was the first time they had been able to see the town centre in any kind of detail. Valdivia stands at the confluence of three rivers – the Valdivia, the Calle-Calle and the Cruces – which converge on the main island just across from the town centre, the Isla Teja. On the other side of the water, wooded hills rose gently in most directions. Valdivia was not unlike Hobart Town in terms of climate. In winter there were clear, cold days, and a watery kind of sunshine prevailed; in summer it was hot but never intensely humid. The town felt like it was being pleasantly cradled by the low hills that surrounded it, which drew themselves up sharply against a blue, cloudless sky. The air was clean and crisp throughout the year, broken only by the smoke that came from the nearby lumber camps and the many town fireplaces. The smell would have been familiar to the convicts and reminiscent of Van Diemen's Land. But it was the sharp, resinous fragrance of freshly cut pinewood, not eucalyptus.

Sparkling in the distance, about a hundred miles to the east of Valdivia, is the massive peak of Villarrica, a white-capped, arrow-headed smoking mountain. The men wouldn't have known it, but they were situated on one of Earth's most unstable tectonic plates. Villarrica is an active volcano. It stands glaring down at the town, so dominant against the flat green plains just beyond Valdivia that it appears no more than a stone's throw away.

Valdivia was built along the same lines as all Chilean towns. The streets were nicely right-angled to each other leading to the main square where Porter was being held, the Plaza de la República. Out from the square the streets narrowed and the feel became far more provincial. For the most part this was a town built of wood, all sourced from the surrounding forests, but in the poorer areas furthest from the centre there were clusters of single-storey houses made of *tapis* (mud walls) or *adoves* (sun-dried bricks).

The wealthier houses had a classically Spanish look. They were made of brick and stone with a conventional courtyard in the front, and an entrance through arched porches. The windows would have iron gratings and shutters – but only the very rich could afford an extravagance such as glass. The entranceway was through heavy folding doors, with a postern on one side. On each side of the front court were rooms for domestics and possibly the younger members of a family. The back part of the house contained a hall replete with antique chairs and leather-backed seats, and a large table often made of oak. This all led to the parlour, the main entertainment area.

The Valdivians were provincials, which meant that in some ways they were closer to classic Spanish Creole tradition than the inhabitants of the bigger cities. And yet they felt themselves to be slightly apart from the rest of Chile and were fiercely independent. 'We are not Chileans, we are Valdivians,' remains the city's best-known catchphrase. Most of the inhabitants were merchants and traders or were connected to the military, but there were a number of extremely wealthy elite. The people, at least on the surface, wanted for nothing and were outgoing and friendly.

The *Frederick* men were ushered into the governor's offices, beautifully appointed in mahogany, with polished floors and a Moorish scent. Scraggly and barely shaved or cleaned for months, they must have felt greatly out of their depth. They were led into a long, high-ceilinged room where the governor sat – 'a fine, noble looking fellow', as Porter describes him – with a number of senior officers at a large table. The governor was José de la Cavareda, though Porter does not name him.

According to Porter, their words were interpreted by Captain Lawson, a British smuggler who had come to stay in Valdivia and reputedly commanded a schooner on the coast. Lawson was the group's spokesman with the governing powers. He repeated the details of the fictitious shipwreck of the *Mary* – how the leak was sprung, how the captain decided to go down with the ship, and why there were no papers to prove the ship's provenance.

The government appeared to have a theory of its own: that skulduggery was in play. In the first letters from Cavareda to his superiors in Santiago, he says he believed that the boat had been deliberately cleaned of any incriminating evidence. It was, Cavareda noted, 'prepared with too much attention'. The investigators must have thought that the captain might have been murdered and these men had pirated the ship, meticulously removing any traces of their crime. The Chileans had in their possession the brig's glass sheaves and blocks that they had retrieved from the longboat, each of which had a British government mark on them.

The governor wanted to know why a merchant ship was in possession of government stores. Porter replied that the government often had a fire sale of old stores and ship paraphernalia, which were often reused on non-government ships. The governor then ushered in Cockney Tom, who said that Porter's explanation was true enough, which astonished Porter. Maybe they hadn't been given away after all.

The governor was silent for a few minutes and then said, 'Sailors, you have come on this coast in a clandestine manner and though you put a good face on your story, I have every reason to believe you are pirates. Unless you state the truth between this and tomorrow at eight o'clock, I shall give orders for you all to be shot.'

Then the governor commanded, 'Take them away.'

Porter, who had become the spokesman for the crew – or later, when writing of this, simply wanted us to believe that he had – then gave a riposte nobody could have expected, least of all the governing powers:

'Avast there,' Porter told the governor. 'We are nothing but shipwrecked sailors in distress and expected when we arrived here to be treated like Christians, not like dogs!'

Porter now pulled out his patriot card and tried it on the governor. 'Would you have treated us this way in 1818 when we British sailors were helping you fight for independence and bleeding for the cause?'

The governor and his adjutants fell silent. Porter was telling them that he had been a part of their independence. He, too, was a compadre. He was referring to the British Admiral Thomas Cochrane, the 'sea wolf' who had delivered Valdivia from Spanish tyranny in a single night in 1820.

Cochrane had attacked the tightly held forts at the mouth of the river under cover of darkness. The resulting confusion disconcerted the Spanish, who gave up all the garrisons the next day. Cochrane's brilliant move on Valdivia was the final stroke in ridding the country of royalist Spanish forces. He hadn't just freed Valdivia but granted Chile its independence as well. Porter had hit upon an emotional subject.

'If you treat us as pirates, England will know of it and be revenged,' Porter continued. 'You will find us in the same mind tomorrow as we are in now, and should you put your threat into execution, tomorrow we shall teach you patriots how to die!'

It was the only brilliant speech James Porter would ever make – if it happened. It hardly fits Porter's style and generally poor use of English. But he had indeed been seconded by the Chilean Navy, which had been under the command of Cochrane, at the time of Chilean independence. He was smart enough to know that the mention of one of Chile's saviours would once and for all dispel any notion that he – or any of his mates – were unruly buccaneers.

*

AFTER THEY WERE sent back to their cells to await their fate, according to Porter, Cheshire broke away from the group and told the entire true story of the *Frederick* to the governor. Cheshire, the coward and traitor – as Porter was apt to describe him – had apparently sacrificed his comrades to save his own neck. This was unconscionable to Porter.

Now that the story was out, the men resolved to confirm the truth with the governor and hopefully gain his mercy. In Porter's account, he was highly sympathetic. Most important to him was that the capture of the *Frederick* was effected without murder, as Barker vowed that nobody had been killed in taking the brig.

The governor also supposedly said that if Cheshire had given up South Americans then 'all the forces I could command would not have stopped the rabble from tearing you apart', but this might be a bit of Porter-speak. Whether Cheshire ever squealed cannot be proven, but Porter always described the man in purely derogatory terms. Lyon, too, incurs Porter's wrath. Shires and Barker, by comparison, are depicted as gentlemen in the memoir. Porter may have been creating heroes and villains for his story, but more likely he was indulging his own grudges.

It was Barker who requested clemency. When the governor asked why the convicts had chosen Valdivia in the first place, he was ready with the answer. 'Because we knew that you were patriots, and had long ago declared your independence. We throw ourselves upon the protection of your flag, relying on your clemency.' The governor told the men he would liberate them at once if he could be assured that they wouldn't escape. Barker did not reply squarely to him. He simply said to the governor that all of them 'would rather be shot dead in the palace square than be delivered up to the British government'.

The governor took the path of least resistance. There was a growing movement among the townsfolk to free the *Frederick* ten, and a petition asking for the convicts' release had been sent to the governor. Of course, the other side had to be factored into the politics too. Cavareda knew that when the British came calling for these men, he would be placed under enormous pressure from his government in Santiago to extradite them. But according to Porter, the governor said he would do everything he could to guarantee their freedom. Escape was the only thing he wouldn't countenance.

The governor added that given the enmity between Porter and Cheshire, he was duty-bound to protect Cheshire, whom Porter might harm. Cheshire would have to be kept close to the governor's quarters, away from the others. To this, Porter said nothing. Lastly, the convicts would be given work so that they could repay the money lent to them while they were incarcerated.

*

BEFORE ANY OFFICIAL inquiry had been convened, and before all the evidence, affidavits and examinations had been submitted, Governor Arthur had made up his mind about who would be blamed for the Frederick fiasco. So it was that on 5 March, the very day that the Frederick ten had come ashore at Valdivia, a board of inquiry sat in Hobart knowing full well who would be indicted. Before them was Taw's affidavit and the details of Hoy's examination. The board found:

> ...that no culpable blame attaches to the guard, it having placed
> itself under the direction of Captain Taw. The loss of the vessel
> can be accounted for only by the number of resolute convicts
> having associated together as to have enabled the organisation
> of the plan to take the Frederick and to the blind confidence
> placed in these people by Mr Hoy added to a like confidence
> on the part of Captain Taw whilst considering them as crew to
> which misfortune (this misplaced confidence) the court are of the
> opinion the success of the attack so easily carried is attributable.

Arthur had his court-martial, of sorts – it would not be an army man, despite the obvious laxity of the soldiers in the *Frederick* episode. Captain Taw, the drunken sailor, was the easy target. He was summarily dismissed from government service.

Hoy, whom Arthur perhaps secretly believed had helped the convicts, would be punished in a more subtle way. Instead of taking up a post as master shipwright at Port Arthur, he was 'banished' to South Bruny Island to help in the construction of a lighthouse.

But these were only little victories for the governor, designed to target the easiest scapegoats and ensure no blame was attached to either himself or his unimpeachable army.

On 9 May 1834, the convicts' entire story was recorded in Valdivia's regional newspaper, a copy of which was eventually sent to Arthur. Any cover they still had was now completely blown, but the men retained their aliases. The *Araucano* newspaper reported that the story of the *Mary* had never seemed satisfactory to local officials and that orders were made to 'make a new and more rigorous' examination.

It became clear that the shipwreck was false, that the individuals were criminals escaped from Van Diemen's Land in New Holland. By that which they have since disclosed it appears that they were occupied in the construction of vessels on account of Government in Port MacQuarry [sic]; that the last being finished, which was a merchant ship called the Frederick, of little more than a hundred tons, all the prisoners embarked on board of her, with the Captain, the Mate, four soldiers and one free mariner.

The newspaper account then related their taking of the *Frederick* and the voyage to South America, including the sinking of the brig, but added: 'It is not known to what extent the truth of this statement can be depended upon.'

There was now nowhere for the men to hide, but they had another option. This was to throw themselves at the mercy of the Chilean republic and beg for asylum on the basis that they'd been cruelly abused by the British government for years.

Their new friend, the governor, strongly sympathised with their plight, but as an official he would always be subject to political persuasion. He promised he would do all he could to convince the Chilean Secretary of State for Foreign Affairs in Santiago that if the men were ever handed back to the British, they would come to serious harm. On 13 May, he sent the convict's request for asylum to the interior minister.

The governor freed them on parole, which required them to remain in Valdivia and report regularly to an officer of the *cuartel*. It was the best kind of freedom the ten could have expected.

Chapter 15

THE CONTRAST BETWEEN how the British viewed rebels like Porter and his companions, and how the Chileans perceived them could not have been greater. On one side of the Pacific they were convict mutineer scum; on the other, *bandidos enamorados*: beloved rebels. They were strangers to their new society and scandals to their old.

The people of Valdivia had not yet met the ten men, but that didn't seem to matter. They didn't have to slink about like wanted men, even after the publication of the *Araucano* article. They were ennobled by virtue of their circumstances. There was no doubt in Chilean minds that these men were heroes, a little like themselves. If the governor had kept them under lock and key, there would have been an outcry. These were men who had shaken off the old world with its inherent injustices and its exploitation of working men and women. The convicts had taken the only honourable course: that of the freedom-loving patriot.

The men quickly learnt about the city's founder, Pedro Valdivia, an aristocratic Spaniard who had attempted but failed to defeat the Mapuche. Legend had it that he was captured by the Mapuche and put to death, forced to drink molten gold. Another figure who loomed large in Chilean history was the arch-patriot Bernardo O'Higgins, half Spanish, half Irish, who'd played a crucial role in the liberation of Chile. Admiral Cochrane, too, had a special place in Chilean history.

The Valdivians weren't strangers to penal servitude. In the previous century the town had been a military base where convicts were used as an unpaid workforce under Spanish rule. To the Valdivians, convicts were victims of their despised royalist past, so a reverse snobbery came into play: convicts were patriots and brothers, imbued with the spirit of freedom under which many of them had suffered.

The ten men had also experienced great adventures on the ocean as they sailed six thousand miles in a leaky boat to seek their liberty. In Chilean eyes, these men were being accorded legendary status in their own time.

And so it was that these scrawny convicts, most of whom were small and not at all beautifully formed, were apparently considered brave, attractive and gentle by Chilean women, and heroic compadres by the men. As can be expected, the convicts took full advantage of the situation.

The nineteenth-century Australian author Marcus Clarke, who used the men of the *Frederick* as the basis of his novel *For the Term of His Natural Life*, gave his description of their new circumstances, particularly with regard to the women:

> Spanish America is noted for the beauty of its women – the
> Chilian [sic] ladies are even now the belles of the seaboard and

our adventurers jumped at the offer. The attraction of the gossip
by the fountains, the chatter of the quaint old market-place, the
dances by night under the orange-trees, were too strong to be
resisted. The fierce black eyes of the manolas; for in those days
there were yet manolas in Spain and griselles in France; the more
golden glory of the Malaguena, transplanted from the sultry
seaport of Old Spain two generations back; the sparkling purity
of the Andalusian granddaughter of some brilliant adventurer of
Seville, conspired to capture the hearts of the escaped prisoners –
all honest English sensualists, I have no doubt.

The fact is that Valdivian life wasn't quite this quaint and simple.
Clarke makes the Chilean women appear to come fluttering out of
the pages of Cervantes, but life for Criollos (Spanish descendants
born in South America) women in Chile, even among the wealthiest,
wasn't easy. The most elite women of Valdivia were rarely allowed to
venture out and were the chattels of their husbands. They were also
expected to adhere to the old Moorish customs. At home they did not
sit on chairs but sat cross-legged on cushions. A male visitor known
to an upper-class family would take a seat on a stool or even cross his
legs and sit in their midst; he might be expected to play the guitar or
sing – these were considered the most honourable accomplishments
of the *gentilhombre*.

For centuries the ruling Spanish and wealthy Criollos throughout
South America had relied on indigenous people and slaves for labour,
and the men had turned to lower-class women, indigenous women,
so-called 'mulattos' and 'mestizos', and slaves for sexual conquest.
This practice in eighteenth- and nineteenth-century Spanish
America was so common that one writer noted that 'it is considered

a shame to live without a concubine'. Of course, the wealthy expected their daughters and wives to remain 'pure and honourable' and live extremely sheltered lives.

William Bennet Stevenson, an English writer, who recorded his travels throughout Chile a few years before the arrival of the convicts, described the women as wearing 'a bodice fancifully ornamented and over a large round hoop, a plaited petticoat of coloured flannel, black velvet or brocade'. In his book, *A Historical and Descriptive Narrative of Twenty Years' Residence in South America*, he wrote that the hoop was not essential in Chile but was favoured as it 'shews their slender waists to advantage'. Normally women would cover their heads with a piece of brown flannel but if 'on pleasure of a visit' a black hat was worn. The hair would be braided or plaited, hanging in loose tresses down their backs.

By the 1830s, the Chileans' former masters, the Spanish, were popularly described as *saracenos* (saracens) or even *godos* (goths), no doubt a reference to the warring and thieving undertaken by the conquistadors under the Spanish crown. To be Spanish was considered thuggish and slightly retrograde, part of an old world order, not the new, thrusting Chile the nation was hungry to become. France and most particularly the United States became the models by which Chilean progress would be measured. But fantasy ruled, as it does so often at times of national fervour.

The Chileans – and perhaps the Valdivians in particular – felt that they were descended from two honourable races: the Basque people of northern Spain and the Mapuche. The Basques were looked on as having an almost Protestant-like ethos: they were not ashamed to work the land they had mastered with their bare hands. They had done this in an almost permanent state of war with the Mapuche.

Valdivians were now proud that many of them were descended from indigenous people who had flung back Spanish attempts to take their lands. Chileans named children after Mapuche leaders such as Lautaro, Lincoyán, Tucapel and Caupolicán.

The history of the Mapuche and their long and successful struggle against Spanish imperialism became – at this time – something to be glorified. 'What are the demi-gods of antiquity alongside our Araucanians?' wrote one local writer. It seemed to have been conveniently forgotten that while the Mapuche may have at one time fought the Spanish and stopped them from taking their lands, they had also made pacts with them.

Compared to other South American indigenous people, the Mapuche were light in complexion. Perhaps this is the main reason why people of mixed race, called the 'mestizos', were never treated with the same contempt that was found in other parts of the continent. Being a mestizo, acculturated by Chilean society, was less of an issue in Chile than in Peru, Argentina or Brazil. However, native Mapuche, who did not mix with Chilean society, were not treated with similar reverence. They may have been praised in Chile's national mythology but they were largely discriminated against by the rest of the population; they were then – and still are – the most economically disenfranchised of all Chileans, usually working in the lowest paid jobs.

The fact was that the real beneficiaries of independence had been the nation's small and cohesive upper class, not the mostly illiterate rural poor, all of whom may have been independent from Spain but remained, at this time, banned from voting. The Chilean common people's reverence for their mixed background was anathema to the white Criollo upper class that remained loyal only to itself. The new order brought in very few benefits and virtually no improvement in most Chileans' material circumstances. In reality, the revolution had little to do with the common people – it was a conservative struggle between warring elites.

Valdivia wasn't a town of wealthy people, but it was not a poor one either. It had plenty of bourgeoisie made up of merchants and traders, as well as hardworking fishermen, sailors and soldiers. The men dressed like Spaniards with the exception that a poncho was the normal outer garment. The poncho was ubiquitous because just about every man (and many of the women) rode a horse, and this was the classic horseriding gear. The Valdivians were expert horsemen from an early age, and the convicts would have seen the locals able to lasso bullocks by the horns, and sheep and horses around the neck. Anyone who travelled by horse had a lasso attached behind the saddle, and children used lassos to catch chickens, cats and dogs. In the heyday of the revolution, Spanish soldiers were brought down and killed – by the lasso.

The Valdivians believed that their newfound freedom should be best expressed by transforming their original plaza, hitherto the military-sounding Plaza de Armas (Parade Square), into the more progressive-sounding Plaza de la República. The plaza retained all its functions from before the revolution – it had its law courts, government offices, military barracks and a cathedral – but it also became the hub for all major festivities and a natural home for the arts. At its centre stood a garden surrounded by four Romanesque statues bearing candles, which represented commerce, industry, science and the arts. Within the garden was a stage for the theatre and musicians.

*

To the British convicts, the Valdivians seemed to have a carefree lifestyle. Their evenings were dedicated to promenading along the banks of the river or around the main square, and afterwards to 'friendly visits'. 'The luxury of harmony and friendship is enjoyed in all its extent,' William Bennet Stevenson wrote. 'The guitar, the song, the dance and refreshments are to be found in every street.' This may have been a nineteenth-century genteel way of saying that the *Chilenos*, like most South Americans, did not need to find cogent reasons to throw a celebration.

A party, *una fiesta*, was something that happened spontaneously, and there may have been psychological reasons for this. Regular natural disasters, especially earthquakes, have left their mark on the Valdivian mindset, as they have in other parts of Chile. The people had learnt to savour life from one day to the next.

When the governor's boat was being launched, all the convicts were invited to the big celebration and were naturally the guests of honour.

The Chileans drank a lot of wine, but they also had their own alcoholic variants, including the popular drinks chicha and theca, wild cherry liqueur. These were very strong and sweet alcoholic drinks which the rum-swigging and beer-swilling convicts would have found strange to the taste. Porter knew his chicha from his earlier period in Chile and took his enjoyment of it cautiously, it was not to be consumed quickly, nor in vast amounts by the uninitiated. The chicha was derived from pea-sized, purple-black *maqui* berries. It could also be made from the fermented juice of grapes, apples and just about any fruit the Chileans desired. There was, of course,

THE SHIP THAT NEVER WAS

nobody to put a brake on the convicts' alcoholic consumption, many of whom had not drunk for months – if not years. Freely available at the party was the heavy grape brandy known as pisco, common throughout Chile – indeed, in many parts of South America. The convicts drank what they could get their hands on. They were hardly discerning. Later that night and the day afterwards, they would pay the consequences.

Then there was the food. There were fruits of all kinds and all manner of colours. Apples, pears, plums, cherries and figs were produced so easily in the temperate climate of southern Chile that they were practically given away. Figs and strawberries grew around the town and its vicinity in wild bushes. The strawberries would have made their English counterparts blush – they were the size of hen's eggs.

As a main course there were *porotos granados*, a stew with ingredients that are native to the region flavoured with Spanish-style condiments such as onion and garlic. Maize, potatoes, squash and *poroto* beans became as essential to the Chilean diet as they had been to the Mapuche, who first cultivated them.

Laden on tables were Spanish pastries such as *empanadas* filled with mince and onions. Beef was also on the menu, but not in the form or taste the convicts might have been used to – it was consumed mostly in a jerked form known as charqui, which spawned national dishes in the form of *charquican* and *Valdiviano*, both of which are liberally spiced with *aji* (chilli).

Well fed and enjoying the abundant drink, the convicts were about to experience a party that only South Americans could produce. There is a story, perhaps apocryphal, of the men at the launch: while the chicha and pisco were flowing liberally the Chilean men were

186

dancing *La Chilena*, a local variant of the *fandango*. The already inebriated convicts looked on slightly puzzled as every dance ended up with a man kneeling in front of a woman, her foot placed rather flirtatiously on his knee. Indeed, some say the dance has no Spanish derivation at all – it more approximately resembles the mating ritual of a rooster and a hen.

As the party's intensity increased, a number of young local women were heading straight for the 'attractive' foreign guests. Barker was reputedly accosted by a rather corpulent middle-aged widow named D'Oliveira, allegedly the richest woman in Valdivia. By contrast, Lyon became friendly with a very beautiful Mapuche woman, an outcast from her tribe who had been expelled by her family. She was said to be deaf and mute, known only as La Silenciosa. It's not known if she was outcast for her disabilities or for the fact that she had taken up with white society.

In the months that followed, the men found employment. Porter says that he started out working on a government boat. Some of the men worked for the governor's vessels, while others worked in the local shipyards. The three Johns – Dady, Jones and Fare – were apparently employed at the port to build a sloop.

Given their quick and deep immersion into the fabric of Valdivian life, it's hardly surprising that within a matter of months, five of the ten were said to be betrothed. Secondary sources say that Barker was the first to marry, and the governor and his wife were there to celebrate his grand nuptials – paid for, apparently, by his wealthy wife. It didn't seem to matter to Barker that he was already married with two children; as the newly minted Benjamin Smith, he was allowed to do as he liked. Leslie (aka George Fortune) was also said to have married, despite the fact that he too had a wife and child in England. He and Russen became instantly related when Russen (aka James Price) became betrothed to the sister of Leslie's spouse. William Shires (aka William Jones) married the daughter of a blacksmith, Senorita Catalina, who was already on the way to having his child. Even the pint-sized William Cheshire (aka William Williams) was married to a Maria Belasco.

Two hundred years on, it is hard to verify exactly who married whom. It appears that some of the men married under their real names. Records found in the parish of Valdivia reveal that a 'Juan Barker' married Carlota Jiminez (not, apparently, the widow D'Oliveira as some have stated) on 25 July 1834. The registry describes him as: *'Juan Manuel Barker, natural de Liverpool, Inglaterra, soltero, hijo de Jorge Barker* (John Manuel Barker, born in Liverpool, England, single, son of George Barker).' Likewise, there's a record of a Guillermo Thiers (Shires?) marrying Catalina Cabello in October that year. There is another record of Guillermo Loabtes (possibly William Cheshire?) marrying María Belázquez (Belasco?).

There's also a question as to how the men married into the Catholic faith, the only possible option in Valdivia. Single men had to produce a certificate of baptism – quite impossible for any of the *Frederick* ten – or be baptised prior to the marriage. Or the intended spouse could find two witnesses prepared to declare the man was both a widower and baptised: this was enough to be married as a Catholic.

*

ARMED WITH THE article in the *Araucano* newspaper, Governor Arthur sent instructions to London to retrieve the men at all costs.

From there, the news was sent immediately to the British vice-consul in Valparaíso, Colonel John Walpole. But it was hardly news to him – the story of the shipwrecked British convicts was well known along the coasts of Chile and Peru.

When Don Joaquín Tocornal, the Chilean Secretary of State for Foreign Affairs, received Cavareda's petition from the *Frederick* ten for asylum, he was placed in a difficult bind. He would have to weigh up the popular view of the men against the political realities of international diplomacy.

Tocornal knew the people of Valdivia had taken the convicts to their collective bosom. Within weeks the men had merged seamlessly into the local economy and become model citizens. Everybody was convinced they were patriots, not pirates. Of course, the niceties of the men and their situation had negligible political value. If the British pushed hard enough, it was almost certain that the Chileans could not hold out.

In the correct diplomatic fashion, Tocornal sent Walpole a missive explaining exactly what had transpired. On 25 May 1834, Walpole wrote to the foreign secretary in London, Viscount Palmerston, about the case. The convicts had admitted who they were and that they had taken forcible possession of the *Frederick*, Walpole told Palmerston. This not only rendered them guilty of escaping transportation but 'adding to the catalogue of their crimes, the act of piracy'.

When British officialdom referred to the ten men, the words 'pirates' and 'piratical' were never far away. The taking of the *Frederick* wasn't just a theft, it was a 'piratical theft'. This left little doubt in anybody's mind, Chileans included, where any legal trial would lead – directly to the hangman's noose.

Walpole was not a man to bother with niceties. In fact, it seems there was nothing nice about him at all. He was the kind of diplomat Governor Arthur would surely have appreciated, as there were no shades of grey in his thinking. What these men had done was 'one of a list of atrocious crimes' that all nations punished, he wrote to Palmerston. Walpole was expressing disgust and indignation that these men were apparently roaming around Valdivia as freemen. He would petition the Chileans to have them placed in chains 'until further intelligence to confirm their innocence or guilt shall be received'.

It seems Walpole didn't bother to visit the men or personally discover more about their situation and background. This wasn't a time when diplomatic staff called on their nationals, inquiring after their health and condition. As far as he was concerned, these men were renegades from British justice, which he seemed to think could be applied and directed well outside British jurisdictions.

Walpole told Palmerston that he would demand the specifics of the men – their full names, backgrounds and identifying marks. This information could then be sent to both London and Hobart to confirm these were indeed the men they were looking for.

Of course, Walpole would have to wait months for a reply from the foreign secretary, even if a boat was to leave Chile the next day. However, Walpole believed that he could influence events in Chile simply by applying pressure. In this, he was to be very mistaken. Tocornal would play the slow game, using all the diplomatic wiles he had to thwart the British.

He wrote back to Walpole in June, explaining that a petition for their asylum had been received and was being considered. He added that this was understandable, given the deplorable conditions they

THE SHIP THAT NEVER WAS

had been subjected to in Van Diemen's Land. It was a direct swipe at the British. The Chileans felt the convict system was little more than slavery, and they wanted to know exactly what crimes each convict had committed for them to have been expelled from Britain in the first place:

'*Como el Gobierno de Chile ignora hasta ahora la clase de debitos por que fueron condenados a aquel presidio, nade puede resolvar acrcea de la suerte futurade estos desgraciados; y no esparar adquirir datos ciertos sobre el particular, sino per el conducto de VD.*'

'As the government of Chile has yet to be apprised of the nature of their crimes and the reason why they were condemned to the place where they were expelled, it cannot make a determination about the future fate of these wretched individuals; there is no other means by which we can arrive at the facts of the case other than via your proofs.'

Tocornal was turning the British desire for information back on them and, into the bargain, was showing his disgust at the treatment the *Frederick* men had been subjected to. If these men were the thieving pirates the British said they were, the Chileans would be only too pleased to receive specific proofs of their crimes in Britain and elsewhere.

The new, free Republic of Chile had a far more modern sense of how punishments should fit crimes. Since their constitution was written in 1822, all Chileans in public life were now proclaiming their belief in the rights of man – 'natural and imprescriptible rights: equality, liberty, security and property'. The Chileans were prepared to make the British work very hard to prove the guilt of these men and, to his great credit, Tocornal would not let the British dictate terms to him.

Walpole's response to Tocornal is quite laughable, given the easygoing freedom the convicts were enjoying while the diplomats were crossing pens. On 21 June, Walpole said he trusted that 'the government of Chile will admit of their continued confinement until their guilt, or innocence, of the atrocious crime can be accurately ascertained'. In other words, the escapees should be locked up on the presumption of their guilt until the British had furnished the Chileans with the men's identities and crimes. Walpole also said that he would lose no time 'in communicating the facts to his government and to others who might help him to circulate the history'.

Walpole, by any standards, was either plain stupid or plain arrogant. He could not exert any pressure on the Chileans until he returned with strong evidence. Tocornal, by contrast, could afford to wait. By playing for time he would be appeasing the people of Valdivia. While the *Frederick* ten remained the flavour of the month in Chile, they were untouchable.

Chapter 16

I T's NO EXAGGERATION to say that the convicts had ended up in a land of plenty. Everything in Valdivia revolved around food – acquiring, selling and preparing it. And the food couldn't have been more different from the British fare the men had grown up with, not to mention the convict gruel they had endured for years.

Just off the main square along the river was the *mercado fluvial* (riverside market), which sold some of the area's most exotic fish, fruit and flowers. Here is where the Valdivians conversed and gossiped, children played and animals of all descriptions congregated. Sea lions hauled themselves up close to the market stalls to scrounge for bits of discarded fish. Vultures and hawks hovered around, zeroing in on loose scraps. The *mercado* was the hub of Valdivia.

Beyond the abundant fruits, there were other stranger fare, they had probably never eaten. The colonists had learnt from the Mapuche that the best way to prepare the tiny coconuts harvested from the Chilean cocopalm was to feed them to the cattle. The digestive process would rid the coconuts of their outer shells, and once 'voided' the nuts were clean and ready for the markets. The cocopalm tree was also exploited for its honey-like sap, the extraction of which was another skill that the colonists learnt from the Mapuche. They would cut down a tree and burn it from the branches to the roots. The sap would escape the heat and run down the tree, oozing out of the roots into waiting calabashes. As much as forty gallons of nectar could be collected and sold at good prices.

Porter never mentioned the food, but given his seafaring background, he must have appreciated where the convicts were located. Seafood, too, was a prominent part of the diet – they would have eaten *locos* (abalone), *machas* (razor clams), *erizos* (sea urchins), and even *cochayuyo* (seaweed). It's possible they had the chance to sample another favourite in the southern parts of Chile: the *caldillo de congrio*, a soup of conger eel, tomatoes, potatoes, onions, herbs and spices.

Yet another obvious cultural difference for the British-reared convicts was the local tea – and this one was likely abhorrent to them. Tea from East India had no place here. The Chileans had a preference for mate, with its strong woody taste.

Porter says nothing about how the other men grappled with the culture, nor how they mastered the language. When a great Spanish polymath, Andres Bello arrived in Chile in 1829, he pronounced that its citizens spoke the roughest version of Castilian on the continent. There is evidence of Mapuche influence on the tongue, along with a propensity for coarseness that the convicts might have appreciated – if they understood it. The Chileans used slang as part of their everyday vocabulary. They used the word *huevear* (to piss around) and its many variants habitually in social intercourse, a word considered gross in most parts of South America.

*

WHILE THE ABUNDANCE of food and drink would have helped the men to overcome the depredations they'd suffered as convicts, it must have become increasingly obvious to them that this amounted to nothing without recognition of their freedom. Despite their perfect immersion in Valdivian life, they never felt secure. By late 1834, there was still no guarantee they would be allowed to stay in Chile.

In time, the smarter convicts, Barker in particular, realised that they were living on borrowed time. They surely noticed that the genial governor wielded little political power – after many months he'd failed, despite his assurances, to confirm their bid for asylum. Silence on the subject was enough to stoke suspicion. Barker almost certainly realised that the wheels of extradition were turning between London, Hobart Town and Santiago. As was Barker's wont, he was always on the lookout for the next opportunity. When he heard that a boat had been impounded in the harbour, he sniffed a chance.

Late in 1834, the Chilean-registered *Ocean* arrived in Valdivia. On inspection it was found to be carrying contraband goods. The brig was impounded, and Captain West, an Englishman sailing under Chilean colours, wasn't allowed to leave the port until a fine was paid.

The story, told through Porter, was that West paid a visit to the chief gunsmith in the town – who happened to be John Barker. Angered by the fact that some of his crew had snitched on him, alerting the authorities to his illicit cargo, West approached Barker bent on some form of bloody revenge. He asked the convict to repair his guns.

But it seems Barker diverted him from his quest for vengeance, proposing to West that if Barker could put together a crew of his men, they could take the impounded brig from under the battery 'or perish in the attempt'. It would be another *Frederick*-style breakout. But for reasons unsaid, though likely due to a collective mistrust, Cheshire wouldn't be included in this particular venture.

According to Porter, Captain West considered the proposal and agreed to take them all on. The nine men prepared for a getaway.

Despite the attractions of their newfound surroundings, and although Barker and Shires had children on the way, the men were entirely willing to escape. It wasn't only Porter who found freedom more attractive than family life. Of course, the situation was different for Barker and Shires. They had to make a very difficult choice: they could remain with their new families while running the real risk they would be deported and hanged ... or they could escape.

While the men waited for the captain's go-ahead, the *Ocean* was released. The captain had managed to raise the money through the help of foreign bondsmen. That Sunday night, two sets of men in two different boats were to make their separate ways to the *Ocean*, which was bound to sail the next morning.

It would not be difficult for Porter's group of six men to steal a boat – dozens lay idle along the riverbanks of the Río Valdivia – but it was going to be a long haul down to the port roughly ten miles away. At the appointed time, Porter, Lyon, Barker, Shires, Russen and Leslie met furtively, then stole over to the water's edge.

They picked up a small dinghy and, in the dead of night, rowed as quietly as they could. They would have preferred to go with the tide, but it was running against them that night. The night was moonless, so they were less likely to be seen by any passers-by. But that had its hazards as well – their own visibility was impaired.

Their main problem would likely be downstream at the river's estuary, where there was a 24-hour watch at the southern fort on Isla Mancera, which had views upriver, across the bay and out to sea.

The three Johns – Dady, Fare and Jones – had the easier part of the escape. They were safely ensconced at the port, hiding aboard the very sloop they had been constructing, waiting for the right time and tide to take the small, single-masted sailing boat out to meet the *Ocean*.

Meanwhile the six men in the dinghy were making the best time they could, but the lack of light and the river currents made things difficult. They took the boat just past the meeting point of the Cruces and the Valdivia rivers, and a little further on they had to contend with a maze of rocky outcrops and islands. The men were steering the boat on the far side of the river to avoid the islands that littered the city side.

Before dawn on the Monday, they reached the river's mouth unseen by any lookout – but what they saw ahead at first light filled them with frustration. The normally placid waters just beyond the river outlet were raging. There was a heavy onshore wind and a huge surf at the bar. Even experienced sailors like Porter and Lyon, who could manoeuvre their way out of the most turbulent waters, knew that their small, fragile dinghy couldn't cross where the surf was breaking.

And yet this didn't stop them from trying. 'We got to the bar in the foaming surf and had to pull before it for our lives which was the means of our not getting to the brig,' Porter recounted. They had tried to pass the bar with all their strength and sailing ingenuity, but it was too much. That morning, the six men sat haplessly at the mouth of the river while they watched the other three men sail out to the bay, abandon their sloop and swim steadily towards the waiting *Ocean*.

This time, the gods of flight were not on Porter's side.

It was a huge blow to the luckless convicts who could see liberty just a few hundred yards offshore. They now had to return upriver clandestinely, while dwelling on the fact that their best chance of a neat escape had disappeared. They reluctantly returned to their work that morning 'fatigued and vexed'. At least nobody else in town was the wiser for their failed escape.

The three Johns successfully boarded the *Ocean*, and in so doing slipped away from the history books. It is believed they made their way to the port of Callao in Peru, and that two of them eventually boarded an American vessel. Three of the original *Frederick* ten had now found real liberty.

The seven left behind were placed in an even more difficult situation. They feared they might be placed under lock and key or, at best, forced to live under more rigorous parole conditions. But remarkably the governor showed no interest in the escape of the three Johns, and there were no immediate repercussions. It may have been that the Chileans had yet to receive any real pressure from the British to extradite the men, or they were glad to have fewer escapees to deal with.

Life in Valdivia went on. But across the oceans, in London and Hobart Town, the machinery of extradition was moving. The newly formed Chilean republic had no idea of the diplomatic fight they were about to have on their hands. The British would go to the ends of the known world to hunt down rebels, pirates, bushrangers and bandits. Crossing jurisdictions meant nothing to this great naval empire.

*

As far as historical records show, Governor George Arthur never again mentioned the *Frederick* ten. In his mind, their plight was now a problem for the British Navy. No doubt, though, he relished the fact that they had been located. British justice, he may have thought, would eventually find its way across the seas to Valdivia, and in good time the thieving pirates would be brought back under his purview. But Arthur was running out of time.

The Van Diemen's Land colony in late 1834 and early 1835 was not a happy one. There was a growing call for rights and proper political representation, which the governor ignored. Van Diemen's Land was, Arthur insisted, a penal colony where rights to assembly had never existed. As threats to people's livelihood and wealth diminished, Arthur reacted inversely, increasing rules, regulations and police powers. As the number of newly freed and non-convict settlers grew, Arthur's hold on Van Diemen's Land did not bend with the zeitgeist but tried to resist it.

By the mid-1830s Arthur had assembled what has often been described as 'one of the most heavily policed countries in the world': a constable for every eighty-eight people. He'd also introduced strange laws that owed more to his religious piety than any social good. The *Licensing Act 1833*, for example, made it an offence for 'a publican to allow ticket-of-leave holders to play skittle, bowls, ninepins or any game of chance in a public house'; even if they (the ticket-of-leave holders) weren't involved in the game, the law required them to leave the premises if one was in progress. This kind of petty manipulation of an already over-regulated society made Arthur extremely unpopular.

The governor had no time for trial by jury and supported stronger powers to magistrates. He lost that battle: a jury trial system for all civil cases was established in Van Diemen's Land in 1834.

In the popular opinion stakes, perhaps most telling count against Arthur was his massive accrual of wealth. He made himself extremely rich with some shrewd land investments. From the late 1820s until his departure, he took control of about fifteen thousand acres of land. There was always the whiff of scandal about his business ventures, but nothing ever stuck. He was also a supreme usurer, lending many thousands of pounds to settlers and officials, then enjoying a lucrative interest rate. There was a nice capital gain for Arthur's landholdings as well, as property values soared well into the 1830s.

He invested in speculative schemes and, while he was never found guilty of any misdemeanour, the nineteenth-century Australian historian John West – who would become a prominent opponent of convict transportation – put it this way: 'The moral weight of government was compromised by the air of mystery which veiled it.' West, who never experienced the Rule of Arthur first hand, nonetheless wrote his two-volume history of Tasmania about fifteen years after Arthur's departure. West opined that Arthur had so much control, over so many aspects of the colony's life and economy, that it would have been easy for him to profit from his foreknowledge.

The governor's personal wealth was one of the whispers that

accompanied him everywhere, and just as telling – and just as resented – was his patronage. If you agreed with Arthur, you were likely to have an easy life filled with graces and favours. But if you did not, he would remember. He was the kind of man who made a note of anyone who showed the slightest opposition or disagreement. He had a physical black book for convicts who misbehaved, and a mental black book for disruptive or non-compliant settlers.

Under the late reign of George Arthur, Van Diemen's Land was an autocracy verging on despotism. The elite few owned huge tracts of the best land and had divorced themselves from most taxes, and there was virtually no aspirational middle class. By the mid-1830s, the public was calling for a more just apportionment of the colony's wealth: former convicts were denied a share of any profits, and new free immigrants were kept out as well. At this point, Arthur – like the ten convicts he sought to capture – was living on borrowed time. As one prominent lawyer said, writing to the Home Office in London, people were 'ready to use their power, and assert their rights, if necessary by force of arms'.

Still, Arthur had won at least one public relations battle by late 1834. The government wanted the colony's citizens to believe that the remaining Aboriginal people had become a prosperous and thriving community, albeit out of sight. On Flinders Island in the Bass Strait, far from contact but not from control, the Palawa were supposedly becoming model citizens and devout Christians. Now that the colonists, assured by government propaganda, believed themselves unburdened by the 'Aboriginal problem', they simply washed their hands of the Palawa. By the end of 1834 nearly all remaining Indigenous people had surrendered to George Augustus Robinson.

In October that year, Robinson was appointed commander of Flinders Island.

Trapped together, the various Palawa clans were anything but homogenous. Members of different clans were in conflict, respiratory disease was taking its toll and the entire population refused to work. Virtually no children were born during this time. Robinson wrote that the mortality rate was cause for regret but this was the 'will of providence'. It was, he wrote, 'better that these people died here where they are kindly treated than shot at and inhumanely destroyed by the depraved portion of the white community'.

*

As 1834 NEARED its end, the British vice-consul in Chile devised a plan. Colonel Walpole would not be put off by the Chileans' obvious high regard and fondness for the men of the *Frederick*, whose freedom to roam was not just an insult to the norms of international justice but also a slur against the British Empire. Nor would Walpole be told what to do by the powers that be in Santiago. He wanted to make a point.

In October, he summoned Commodore Mason to his office, the captain of the 46-gun British frigate the *Blonde*, who had anchored in Valparaíso about four hundred and fifty nautical miles north of Valdivia. Walpole asked the commodore to sail to Valdivia and make his presence known. Mason was going to engage in a little gunboat diplomacy, and Walpole expected the Chileans would fold immediately in the presence of a mighty British warship.

But there was something important that Walpole did not yet know. When the *Blonde* entered the harbour in Valdivia in November, with full British regalia blazing, only seven of the *Frederick* men remained.

Porter describes the slightly comic scene when the frigate sent out a boat that endeavoured to pass the outer fort of the harbour. The Chileans 'let drive a 32 pounder across her [the *Blonde*'s] bows which caused the boat to return to the frigate'. The British ship was obviously unwelcome – it had been neither invited nor scheduled to arrive. The governor reacted to the news of the frigate's arrival by locking the seven remaining men up again. They must have feared that they would be delivered into the hands of the British.

Later that night when the governor, Cavareda, arrived at the *cuartel*, he made his intentions clear. According to Porter, he had confined them for their protection, not for any crimes. They might have bolted into the forest, the governor said, where they might be killed. 'The Commodore has sent for you to go on board his vessel, to give an account of yourselves,' he said to the seven men assembled. 'Is it your wish to go?'

When the men protested that they would never render themselves to the British under any circumstances, the governor said he would send a letter inviting Commodore Mason to government house where he could interview them all. 'But I will not allow another person to accompany him,' Cavareda told the men. He added that if the British were to somehow force their way in to capture them, he would 'send you all away in to the interior and let the sealions find you if they can'. By 'sealions', he meant the British.

When this message was delivered to the commodore, he did not take kindly to it. He didn't bother to come ashore but simply set off the next day, heading back to Valparaíso. The remaining *Frederick* men were still in the ascendant, enjoying the protections of a sympathetic country and a congenial governor. As soon as the *Blonde* left they were released from gaol.

But the fears of all had been aroused. The British weren't just coming – they were already here.

Chapter 17

JAMES PORTER MAY have changed his name to O'Connor, but to his newfound friends in Chile, he was their beloved Don Santiago – the Spanish form of his name. Like all the others, he took his freedom very seriously. The old James, the one on the lookout for the next lark and a slice of the action, was now a man about town, well liked, affable, gentle and kind. This was the way the new James depicted himself – he had discovered noblesse oblige.

In his account of this time, he depicts himself as a defender of the poor, helpless and weak. His commentary seems only half-believable, but this means there may be truth in the other half. Place a man in better circumstances, and he may show himself to be, indeed, a better man. Porter had previously only looked out for himself; now, for the first time in his life, he found himself being looked up to and depended on. James Porter was a somebody.

It's likely Porter started work in the Valdivian shipyards as a caulker and possibly – given his knowledge of sailing – a rigger. When caulking a vessel, he would have worked with oakum or cotton, following a process similar to what he'd helped to do for the *Frederick*. When working as a rigger, Porter would have known where to place the ropes, wires or chains for the standing rigging on the ships' masts and yards, and how to correctly thread the running rigging, which used rope blocks to hoist and lower sails and trim them to the wind.

Somewhere along the line, he caught the eye of his landlord, a certain Don Lopez, who thought him an exceptional talent. Lopez, a successful local furrier, plucked him from the shipyards to become his fixer. Santiago was a part of the family, Don Lopez declared, and that was that.

There was a strong sense of deja vu in all this. Just as Porter had been assigned in Hobart, he was being assigned here. But for once in his chequered career, he was moving up the ladder: Lopez was a wealthy merchant who sold valuable skins he bought from poachers in the interior of the country. He asked Porter to retrieve a great quantity of these skins waiting upriver.

Porter, ace sailor and former boatswain (who had once stolen beaver skins) obliged. The two of them travelled in a launch to the Río Primero, about twenty-five miles upstream. Another twenty-five miles onwards, they located the cargo, loaded up and returned. Porter realised a rudder was useless in fast-running water and used a long oar to steer through rapids and whirlpools. If help was needed, he had a Mapuche man on board who was ready to assist should the whirlpools prove too strong. In the end, Porter's sailing expertise brought the entire cargo downriver without loss. According to Porter, this was the first time Lopez's cargo had been delivered safely.

The new James Porter was in such demand, he had to be shared. A certain Lady Donna Inez Ascension, as he names her in his memoir, asked Lopez if she could 'borrow' Porter for the cider-making season. Porter happily obliged, and within a few days he was nicely ensconced up-country, living in the house of a wealthy widow, ostensibly to protect her young son and the property. Porter supposedly agreed to take on the job because he felt for a vulnerable woman.

But he soon realised his mistake. This woman, in his words, was a 'spitfire'.

The lady Ascension ran a property with more than twenty servants, who she ostensibly treated as her property. One of them was a handsome sixteen-year-old Mapuche girl, Antoinetta. She had, according to Porter, been exchanged for a cow and an axe. Slavery was outlawed at this point, but the Mapuche were treated, especially by the Criollos, if not as slaves then clearly as third-class citizens. Porter says that the morning after he arrived, Ascension assembled all the servants in the forecourt 'and gave them to understand I was their master ... everything was in my charge'. Porter was now on the other side of the punishment ledger.

He'd only been in the job a few days when one morning he looked out on the front yard to see Antoinetta hanging from a wooden block. She had been strung up by the thumbs to a cross pole for no other reason than being 'too nice' to Porter – whatever that entailed. Aghast, he ran into the yard, perhaps remembering how he had been strung up more than once to the Macquarie Harbour triangle.

Within a few seconds, he had cut Antoinetta down – but he had overstepped the mark. The lady Ascension may have given him mastery over all he surveyed, but not punishments: that was her domain. When he returned to the yard a few hours later, the hapless Antoinetta had been restrung doubly tight and was suffering excruciating pain. Porter did his duty and cut her down again.

When he entered the house, Porter was confronted by a very angry widow charging at him with a very large carving knife. Before she was able to lunge and plunge the knife, he had tripped her up. He was, after all, a street fighter of some repute. With a little sleight of hand he had also taken the knife from her grasp.

She lay on her back gasping, but the lady was not for turning. While Porter backed away, signalling for her to calm down, an even angrier widow came at him. She had found another knife, but Porter was even more prepared this time. As she made her next lunge, he struck her on the head with a chair, lodging her hair comb in her skull. Knocked cold, the lady Ascension fell senseless to the floor.

Porter didn't wait to discover the repercussions of his actions. He and Antoinetta fled to the local magistrate. In this strange new world, Porter confessed his crimes to the constabulary, which makes his writings – at least those covering this point in his career – suspect. The old James would have skipped town without asking questions and fled for the hills.

Normally a magistrate would have held Porter for questioning at least, but this one, according to Porter, was highly sympathetic. He told Porter that her ladyship deserved to be chastised, even with a serious knock to her head. She was well known to have a cruel disposition, the magistrate said – so difficult was the lady's temperament, her husband had shot himself in desperation.

Ultimately, the lady Ascension coaxed Porter and Antoinetta back, promising to change her ways. For some time after, she remained carefully congenial.

A little after the fracas with her ladyship, four soldiers attempted to steal alcohol from her cellar. Porter recounts that he single-handedly fought them off, then dressed the wounds of one of his attackers. Three of the soldiers then arranged to have him killed, and Porter beat up the local sealer who had attempted to murder him.

When the sealer's wife pleaded with Porter to save her husband's life, Porter was all affability and condescension. He told her he would do the right thing and spoke to the court with the gentility of a forgiving knight:

> It is true I am an Englishman, the only one among you, yet I look with the same degree of pleasure on all around me as though it were my native soil I stand on. Gratitude, for the kindness and protection I have received since my arrival on this land from the Cavaliers residing in the province of Valdivia compels me to express my feelings that I consider myself thus far a true Patriot, that I am ready at any moment when required to fight, and rather than flinch expire under it.

Porter, it seems, managed to conjure up the knights of Valdivia – while, presumably, he was becoming one of them. All eyes were upon him as he spoke for the sealer's life: 'I freely forgive yon mad-brained sealer striving to take my life when in a state of intoxication. I hope Gentlemen you will Coincide with my feelings, and Acquit him for this time for the sake of his Wife and infant Child.'

The courtroom was in a state of disbelief, or so Porter later reported. As one of the judges remarked, it was only yesterday that the defendant was contriving to take Porter's life. 'Now he is supplicating to save yours,' the judge said to the sealer. 'For shame on you! And from this moment, never, never, forget the villainy on your side and the compassion of this foreigner on the other.'

This scene of infinite mercy and kindness was not quite over yet. According to Porter, the three soldiers who'd paid the sealer to kill him then stepped forward and delivered themselves to the court. 'I, of course, spoke on their behalf as well as the sealer,' reported Porter. 'And they being military men, the officers were very glad to let them off.' The men were handed minor punishments and the sergeant was suspended for six months. Porter had done his duty and set the world to rights.

For a brief moment, James Porter became Don Santiago, the most magnanimous man in Valdivia. He found himself living in an alternate universe. In this magic land, he had the ear of a sympathetic magistrate, and those who were tried for capital punishments were readily absolved by the courts, especially when their victim stood up for them. In between, fair ladies were being saved, evil ones got their comeuppance, rogue soldiers received just punishment, and chivalrous Englishmen did it all for the love of fairness and justice.

Porter wasn't just writing his memoir: it seems he was also indulging a few fantasies. The new James, he wanted his readers to believe, was a man of repute and high standing. It was a role he cherished.

Decisions in much higher places were now taking shape. The time for chivalry and courtly *gentillesse* was coming to an end.

*

WHILE PORTER WAS apparently busy saving lives and showing mercy to all he graced, there were others, particularly among the British foreign administration, who were far less inclined to such largesse. At least not towards the *Frederick* ten.

The two warring diplomats, Tocornal and Walpole, had now dropped all pretence to politeness. This situation was becoming a diplomatic incident of international significance, according to Walpole. He was enraged that the Chileans had reacted to Commodore Mason with such unseemly alacrity. In Walpole's eyes, the commander of a British naval vessel had been viciously fired upon – Walpole seemed to forget that the ship had come unbidden and rolled out her full military regalia. In Chilean eyes, they had responded naturally to a country sending out a ship to flex its muscles.

When Tocornal later told Walpole that three of the ten men had escaped, things took an even nastier turn. On 1 December 1834, Walpole responded to Tocornal, incredulous. He wanted to know about the circumstances and mode of escape, and to ascertain the 'degree of negligence' in the execution of the duty of the officer who was charged with overseeing them.

It was Arthur all over again. Someone's head had to roll. Walpole wrote that it was almost beyond belief that nobody on the Chilean side had gone unpunished. Even worse than this, how could the remaining seven not be under lock and key 'until their innocence or not is ascertained'? Walpole had even heard a more shocking revelation: that the men were at large, reporting just once daily to an officer and had – shock, horror – 'been permitted to intermarry with Chilean natives'. Walpole was all anger and spittle but this was no man of action, just a man of bluster. The idea that he should go in person to check on their situation – or even confront the governor who kept them – seems never to have occurred to him.

Walpole was convinced that the state of freedom in which these men were allowed to exist was 'inconsistent with the expressed intentions of the [Chilean] government'. To him, there seemed to be no proper line of command – necessary, the British believed, to enable any social system to work. There was 'a want of vigilance on the part of the authorities of Valdivia'. Walpole was essentially accusing the Chileans of being lax and incapable of carrying out the most basic of duties.

Tocornal, no doubt embarrassed by the news of the escape, could only offer a lame response. The Chilean government, he said, didn't feel itself authorised to confine the men in prison during the 'long time that must transpire before certain intelligence could be received of the nature of their crimes'. It was most reasonable, he said – with 'consideration of humanity and justice – to let them go free'. He did, however, offer to investigate the circumstances around the three men's escape. As for the remaining prisoners, Tocornal used the most delicate language he could muster, which actually had no real meaning at all: these men, he said, would receive no more liberty 'than that which may be evidently compatible with their security'.

It's understandable that by early 1835, diplomatic relations between Chile and Britain were somewhat tense. The seven men weren't just allowed to be free – they seemed to be receiving protection. But the smartest of the men still knew that enjoying the graces and favours of their host nation was unlikely to last forever. For the remaining seven, the urge to cut and run was growing by the day.

James Porter's instincts had told him all along that the governor was a man he could trust. But early in the new year, the news came through that Governor Cavareda was being recalled to Santiago. He would be replaced by Don Isaac Thompson, whom Cavareda recommended highly. When Cavareda introduced Thompson to the men, the new governor assured them it was business as usual: he would be just as hardworking for their asylum and as sympathetic to their cause. Porter says he clocked this man from the start – he was 'a complete Nero, which he proved to be'.

It may not have helped their cause that Thompson was a Chilean of British descent. At their first meeting, Thompson told them that the courier carrying letters confirming their asylum status had been unavoidably detained by the Mapuche. The courier had, he said, entered their territory during their 'drinking season' and would not be allowed to leave. Porter's and Barker's suspicions were undoubtedly aroused, even if they didn't know the real reasons behind the 'delay'. It had everything to do with the ongoing spat between Britain and Chile, nothing to do with indigenous customs. The seven men were being held in a state of diplomatic suspension.

Porter wrote of Thompson that they were all being left 'in the disposal of a tyrant', and before long he was pretty sure his gut feelings about Thompson were correct. The new governor tightened up their daily reporting requirements: they would have to present themselves at government house at six each night. 'This looked as much like Macquarie Harbour discipline that we determined with the first slant of wind we got we would take French leave for it, and sail clear of him,' Porter wrote. On a subsequent trip to help fit out a barque, he was astonished to find that he was being tailed by two of the governor's men. 'This grieved me to the heart,' he wrote.

The growing collective unease could only have been compounded by the arrival of another ship that sailed into the harbour streaming British colours. On 8 February 1835, HMS *Beagle* anchored at the outer forts, skippered by the eminent Captain Robert FitzRoy. The *Beagle* was a medium-sized barque fitted with seven guns, which had rounded Cape Horn en route to Concepción and Valparaíso. On board was a young naturalist, Charles Darwin. Whether the seven escapees met and spoke to FitzRoy, Darwin or any of the crew is not known, but FitzRoy presented as a uniformed British officer, which could only have triggered some anxiety among the men. Undoubtedly FitzRoy had been asked by his superiors to make inquiries about them. He wrote he observed (or spied?) two of them at work – at a distance:

> *I was told by the Intendente that some Englishmen had arrived in his district a few months before we came, whose character and business he did not understand. Rumours had reached his ears of their having escaped from one of our convict settlements at the other side of the Pacific, and he was inclined to believe the report. Three of these men had married since their arrival, and all but one were industrious members of the community: indeed I saw two of them hard at work on a boat belonging to the Intendente. Having no proof of their delinquency, I did not deem myself authorised to ask him to have them arrested and delivered up to me, in order that I might convey them to the senior British officer in Valparaiso.*

FitzRoy then recounted that only afterwards did he learn that they had escaped from Van Diemen's Land. But the whole passage seems disingenuous. Thompson was pretending to know very little about the men, because if he were to tell FitzRoy the entire story, he might feel compelled to deliver them to him. FitzRoy, too, appeared to be feigning a lack of knowledge, because he either wasn't willing to take the men or didn't want to be entangled in a diplomatic wrangle. Either way, the story of the *Frederick* was well known in all the South American ports that the *Beagle* visited.

TOWN SEEN ACROSS THE RIVER.

OLD LOOK-OUT TOWER.

VALDIVIA.

Three views of Valdivia by Philip Gidley King of the Beagle *expedition.*

The young Charles Darwin, at least, seemed better informed than his captain: 'They stole (or made) a vessel and ran straight for this coast. When some distance from the land they sunk her and took to their boat.' He added, sardonically, that 'they all took wives in about a week's time'. In Darwin's eyes they were notorious rogues, and he believed the Valdivian governor had entirely overlooked this for the 'advantage of having some good workmen'. The naturalist's take on all this was that the people of the former Spanish colonies seemed to forgive anyone who committed a crime. It must have been something about their Catholicism, he believed – what he called 'a consequence of their absolving, forgiving religion'.

It's interesting to note Darwin's response to the men working in Valdivia. In a later passage in his writings, he visited Hobart Town, strongly commending the advantages of the convict assignment system: 'As a means of making men outwardly honest, of converting vagabonds, most useless in one country, into active citizens of another, and this giving birth to a new and splendid country, [assignment] has succeeded to a degree perhaps unparalleled in history.'

Presumably assignment worked splendidly in Van Diemen's Land under British rule, but not in Chile.

The naturalist had more interest in the local flora and fauna than in politics and scandals, and paid no more attention to the escapees. But this interest was rudely diverted just a few days later. On 20 February 1835, Darwin was idling on a beach near the port and felt the shocks of an earthquake: 'I happened to be on shore, and was lying down in the wood to rest myself. It came on suddenly, and lasted two minutes, but the time appeared much longer.' Darwin described the rocking of the ground as 'very sensible'. Neither he nor his companions could discern where it was coming from. Some thought east, others thought the south-west. In fact, its epicentre was in the vicinity of Concepción, about two hundred miles north of Valdivia.

'It was something like the movement of a vessel in a little cross-ripple,' Darwin wrote. 'Or still more like that felt by a person skating over thin ice, which bends under the weight of his body.'

Darwin was lucky to be many miles from the earthquake's worst ravages. On 4 March, the *Beagle* travelled north to Concepción, and there he surveyed a scene of absolute destruction, the worst the region had experienced in sixty years. 'Not a house in Concepción or Talcahuano [the port] was standing; that seventy villages were destroyed; and that a great wave had almost washed away the ruins of Talcahuano.'

Darwin saw a coast strewn with timber and furniture 'as if a thousand ships had been wrecked': 'Besides chairs, tables, book-shelves, etc., in great numbers, there were several roofs of cottages, which had been transported almost whole.'

In his memoir, Porter says nothing about the earthquake. FitzRoy was in Valdivia when it hit and reported that many of the houses were shaken. 'The boards [of the houses] creaked and rattled together,' FitzRoy noted. 'The people rushed out of doors in the greatest alarm.' But the quake caused little damage to the town. And at the time, Porter was surely much more alarmed at the thought that he might soon find himself in chains again.

Chapter 18

JOHN BARKER AND James Porter were very different men, but they both possessed a sixth sense. They knew when trouble was brewing. Barker could point his finger to the wind and sense a change. In such circumstances, his style and methods were clear: apply expert subterfuge, plan the exit meticulously and execute it coolly. Porter, too, was able to sniff out people – in particular, certain kinds of authority figures – but his methods were less developed. He had no talent for subterfuge or planning. As for his style of execution, it was always figured out on the run.

A new escape plan was afoot, and Barker was again at the centre of it. He went to Thompson and pitched the idea of constructing a whaleboat for the new governor. Thompson eagerly agreed, knowing of the men's shipbuilding abilities. Barker, who did not need to work, suddenly became highly industrious; within three weeks he had overseen the building of a very sturdy and eminently seaworthy whaleboat.

The plan to hoodwink the authorities was simple. Barker told Porter they would take the boat downriver to the harbour and slip away unseen on the following Sunday night. This time, the escape would be for a select few: Barker, Russen, Porter and Leslie. Shires, who was now a father to baby Bernardo, was perhaps not invited or may have even declined the offer. Cheshire and Lyon, we must presume, weren't offered an invitation.

Porter went to sleep on the Saturday night expecting it to be his last in Valdivia. But the other three men must have had second thoughts about bringing Porter. They left a day early.

In a repeat of their quest to reach the *Ocean*, they took the whaleboat and stole quietly down the river, dodging the islands and rocky outcrops on the city side. They rowed all night until they reached the bar, and this time they found no raging surf to prevent them from passing into the ocean. Like the three Johns, Barker, Leslie and Russen were never seen by the remaining convicts again.

They had been allowed to rig the whaleboat, fit it out and make it highly seaworthy under the auspices of Governor Thompson himself. The problem was, this time they had stolen government property. Someone would have to pay.

Porter awoke on the Sunday morning to find soldiers hovering over his bed. He was frogmarched to the barracks at the Plaza de la República and incarcerated. He had only one small consolation: Lyon and Cheshire, the Judases in Porter's writings, were chained as a pair, while he would be chained with his mate Billy Shires.

Barker had left behind his wife and child, while Russen and Leslie had left their wives; such was the allure of freedom to these three that friends, wives, children and fellow travellers were all discarded. Porter, who surely felt totally betrayed, did not mention them in the rest of his memoir. Of course, we don't know how any of the three felt about Porter – there could have been cogent reasons why he was left out.

The *Frederick* ten's most skilled escapologist was now gone. 'I then gave up hope of ever regaining my liberty,' Porter says in his memoir.

*

WHEN WALPOLE HEARD in April that yet another three men had escaped Valdivia, he was apoplectic. It was, Walpole said, nothing less than a 'culpable remissness in the execution' of the directions forwarded to Tocornal. And there was little Tocornal could do to argue against this. His excuse was poor: supposedly the governor of Valdivia had never received his instructions that the men should be kept under lock and key. It's understandable that Walpole was never quite sure whether he was dealing with the incompetence of the Chileans or their complicity with the prisoners. He almost certainly would have suspected both.

At least he now had his long-held wish: the remaining four men were firmly under lock and key.

The two diplomats had made very little progress. Tocornal could hardly argue, when he finally met with Walpole in September 1835, that the convicts had been properly supervised and overseen – that argument had been lost. Also, by this time he had received all the particulars of the men from the British: their provenance and histories were no longer in doubt. But at the meeting with Walpole he launched into a new argument. His conscience would not allow him to hand over men who would be automatically condemned to death. Tocornal told Walpole that 'international writers on law' would not necessarily construe the actions of the escapees as piracy. This was no more than a bid for their freedom.

The meeting was well documented by Walpole soon afterwards,

when he wrote to Lord Palmerston on 29 September. Walpole said that the Chileans believed that the act had not been committed 'with a view to profitable plunder': it was solely for the purpose of effecting escape. Walpole, of course, disagreed, telling Palmerston that he had told Tocornal that 'seizing by force and carrying away [a ship] for their own purposes, whatever these may be, constituted a crime'. Walpole conceded very little, except to remark on 'the very loose manner in which, from benevolent and human but mistaken notions of the Chilean government, they had been confined'.

Walpole's arguments wore the Chileans down. They eventually conceded the point that what the *Frederick* men had done was indeed a crime. The Chileans would recommend the government 'to acquiesce in the request of His Majesty's Government and authorise the delivery of the prisoners to the officer commissioned to receive them'.

One of Tocornal's last acts before he retired in November that year was sending a final letter to Walpole. In it, Tocornal requested that if the escapees were not pronounced guilty of piracy, then would the British permit them to enjoy the benefits of asylum 'which the government of Chile would not have deprived them of ... if not for the protestations of yourself that they were guilty'? He now appeared to be offering them a future in Chile – but only if they were cleared of all charges.

Just before Christmas 1835, it was revealed that Leslie and Russen had been recaptured in Concepción. Within a week, Leslie had escaped, allegedly bribing a prison guard. While Walpole was fuming at this latest lapse in Chilean security, Russen also escaped. Inquiries by Walpole were along the same lines as before. When writing to Ramón Boza, the governor of Concepción, Walpole demanded an explanation as to how Russen had been allowed to get away. Boza replied that Russen 'was not allowed to be rid of the irons' but did so himself and 'scaled the prison wall built of wood'. Walpole may have won the arguments but he had lost six men, had two recaptured and then watched aghast as he lost those two again. In the strongest possible terms, he made his view known to Governor Boza that the Chilean 'power to carry [its intentions] into effect appears essentially deficient'.

Yet another inquiry ensued, this time directed at the governor of Concepción, but it yielded no results. The men were gone and there was nothing Walpole could do about it.

*

WHILE THE DIPLOMATS and politicians were parrying with each other over whom and what to blame, James Porter was still suffering in much the same way he had been for more than a decade. He says in his memoir that he and Shires had been 'chained together like dogs' for the past seven months.

Sometime late in 1835, he was told by his friend and former employer Don Lopez that a British vessel was on its way to pick them up. After months in chains, there was little left of the affable Don Santiago, and the old James was looking for any chance to take 'French leave'.

This time he concocted a plan that he hoped would allow him to lose himself in the hinterland, never to be seen again. First, he complained he was sick so that he and Shires would no longer be chained together. The warders fitted a pair of bar irons to his ankles, which prevented him from stepping more than four inches at a time.

He endured this for seven weeks. Then, according to his memoir, the girl he'd saved from the lady Ascension came to visit him.

Antoinetta was crying over his predicament, but Porter calmed her. He had summoned her for a task. There might be a way out, he told her, but he would need her help. Would she be willing to give it? 'I could see her dark penetrating eyes sparkle again at the base recital, she quickly answered "yes".'

Porter asked her to find a thin knife and a file – and to not breathe a word to anyone. In recounting this story in his memoir, he seems to be telling his readers, who may have been in some doubt on the subject, that actually, in his experience, he'd found many of the fairer sex to be just as trustworthy as men.

Antoinetta was as good as her word, secreting a file in her hair and a knife up the sleeve of her gown. Porter now had his chance. Within less than an hour he had cut through the bar by notching the knife with the file. He could now remove the irons at will. At eight that night, he got permission to use the privy. As he shuffled past in his irons, he squeezed Shires' hand.

Within minutes, Porter had placed a plank of wood against the prison wall, leapt to catch the top of it, and was up and over. Just outside the *cuartel*, he saw an old woman carrying a lantern. 'I knocked it deliberately out of her hand. She screamed but I cared not. We were in darkness and that was all I wanted.'

Don Santiago was now nowhere to be seen. James Porter was back.

Chapter 19

Porter's guards had seen him scale the wall and were not far behind. Just outside the gaol, he found himself at the edge of a swamp and figured that it would be best to camouflage his white prison clothes with mud. Black all over, he left the swamp, crossed over a few small farms and made for the road out of town. But this proved to be a mistake – the soldiers chasing him were now on horseback. Just before they came upon him, Porter jumped into a ditch.

With the road out of town being watched, his next move was to travel north of the river, under cover of the woods. First, he needed a vessel to cross the water.

Normally a boat was easy to come by on the city side of the Río Valdivia, but the only one he could find was moored just offshore and difficult to dislodge. He also needed a paddle. Combing the riverbanks he found one, but by this time he had been spotted. As he put it, he was accosted by 'a lump of a Spaniard', who must have seen him trying to prise his boat from its moorings.

Porter, the self-proclaimed street fighter extraordinaire, knocked the man out with the paddle – 'I would venture to say he did not put his head out again until daylight.' His assailant suitably neutralised, Porter returned to the boat, successfully dislodged it and climbed in. A fog was now moving across the river and he was already feeling cold. The next thing he heard was an alert coming from the *cuartel*. Concealed by the mist, he managed to paddle across the river despite growing colder and getting a cramp.

By now Porter had absolutely no idea where he was. As ever, he was playing it by ear. He knew he should make for the interior where the Chileans were scarce, but there were other dangers – the Mapuche were the masters inland and might prove dangerous to a wandering white man. Not for the first time, he would take a chance on the basis that anything was better than prison. He kept moving through the woods, seeking out some form of habitation. 'All that I had about me was a knife in a sheath, a half pound of tobacco and five dollars of money, but nothing whatever to eat.'

In the morning, hungry and tired, he spied a young boy herding some cows – and, beyond him, a small farmhouse. There was nothing for it: Porter had to go there and plead his case. An old lady opened the door and ushered him in; there was plenty to eat and he would be welcome to it, she said. Porter was being given a Chilean-style reception: *estranjeros* are always welcome, no questions asked.

But the lady was no fool. She waited for him to finish eating before she demanded to know point blank where he had escaped from.

Porter dreamt up a new story. This time he was a Frenchman who had escaped a whaler that had been anchored at the heads.

'I know you – you are Santiago,' she replied. She was Carmaletta Ray, the mother of the woman married to Cockney Tom. Porter started at the name: Cockney Tom was still the governor's chief sneak. The lady assured Porter he was safe – she had no love for her son-in-law and never allowed Tom anywhere near her premises.

Suitably refreshed, Porter started out the next morning in a fresh set of clothes and with a few days' supply of food. He was heading north towards the town of Concepción, but that was still more than a hundred and fifty miles away. He came across another farmhouse but this time didn't stop to meet its inhabitants; he did, however, steal a poncho.

By the third day he was on the llanos, the great plains north and east of Valdivia. This landscape has only two temperatures: baking hot in the day and bitterly cold at night. The plains stretch as far as the eye can see, like an ocean covered with light-green seaweed, and the air is clean and the sky usually a vivid blue. Porter crossed the Río Pichoy, heading inland, where he came across small lakes dotted around the river. Further north-east, he found himself among great Mapuche-grown cornfields. Mountains came into view. As he approached them, the land filled out with trees, the trees became woods, and the woods thickened into forests.

On the fourth day he made it to the lakeside town of Pucón, which stands at the base of the great smoking mountain Villarrica. Beyond it, to the east, are more white-capped volcanoes and the mighty Andes seeming to stretch into infinity.

Porter didn't stop at the town. As he was crossing one small mountain, he didn't realise that the path was circular and found himself at the very spot he had been six hours earlier. 'Fatigued with walking and vexed at the disappointment I threw myself down on the grass.' He fell asleep in the open.

This proved to be another mistake. He awoke to find a man of 'robust appearance' hovering over him with a knife. The man claimed the poncho Porter was wearing belonged to his father. Porter was in no mood to argue and handed it over.

But that wasn't the end of it: the man wanted to take him prisoner. A fight ensued. Porter was seemingly always able to conjure up a weapon at a moment's notice. He knocked his assailant out with a large stick and, while the man was stunned, stole his knife and took back the poncho.

When the man awoke, Porter forced him at knifepoint to be his guide. Porter was lost – he needed to find the pass through the mountain he had failed to traverse the day before. When they came to a crossroads, Porter let the man go free. One road led to Nueva Imperial, directly to the west, and the other to Concepción in the north-west. Porter now had his bearings. He would head north-west to Concepción.

Two days later, a posse of soldiers found him exhausted by the side of a road. He was suffering from dysentery about fifty miles south of Concepción. It's possible the man he had forced to guide him had tipped off the authorities.

*

IT HAD BEEN another brave attempt by Porter, but it had failed. He had to make the decidedly unpleasant trip back to Valdivia. The sergeant ordered him to be strapped over a horse, with his feet and hands tied under the animal's stomach. According to Porter, he was mistreated throughout the journey, at one point being placed too close to a fire and at another beaten by the flats of the soldiers' swords.

When Porter arrived at the governor's house, Thompson asked why he had run away. Porter did not hold back: 'Two reasons I had for doing: first, the cruel treatment and oppression of a tyrant like yourself, secondly with the hope of obtaining my liberty.' James Porter had lost his Santiago-like courtesy, but given the ill treatment he'd just received, he was hardly arriving in a peaceful state of mind.

The governor was in no mood for words. Porter was to have bar irons welded around his legs – and would be taken to the square the next day and shot.

> I was quite indifferent as to his putting his threat into execution (for to speak candid) I was tired of my wretched life; I was then conveyed to the blacksmith's shop and ordered to stand upon a large anvil. The irons were put upon me and a piece of red hot iron hissing from the fire was placed in the end of the bar and actually welded on to prevent the bar from slipping through.

Thompson was probably only scaring Porter, because it was well known by then that the prisoners were awaiting the next available passage to Britain. Executing Porter would have caused more than just diplomatic outrage between the British and the Chileans, it would have provoked a serious incident. Porter was now effectively under the protection of the British.

Even so, according to Porter, the local townspeople, priests and certain prominent women banded together and beseeched the governor to spare his life. This was, after all, their beloved Santiago. A padre Rosa told Porter that they had managed to sway the governor in his favour, but the prisoner appeared to care little. Sick and fatigued, and no doubt despairing that yet another escape plan had failed, he was surely feeling seriously depressed.

When Thompson finally appeared, he didn't meet a thankful and contrite James Porter. Thompson told Porter that he had his many friends to thank for being alive as Porter 'richly merited death for absconding'. Porter did not mince his words: 'I will not thank you for prolonging a life like mine which has been a life of misery,' he told the governor. 'No. I will not thank you because you are the chief cause of it by your oppression.' Thompson, probably not used to such flagrant disrespect, could only glare back at him. Porter couldn't have cared less. He had nothing left to lose.

In late April 1836, while the town was enjoying its afternoon siesta, Porter, Shires, Lyon and Cheshire were escorted from the *cuartel* in chains down to the port. At anchor around the outer forts lay the cutter, HMS *Basilisk*. The town, which had taken these men to their hearts for two years, never had a chance to see them off.

By early evening they were in British custody. James Porter must have felt that a dozen years of escape attempts had all been for nothing. The long arm of the Royal Navy, so feared by the *Frederick* ten, had proven its extraordinary reach.

*

THEIR ROUTE WOULD be long and circuitous. The prisoners would be treated like freight, carried on whatever British ships were most convenient, until they finally reached Hobart Town. The *Basilisk* conveyed them to a very large frigate, HMS *Blonde*, which was waiting for them about three days' sailing away in Valparaíso. Once handed over to the *Blonde*, they headed north to Callao, the port of Lima, Peru.

There was something of an irony in being picked up by the *Blonde*. It was the very same ship that had tried to pick up the men nearly eighteen months earlier, but which the Chileans had rebuffed with a 32-pound cannon shot across her bows. Back then Commander Mason had departed with his tail between his legs, but now the human cargo he'd sought was in his possession.

Mason was in command of one of the most famous ships in the British Navy, which a decade earlier had been captained by Captain George Anson Byron, cousin of the great poet Lord Byron. Back then it had been given a sacred duty. The Hawaiian King and Queen had wished to meet King George IV, but in England both contracted measles and died. The *Blonde* returned the bodies of King Kamehameha II and Queen Kamāmalu to the Hawaiian islands, then known as the Sandwich Islands.

This 46-gun frigate was about 155 feet long, with three square-rigged masts. She was well manned and well equipped, and a veteran of Pacific travel. By 1836 the *Blonde* was middle-aged but still a formidable vessel.

The four men were securely tethered in the gun deck, one floor below the main deck. All the while, Porter was looking for an exit. Somewhere, he surmised, the *Blonde* would anchor close to a harbour where he could jump ship and make a clean swim for it. The ship was so large that perhaps he could slip away unnoticed.

His opportunity arose when they set anchor on a moonlit night outside a nameless port, somewhere on the northbound journey from Valparaíso to Callao.

Porter knew how to oval the shackles – and they must have been relatively light shackles for him to do so. This was standard fare for convict escapees: they used a heavy object to beat the shackles so that they became misshapen and pliable. Once they had been 'ovalled', Porter could fit his feet through.

The four men were chained to a single bar. The plan was for all of them to escape, because it was barely possible for one to leave without the others knowing about it. But Shires said it wasn't worth the effort for him to go – he couldn't swim, and if he had to be assisted to shore he would only be a burden to them. 'My only request,' Shires told · Porter, 'is that, should you get clear off, you will not forget to see Catalina, my wife and also my little boy, and be a friend to them, for I shall never see them more.'

The nights were getting warmer as they sailed north towards the equator and one still, clear night, with the faint lights of the nearby port several hundred yards onshore, Porter released himself from his shackles, placed his 'jacket' where his body had been (to look as if he was sleeping under his clothes) and crept soundlessly up to the main deck. Porter was meant to take Cheshire and Lyon with him, but according to his memoir, Lyon was fast asleep and Cheshire had decided not to come. Yet again, Porter would have to escape on his own.

As he reached the main deck, he heard voices. He was compelled to crawl along the side of the ship and hide behind as many obstacles as possible. Just a few feet away, the night sentinel was talking to the quartermaster. Porter managed to reach the chain plates that supported the mizzen mast, when he found himself face to face with a marine – and with the marine's pistol.

This escape attempt was one of Porter's least successful, foiled in just a few minutes. Porter attributed the failure to none other than his archenemy Lyon, who had warned the sailors of Porter's escape by clanking his irons: '[Lyon] was the person that aroused the sentinel and caused me to be detected. I am certain I should have soiled my hands with the villain's blood in the heat of my passion, only for the timely interference of my companion William Shires.'

Shires was becoming not just Porter's calming influence, but his best friend. As for the other two, it's hard to know what their motives were. Perhaps they simply hated Porter as much as he did them. They may have been envious of his escape or angry he hadn't taken them along. Schadenfreude wasn't rare among convicts.

The next day, a first lieutenant asked Porter the inevitable question: who was involved and why he had endeavoured to escape? Porter told him that he 'had been a prisoner long enough'. He added, 'I am innocent of any crime and I consider it my undoubted right to escape if I could.'

Porter was now trading under the name of James Connor, a man innocent of everything, vociferously pleading his case to anyone who would listen. It didn't seem to matter to him that he and his companions' identities had been verified in Valdivia. Everyone knew the likely fate of the four men, and this is probably why Mason showed some empathy for Porter's cause: 'It is natural the man would endeavour to make his escape,' Porter reports the commodore as saying. 'It is our duty to prevent him if we can, if they are guilty of the offence they are charged with they are to be treated as men, and if innocent, their case is very hard and aggravating to them.'

Perhaps fearing Porter would be severely punished, Shires offered to share the blame for the escape. As for Cheshire and Lyon, 'the two scringing hounds' as Porter describes them, both denied any knowledge of, or part in, the attempt.

Porter had little hope to save his own skin – he wasn't just chained to the *Blonde*'s gun deck, he was chained to his enemies.

The *Blonde* stayed several days at Callao, one of the least beautiful ports on the South American west coast. That part of the Peruvian coast is famous for the fog that blankets the ocean and well inland. Darwin did not approve much of it either. When he visited in 1835 he said there was hardly any rain in Lima, but a 'thick drizzle of Scotch mist' hung over the coast, known by sailors as 'the Peruvian Dew'.

The *Blonde* then headed back down the coast. For the second time the men found themselves in Valparaíso, where they caught a ticket to England. They were going home.

All four were transferred to the *North Star*, a smaller frigate than the *Blonde*, which soon got under way and moved steadily south towards the barren, forbidding coast of Tierra del Fuego. The *North Star* rounded Cape Horn amid freezing weather, negotiated between giant icebergs and then started its ascent through the south Atlantic, along the east coast of South America to Rio de Janeiro, the last stop before the long haul back to England.

And so it passed that six months after they had left Valdivia, the four men found themselves within sight of Portsmouth Harbour, just as winter was about to break.

Chapter 20

Jᴀᴍᴇꜱ Pᴏʀᴛᴇʀ ʜᴀᴅɴ'ᴛ seen England for over a decade, and it wasn't exactly a sight for sore eyes. Along the quay at Portsmouth were a number of enormous floating prisons, many of which hadn't moved for years. Some of these hulks were tied to the piers and others bobbed in the water just behind them at anchor. They were all rotting, putrid and rat-infested.

The four men didn't board a hulk directly but were sent to a guard ship and handcuffed to gratings, two men apiece for two days. As Porter puts it in his memoir, they were scarcely allowed to fend for themselves. They had their food cut up for them and were 'not even allowed to go to the head [toilet] without a lump of a marine being lashed to each of us'. They were being singled out for special ill treatment; there was no doubt that their piratical reputations had preceded them.

The prisoners were soon boarded on the *Leviathan* hulk, once a proud ship of the line that had fought at the battle of Trafalgar. In her better days she was a majestic frigate sporting seventy-four guns and sailing proudly near the front of Lord Nelson's column, led by his flagship, HMS *Victory*. But for twenty years now she had sat idle in Portsmouth Harbour, a giant wooden bathtub stripped of her rigging, sails and rudders, her two masts converted into clotheslines. On deck there was a rusty, half-broken shed. The only magnificent thing she retained was her immense capacity: she could, if needed, cram in six hundred prisoners.

The *Frederick* men were marched aboard and paraded on the quarterdeck, mustered and received by the captain. Their irons were removed, then they were handed over to the gaol authorities, taken to the forecastle, and forced to strip and take a bath. They were each given a coarse grey jacket, waistcoat and trousers, a broad-brimmed felt hat and second-hand shoes. This garb was hardly sufficient for the upcoming winter and bore no relationship to their weight and height. According to Porter, the clothes 'fitted ... like a purser's shirt upon a handspike'. Once dressed, the men were shaven and cropped and marched to the lower decks.

It was cramped, hot and stank in the boat's crowded, fetid holds. The hulks were famous for their rapid spread of disease and putrid quarters. The lower deck was divided by means of iron palisading, and each division subdivided into cramped cells that could hold between fifteen and twenty prisoners.

Porter and his companions were thoroughly scrutinised. The authorities ushered through a procession of 'old gangers' to see if any of the four could be positively identified. The captains of surrounding hulks were also brought in to see if they recalled any of them. Porter, of course, continued to plead innocence – he was, after all, James Connor. Luckily for the four men, they weren't identified.

In his memoir Porter says little about his experiences on board the *Leviathan*, but while waiting for their transport back to Van

Diemen's Land, it's likely the men were assigned to a mess and allocated to a work gang. Their jobs would have been close to what they'd experienced as Van Diemonian convicts. The men would have been allowed off the hulk for most of each day, labouring on various projects: river cleaning, stone collecting, timber cutting, and embankment and dockyard work. Porter must have missed working in a sunlit apple orchard – he may even have missed the lady Ascension.

*

FOUR DAYS BEFORE Christmas 1836, Lyon, Porter, Cheshire and Shires were transferred to the *Sarah*, a 480-ton former commercial vessel converted into a transport, bound for Hobart Town. She was the fifth ship they had graced in eight months.

In the *Sarah*'s hold, waiting to be carried away, was a rich cast of characters, including some of Britain's most charismatic criminals and political prisoners. Two colourful identities from London were among them. John Perez de Castaños, a Spaniard, was once described as one of the most 'finished swindlers' ever seen in court. He and Piedro Caligani, an Italian, fleeced several Mayfair jewellers and tradesmen before being caught and remanded in custody at Newgate Prison.

Apart from de Castaños and Caligani, the non-British Isles contingent on the *Sarah* were all colonial. They had been transported from their places of trial across the Atlantic to England. They'd been under guard, in horrific conditions, for months and sometimes years. Some were West Indians who had rebelled after their emancipation and found themselves in circumstances almost as dire as they had experienced as slaves. There were also nine Canadians and twenty-two Irishmen, most of whom had been indicted not for sleight of hand but for political crimes.

The *Frederick* four's arrival on the *Sarah* caused an uneasy stir. It wasn't the West Indian rebels, former soldiers gone rogue, political firebrands or fancy thieves who exercised the officers' imaginations – it was the *Frederick* men. In the eyes of the crew, they were pirates with real form, with all the attendant connotations of violence, rebellion and fear.

Just as in the hulks, rumour had played its part in forming perceptions of this now famous convict cargo. While Porter and the others hadn't been positively identified in England, that hardly mattered. Their crimes were famous, even if the exact circumstances of their 'piracy' were not. The general consensus was that the *Frederick* had been captured 'in circumstances of great atrocity' – as a senior official on board put it. They were believed to be the kinds of men who would shed blood at a moment's notice. Aboard the *Sarah*, they were watched closely.

The *Sarah* was a typical convict transport: a large, three-masted ship that used every inch of space to ensure as many people as possible could be crammed into the lower holds. Porter surely remembered his first trip to Van Diemen's Land on the convict transport *Asia*; the *Sarah* was similar – she would strain and creak with every minor tack. Even in moderate winds, transports barely responded to the movement of the sea and air: the winds came, the transport creaked, the sails cracked and then came a pause before the vessel moved. She wasn't the lightweight, responsive *Frederick* – she was a heavy, ponderous boat taking them to a heavy, ponderous life.

*

SECURITY ON THE transports was extremely tight. The tween decks were enclosed in a wall of heavy timbers, and the main and forward hatchways were barred, which meant only one person could squeeze through at a time. The *Sarah* didn't contain the ultimate protection afforded to senior officers against mutiny: on some convict transports a barricade was erected across the width of the ship just behind the main mast, and ten armed soldiers would be stationed there, on watch at all times. Convicts who rushed the barricades would face an even more formidable weapon – cannons filled with grapeshot, a stringent defence against any number of determined mutineers.

The man ostensibly in charge of the convicts was the surgeon superintendent, Dr James McTernan, and he had more than a potential mutiny on his hands. The ship had been sitting for a month waiting for the weather to improve, and throughout late November and into early December, the conditions on board – especially down below – were becoming untenable. McTernan was paid for each safely delivered convict, and it wasn't in his interests to have anyone expire on his watch. The bad weather had given him very few opportunities to let the men take on fresh air and exercise, even while still at port. He noted in the surgeon's log that he expected some form of disease. The enormous rains in November and December 'led me to fear the invasion of some unfriendly consequences'. 'The elements were against us,' he wrote, and that was before the *Sarah* even set sail on December 22, 1836.

There was always a fear of cholera, typhus and scurvy on board convict ships, but by the late 1830s such outbreaks were becoming rarer. The biggest killers were dysentery and diarrhoea – spread, as it was still believed at the time, by airborne miasmas. McTernan was a veteran of convict transports and knew what had to be done: there was a need for ventilation, swabbing, clean heads, disinfection with lime, regular fumigation of the lower hold and regular onboard exercise for the men.

Beyond the big killers he expected the more common forms of sickness that laid so many low. Many prisoners on the *Sarah* were first-timers: they had never seen the sea, let alone sailed on it. Think of the way the *Frederick* landlubbers dealt with far less cramped conditions when they set out from Macquarie Harbour, and multiply that problem a hundredfold – a high proportion of convicts would be seasick in the first few days, and many would simply not know how to deal psychologically with the vast and capricious nature of the ocean. The very idea of being at the mercy of the Atlantic must have caused them severe anxiety. This was made worse when they were sent to the holds, battened down and chained up in heavy weather.

The *Sarah* wasn't equipped with hammocks that swung freely with the roll of the ship; she was fitted with berths arranged in rows like bunks, stacked against the hull. These tiered bunks were rigidly arranged to allow as little body movement as possible. Four convicts would be placed in a wooden berth of around six feet square. Smoke from gas lamps and portable stoves, the only source of heating, accumulated along the sides of the hull bulkhead where the prisoners slept. The hatchways were barred with thick grilles and always secured, resulting in poor air circulation.

The hulls were very narrow in construction, which made living in them almost unbearable during violent weather. Everything would roll together, and in the confined quarters below decks there was no escaping the putrid bilge water. The sea and rain would filter through the hatches and other cracks in the hull, and water would flood from the bilges, bringing a cocktail of slime and filth that was intolerable. The *Sarah*'s convict hold was not just unhygienic, it was toxic.

It was under these conditions – a deep, all-pervading cold and wet, combined with close-packed humanity and plenty of filth sluicing in the bilges – that Dr McTernan encountered his first case of erysipelas. The *Sarah* hadn't even set sail when on 16 December, Convict No. 51, Andrew Sampson, was diagnosed as having 'an erythematous blush extending from the instep to the calf of the leg'.

Sampson, a West Indian, was struggling. There was pain at the touch of his skin, his pulse was weak and erratic, and his tongue was thick and white in the centre. He was the first of several erysipelas victims – his body was being attacked by flesh-eating streptococcal bacteria that began as a rash and imbued the affected areas of skin with the appearance and consistency of orange peel. Also known as St Anthony's Fire, the symptoms McTernan described were 'furry tongues, pulse racing to 100–120, high delirium with excited vascular action, and sanguinous discharge from the scarification'. There were also fevers, shaking, chills, fatigue and vomiting. The infection could be treated if caught early enough, but in these cramped and wet conditions it was more likely to flourish than abate.

*

ON A FREEZING grey day, the *Sarah* slipped through the narrow heads at Spithead and turned west into the Solent waterway. She made good time, moving briskly past the shores of the Isle of Wight with the Needles on her portside, the three giant stacks of chalk that rise off the island's western extremity. The ship's last view to starboard was of Henry VIII's Hurst Castle, a fortress designed by the Tudor king to defend the western bank of the Solent from the threat of French invasion. The *Sarah* then turned south-west and deeper into the English Channel.

The winds and rain had abated somewhat, but it was just a pause. Within a few days the bad weather returned. And according to Porter, as soon as the ship entered the channel, the sickness became endemic.

McTernan described heavy tumbling seas formed by the same unrelenting westerlies, which splashed over the forecastle through the hawseholes, filling the prison and hospital. Water reached the ship's deepest crannies through the hatchways, creeping into the convicts' hold. As the weather worsened, one case of bacterial infection followed another. There was James Entwistle, Convict No. 32, whose erysipelatous blush 'shews itself from the right ankle extending nearly to the knee'; and George Stapleton, whose symptoms were so bad, all McTernan could do was administer large doses of brandy to the dying man. Edward Daniel had a blush of red across his face 'which developed into extensive facial tumefecation and redness'.

Down in the stinking hold, McTernan did what he could in insufferable conditions. He wrote that '18 of my 24 hours were on average passed in the hospital on attendance of the sick, fearlessly using the lancet' and was 'grateful for its results'. His main weapons against the disease were camphor spirits and his trusty lancet. *'Habeo spiritum camphor ad partibus adfectis applicandum* [I have applied spirit of camphor to the affected parts],' he wrote in classic medical Latin. He applied, swabbed, scraped and cleaned patients as best he could. It was his belief that the men who had lived unhealthy and dissolute lifestyles would be less likely to survive. He noted that Edward Daniel, despite his severe facial tumours, was cured as he was 'a well conditioned man'. Sampson, the first man to manifest symptoms, also survived the scourge. James Stevens, a former soldier 'of intemperate habits', did not.

McTernan was under the impression that this disease was not contagious, as he did not know what we know now: erysipelas can be transmitted by physical contact or by touching the saliva, sputum or blood of an infected person. The surgeon believed in the miasma theory and, in a sense, he was right: the infection can also be transmitted through the air and via coughing, and also from affected surfaces, through faecal matter and infected blood and needles. 'What would have been my fate, and that of my hospital men who lived in the midst of this scourge and breathed nothing but it?' he wrote. There would be sixty-eight cases of the bacterial infection, and it is a credit to McTernan's tenacity that only seven men died of the infection.

What may have saved many of them was the surgeon's insistence that the convict hold needed to be thoroughly swabbed and cleaned, and doused with an antifungal powder, chloride of lime. And there doing his duty was one James Porter, now working assiduously as one of Dr McTernan's hospital orderlies.

'I then exerted myself in assisting them all I could, and kept the prison clean from filth, for which I got praise from the doctors and officers on board,' Porter recalls in his memoir. He was now enjoying favour among the officers and crew, and while he was helping to clean and assist, they struck off his irons. All passed well, he wrote, and after a month 'all hands were in good health on board'.

But as was always the case for James Porter, the pendulum soon swung against him again. While mass infection was declining, rumours of mass insurrection were sweeping the ship. One morning, Porter says, he was summoned to the quarterdeck and set upon by soldiers. He was forced onto his back with his legs placed in a block. Heavy irons were then roughly applied. Whatever goodwill he had stored up had all been for nothing. For the second time in his life, Porter was being accused of mutiny.

Chapter 21

O<small>F ALL THE</small> things that nineteenth-century British naval officers feared, the most frightening was rebellion lurking unseen and close by. This fear of mutiny was matched by only one other: an assault by pirates. As far as the captain and officers of the *Sarah* were concerned, the *Frederick* men were both mutineers and pirates.

It was about a month after they'd left the Solent that Porter was hauled up onto the upper deck. He wasn't alone. By eight o'clock that morning, there was a mass gathering. 'There were English, Irish, Canadian, Spanish and Italians,' according to Porter. 'And a poor French sailor that was aboard who did not escape the villains.'

Porter lay hapless on the block, unable to move. Looking down from the quarterdeck were Captain JT Whiteside and the chief surgeon, Dr McTernan, their faces set hard, ready to dispense retribution. Next to them stood Lieutenants Wotton of the 44th Regiment and North of the 80th Regiment.

Shires was pushed to the front of the line and looked half-shocked, half-bemused. He asked meekly what this was all about.

Captain Whiteside said he had reason to believe Shires was the ringleader behind a planned mutiny against the *Sarah*. Shires looked incredulous. He glanced back at the other convicts and then at the captain and surgeon as if this was a surreal joke. Within an instant, he was tied to a grating. An enormous black sailor, the ship's knotted logline in hand, stepped up behind him and drew the lash back for the first stroke.

The sailor must have been ordered to administer the lashing as quickly as possible – many more men would need to be taught law and order that day. Shires didn't scream, but by the tenth or twelfth stroke was moaning audibly. By around the thirtieth, he was begging for mercy, blood trickling down his legs, filling his shoes and despoiling the deck. Porter feared for his life – Porter was an old hand at the cat, having totted up three hundred, while Shires had never experienced a whipping.

Like everybody else on the ship, Shires was weak and under-nourished. By the time he had been lashed four dozen times, he was unconscious, his mouth frothing and his body limp. His back had been sliced thinly, some cuts light and others far deeper, where the cord had found its mark several times. There was skin dangling by a few threads. Porter's best mate was grievously hurt.

While Shires was being untied, Porter was having the bolts removed. Two men pulled him to his feet and stood close on either side of him. Porter was ready to protest his innocence. He appealed directly to the doctor, whom he had worked so closely with over the past month. 'Dr McTernan. I am James Connor, a free man and you'll find this out for yourself when we arrive at headquarters,' he said. 'Punish me if you think this is proper, without rhyme or reason, but you will have to put up with the consequences when we arrive.'

Ordered to strip, Porter did just the opposite. He buttoned up his jacket and stood there in defiance, looking directly at the two 'judges' above. 'I will not accept this punishment, I have been falsely accused. I demand to know the reason for this punishment.'

Seeming to fear that Porter might escape punishment by standing his ground, Lyon and Cheshire stepped out from the assembled crowd. Lyon proclaimed, 'These men are at the head of a vast and dangerous mutiny. They planned to rush the quarterdeck and slaughter everyone in sight.'

Porter's defiance had at least flushed out the accusers. They were, he wrote later, the same old 'snivelling hounds'. Lyon and Cheshire had told McTernan that Porter and Shires, with the help of a dozen Canadians, would put everyone other than their fellow conspirators to death. This is an interesting number given that there were only nine Canadians aboard.

The day before, McTernan had been all grace and light towards Porter. Now he looked down on him like a censorious judge. If Porter was seeking weakness from either the surgeon or the captain, he didn't find it. McTernan signalled to the soldiers.

'Knowing my innocence I stood there petrified. I was seized by the soldiers and seamen, lashed to a grating, and to that degree until the blood hoosed from the parts where the lashings went round different parts of my person. And a lump of a black fellow flogged me across the lines and every other part of the body.'

Porter remained silent throughout his forty-eight, staring contemptuously at McTernan and Whiteside. The message written across his face wasn't just, *You were stupid enough to believe them?* but also, *This won't break me.* He wanted to make them feel as uncomfortable as possible: 'I would not give them the satisfaction to cringe to their cruel torture.' Close to the end he went limp with exhaustion. 'I knew no more about it until I was cast adrift.'

The chief accusers now walked through the ranks of assembled men with the power to name, shame and punish. In all, sixty men were named by several accusers, who included Cheshire and Lyon. It was a witch hunt, according to Porter.

As they were pointed out, some of the accused dropped to their knees. Others were shaking with fear and avoiding the gaze of the accusers as they passed through.

McTernan and Whiteside had swallowed the entire story.

*

THREE HOURS OF floggings ensued, and the top decks ran red with the blood of scores of men. It didn't cease until 'seven bells, half past eleven o'clock'. Porter and Shires, among the alleged ringleaders, were thrown into a makeshift dungeon, a part of the ship that would scarcely contain them. Their feet were chained together, their hands fastened behind them, and their bodies suppurating and bleeding together. The heat in this dungeon was atrocious, Porter wrote later, but it wasn't the physical pain and discomfort that irked him most. Lyon and Cheshire were charged by the captain to stand over Porter and Shires as 'sentinels' to ensure that 'we got neither water, food, nor tobacco given to us by any of our fellow prisoners'.

'It was past description. That was the time, my gentle reader, I craved for death to alleviate my tortured feelings, and when describing this part of the narrative my feelings are harrowed up to such pitch that revenge is uppermost in my thoughts.'

Porter would always swear that he'd had nothing to do with a planned mutiny on the *Sarah*. According to him, Lyon and Cheshire had attempted to curry favour with the captain by being seen to save the ship from a potential insurrection. They were sacrificing Shires and Porter, thinking (quite erroneously) that this might save them from the drop. This may have been the case, or Lyon and Cheshire might have been part of the original plot, only to confess and implicate Porter and Shires.

For three weeks, the two captives were kept together, bloodied, bound and barely able to move, until they looked 'more like anatomies than living beings', in Porter's description.

Most analyses of these events on the *Sarah* have tended to favour the official version – that McTernan caught the mutineers early, punished the protagonists and halted any real uprising in its tracks. The surgeon would later write to the colonial secretary, John Montagu, that the conduct of the four prisoners during the voyage 'justified the necessity of great caution'. But this was perhaps disingenuous: Porter's good works in helping the sick were not mentioned. 'For here they concocted a familiar design and succeeded in bringing many to their views,' he says in his memoir.

In his letter, the surgeon wrote, 'I was made aware of it and in due time checked it with a full exposition of their guilt and timely infliction of punishment of the active members of the plot.' He then explained that a Frenchman named Wilson, one of the sailors on board, was the main perpetrator on whom the other plotters relied for information to relay arms. McTernan said Wilson was 'unequivocally involved'.

McTernan had supposedly uncovered a plot organised by Wilson – a strange name for a Frenchman – who purportedly admitted his guilt 'on his own solemn promise'. McTernan recommended that, on arrival, the authorities should 'direct fresh proceedings' against Wilson, but none against the *Frederick* four. This seems to make little sense: either they were guilty of being part of the mutiny or not. Of course, it is possible McTernan saw no point in charging them for an offence that they were already due to answer in the *Frederick* case.

Although McTernan wrote of their guilt to the authorities, he could never present any solid evidence against Shires and Porter other than accusations made by others – which may have also included those of Cheshire and Lyon, which Porter spoke of. The staged whippings on the top deck were, it now appears, little more than a cruel fishing expedition. If those in charge couldn't coax out the main perpetrators, at least they could put the fear of death in everyone else so that nothing further would ensue.

*

CAPTAIN WHITESIDE WAS no less convinced than McTernan of Shires' and Porter's guilt. He wrote later that the *Frederick* four, Wilson, and the Spanish swindler de Castaños 'as well as two or three desperate characters' were the main perpetrators. Whiteside was so fearful that mutiny would break out a second time that he ordered the ship to bypass Rio de Janeiro. This was where most convict ships needing fresh supplies stopped en route to New Holland, but he feared that the conspirators could rise up and murder everyone, scuttle the ship and seek sanctuary in South America.

Somewhere in the midst of the south Atlantic, the *Sarah* changed course and headed south-east, away from Brazil and towards Cape Town.

By February, Porter and Shires were enduring the worst of the doldrums. So close to the equator, the heat is insufferable; the prevailing trade winds of the northern hemisphere blow to the south-west and collide with the southern hemisphere's driving nor'-easters. There's often little surface wind and intolerable heat.

Down in the tween decks, the cramped and hottest part of the ship, the two men eked out some kind of existence. They were allowed just a quart of stinking warm water per day. They had nothing to keep each other going other than their mateship.

After the convicts' health was compromised in the cold of Northern Europe, it was just as liable to fail on the equator. They were pinned together in an unbearable fug, their bloodied backs unattended and their bodies lying in their own filth. To add insult to injury, the pitch used for caulking the seams of the ship's timbers melted like a rain of hot tar, dripping relentlessly onto the men.

*

AFTER THREE WEEKS, Porter and Shires were led out, more cadaver-like than human, blinking rapidly in the harsh sunlight. It's most likely that after some inquiry, the captain and the surgeon may have reasoned that these two were not the main perpetrators – or that they were simply incapable of anything after their ordeal.

But Wilson and de Castaños were given no such joy. They would be kept in irons for the remainder of the voyage.

Just after they had regained their freedom, the two *Frederick* men tended to each other's wounds. Later that day, Porter was writing on a piece of paper when two soldiers knocked him from behind and snatched it from his hand. Conspirators in the attempted mutiny were believed to have been passing notes to each other.

The soldier hadn't picked up a clandestine message, but a poem:

> How wretched is an exile's state of mind
> When not one gleam of hope on earth remain
> Through grief worn down, with servile chains confined
> And not one friend to soothe his heartfelt pain.
> Too true I know man was made to mourn
> A heavy portion's fallen to my lot
> With anguish full my aching heart is torn
> Far from my friends by all the world forgot.
> The feathered race with splendid plumage gay
> Extend their throats with a discordant sound
> With Liberty they spring from spray to spray
> While I a wretched exile gaze around.
> Farewell my sister, Aged Aunts dear
> Ere long my glass of life will cease to run
> In silence drop a sympathetic tear
> For your Unhappy Exiled long-lost son.
> O cease my troubled aching heart to beat
> Since happiness so far from thee has fled
> Haste, haste, unto your silent cold retreat
> In clay cold earth to mingle with the Dead.

It was hardly first-class poetry, but it was Porter's heartfelt cry to the unforgiving gods.

According to Porter, the soldier who'd snatched the piece of paper immediately apologised and showed remarkable sympathy towards him – but still took the poem to McTernan.

A little while later Porter was summoned to the dispensary where he was asked about the capture of the *Frederick*. The surgeon no longer asked about his alleged involvement in the mutiny on the *Sarah* – he wanted to know who Porter really was. Also present was Whiteside, the first mate, and an army lieutenant.

Three weeks in a dungeon hadn't loosened Porter's resolve. He remonstrated that he was not Porter but James Connor. In his memoir, he explains to his readers that this was his last ploy for escape on arrival in Hobart Town.

I suspected, had I informed them I was the man they represented me, they would have looked sharper after me and prevented my making an escape, for it was my intention, as soon as we made the head land of Hobart Town, to endeavour to make my escape, as I knew every creek and corner of it. This then was the principle cause of my persisting in the falsehood.

Even after all this time, and in these direst of circumstances, Porter was still hopeful an escape opportunity would present itself. He must have known that too many people in Hobart could identify Police No. 324, and it would only take a cursory look at his distinguishing marks – most notably his blind left eye – for an officer to positively identify him. As ever, he was boldly clinging to threads.

If there had been a bolt that could be loosened or something to be thrown overboard that might help a man find freedom, James Porter would have taken the chance. But on a large, crowded ship like the *Sarah*, well guarded and already primed for any form of misdemeanour, there were no loose screws. Porter's assertion that he could somehow find a way out as the innocent James Connor, victim of an international miscarriage of justice, was more hope than expectation. Porter had been through a tremendous ordeal and yet still hung on to whatever threads he felt he still had. He may have known that he would probably be recognised in an instant, given the exactitude of the identification process.

*

THE FREDERICK FOUR passed the final days of their voyage under a rough naval kindness – treated well but closely watched and always in chains. They were, after all, men who had practically been fitted out for their coffins. While Porter had very little hope for his liberty, the sailors knew him as one of their own, and he had their sympathy.

The four men had one thing going for them, which they would discover on arrival: their greatest nemesis wouldn't be there to receive them.

George Arthur had gone. By the time the *Frederick* men had arrived in Portsmouth, Arthur had left the colony under a cloud. His cronyism and self-enrichment had become too much for a growing number of free colonists who wanted a more open, fair and less penal society. It had taken time, but Arthur, the richest man in Van Diemen's Land, could no longer haunt their lives – or their dreams.

The convicts on the *Sarah* would be the responsibility of the new governor. In January 1837, Sir John Franklin had received a message from Lord Melbourne, the British Prime Minister, informing him that the four prisoners taken from Valdivia would be sent as soon as possible to Hobart Town for trial. Porter, Shires, Lyon and Cheshire would not arrive unannounced. The *Frederick* four were expected.

For James Porter, the days of loosening bolts, ovalling irons and filing chains were over. The only way out now was through a court of law.

Chapter 22

T HE *SARAH* ROUNDED the Cape of Good Hope and gathered speed, its topsails hoisted as it slipped into the blustering roaring forties. The ship made excellent progress across the Indian and later Southern oceans. By late March 1837, land was sighted.

Most of those on board had no idea what lay in store for them in the colony's nether regions, but for men like Porter, Shires, Lyon and Cheshire, there must have been a heavy sense of deja vu. The ship had to adjust its course several degrees south as it approached Van Diemen's Land, and for a short while was approximating the flight of the *Frederick* from Macquarie Harbour almost exactly three years earlier.

The *Sarah* made the heads of Hobart Town on 28 March 1837 after a voyage of ninety-seven days, one of the quickest ever made by a convict transport ship from England by sail. The ship's speed was possibly the only positive thing to come out of that journey. As it sailed into Hobart, the legacy of the previous three months was sitting motionless between the decks, either holed up sick or in chains. Of the 254 convicts, 134 had been sick, 115 discharged to duty and ten sent to hospital. Nine had died. That there weren't a greater number of mortalities was a tribute to McTernan's surgical skill and tenacity.

The *Hobart Town Courier*, 31 March 1837:

> *The ship Sarah, arrived on Wednesday with 253 male prisoners under the charge of Dr McTernan … Amongst the criminals are four men, viz: Shires, Connor [sic], Lyon and Cheshire, who have been sent here to take their trial for seizing a vessel, the Frederick. During the voyage, a plan was formed, in which a freeman, a sailor on board, is involved to take the Sarah; but as is invariably the case, the plot was disclosed to the officers and accordingly frustrated.*

The four men knew they were about to have a date with destiny, a final parlay with the authorities. James Porter may have boasted that he knew every 'creek and corner' of Hobart Town, but it was bigger and more prosperous than when he had left it.

The colony was now selling itself overseas as the 'Sanatorium of the South', famous for its flowers, fruit and healthy inhabitants. English novelist Anthony Trollope declared that the colony was a better version of England than England itself – just about everything was now being described in English terms. Houses, gardens, fruit trees and rivers were all delightfully Anglicised. No doubt this was part of the propaganda to bring as many of the best and brightest from the old country, but there was some truth in it as well. Van Diemen's Land, now increasingly being referred to locally as Tasmania (although the name change didn't occur until 1856) was considered a far more pleasant clime than its northern counterparts Brisbane,

Sydney and Melbourne – here was Arcadia in the Antipodes, sans its noble savages.

But in the world of recidivism, some things hadn't changed. The mechanisms for identifying, qualifying and characterising convicts remained in place. As soon as the ship was docked just outside Sullivans Cove, a party boarded. There to greet them was the chief police magistrate Matthew Forster, one of Arthur's long-time lieutenants and, like Arthur, a stickler for detail and an able 'top-down' manager of his convicts.

Forster knew Porter well enough. Once Porter saw the chief police magistrate stride up, he knew his cover would be blown. The man Forster had known well from 1824 to 1830 was a little older and more grizzled, but it was Porter right enough. Within a few moments Porter's ruse, on which he had staked so much, crumbled. James Connor was consigned to history, his place taken by the one-eyed man from Bermondsey. This time at least, Porter wasn't having a lark – the lark was on him.

Over the course of several hours, they would be heavily scrutinised. Police Numbers 324 (Porter), 299 (Lyon), 280 (Shires) and 819 (Cheshire) were all duly stripped to the waist and thoroughly checked by clerks for height, scars and tattoos, all of which were duly entered into the massive convict record books. There for the clerks to check were Porter's dimpled chin and tattooed pugilists, and Charles Lyon's scar on his left brow and anchor on his left arm. In the thirteen years since he had first been checked, Lyon had acquired a few new tattoos – a lady on his left arm and a crucifix on his right.

Some observations were adjusted. Shires was noted as having a sallow complexion, narrow visage, large nose and hairy arms. Porter was no longer a beer machine maker but a seaman. He was recorded as aged thirty-seven, which doesn't square with his earlier record that had him aged thirty-four. It wasn't uncommon for convicts' ages to 'change' – some didn't know their correct age and just picked an approximate figure.

There was one strange quirk about Porter's second identification, though: the blindness in his left eye wasn't recorded.

According to the records, the four men were simply labelled as 'absentees returned'. The next day, they were all marched off the ship in single file. The four *Frederick* men – as well as the French sailor Wilson – were chained together, with two soldiers, one on either side of them. The five men did not have far to go. They were conveyed from the Old Wharf in the Wapping area, up towards Macquarie Street, where they turned sharply left and were marched to the corner of Macquarie and Murray streets. Porter always believed that Wilson was innocent and later wrote that he felt for him 'from his heart': 'His haggard appearance occasioned by fretting caused him to have a ghastly appearance. He held his head down, the only foreigner among us. I knew he was innocent.' De Castaños, meanwhile, now deemed a lesser protagonist of the attempted mutiny, had been sent directly to Port Arthur.

The twelve-foot wall of Hobart Gaol was the most prominent feature of Murray Street. The best that could be said of the prison was that it had a sense of space and was more capacious than one might expect, but it was hardly adequate given the growing number of convicts in the colony. Some said that it looked more like a hospital than a gaol. When it was first built in 1815, a report on public buildings emphasised that it was in 'an elevated and airy part of town' that didn't look like a place of punishment and coercion. With an entrance fifteen feet high and twelve feet across, it took up an entire block, dominating the southern side of Murray Street. It faced three of the more substantial buildings in the town: the treasury, Supreme Court and police station. Not far opposite was St David's Cathedral, with its three-sided clock and dome capped with grey-green lead.

The gaol as a whole was roughly divided into cells for felons and for debtors, the two most common classes of criminals. They, however, were led out to the yard where there were four cells: two that attracted light, and two that courted the darkness. Porter and Shires were placed in one of the light cells, Lyon and Cheshire in the other. They would not glimpse the streets of Hobart for nearly a month.

*

IN 1824 PORTER had arrived a few months before Arthur, and now in 1837 he had missed him by several months. With Arthur gone in October 1836, there was great rejoicing – and not just from the four accused. Porter thanked providence that the cause of his misery was no longer there to press his final misery home. Everybody knew that Arthur practically made the laws; he hadn't just been judge, jury and executioner but supreme legislator. It's not speculation to say that he would not have countenanced any mercy in this case.

Hobart Town – and the colony as a whole – was enjoying a new lease on life. Sir John Franklin was the people's deliverer from despotism almost by default. When he was appointed in January 1837, it was believed that he would usher in a new age – the autocratic bureaucracy created by Arthur and his faction of favoured men would be dissolved and replaced by a more liberal, freer-thinking and fairer regime.

Franklin was almost the perfect English hero. As a child, he had sailed with Matthew Flinders to Australia and had been an extremely capable soldier in the Napoleonic Wars. In 1819, he led an arduous 500-mile expedition across arctic Canada in search of the North-West Passage; and from 1825 to 1827 explored the north-west rim of the North American coastline, from western Canada to the southernmost parts of Alaska. By his early forties he was feted throughout the dominions as a great polar explorer and dubbed a knight of the realm. By the mid-1830s he needed a role that fitted

The people of Van Diemen's Land initially viewed Sir John Franklin as a saviour. As a former polar explorer he had all the attributes of a hero, but despite his best intentions, he was not able to transform the colony as the people had hoped for.

his talents, and it was suggested to Lord Melbourne that Franklin was the man to replace the now much-maligned George Arthur.

In early 1837 there were balls, teas, meetings and parties to honour the great polar explorer whom many thought was about to usher Van Diemen's Land into a golden era. When he travelled to Launceston in February 1837, three hundred horsemen and seventy carriages turned out to escort him.

Nor had he come alone. With him was his wife, the strong-minded and indomitable Lady Jane Franklin, who would become almost as powerful a presence in the colony as her husband. Franklin may have been the governor, but the real intelligence behind the throne was his private secretary, Captain Alexander Maconochie, who would go on to have a very important – if somewhat contrarian hand – in the fortunes of the colony. If there was one man who was against Arthurian thinking, it was Maconochie. He didn't mince words about the convict system that he and the new governor had inherited; in his view, the settlers who had convicts assigned to them were no less than slave-holders and the assignees 'slaves'.

The local gentry thought Franklin would be the man to dispense with Arthur's despotic theocracy and reforge Van Diemen's Land into the democracy it so plainly deserved to be. Among the more bizarre beliefs floating around was that Van Diemen's Land would become its own country, able to determine its own fate and answerable to no higher power – this, of course, was never even vaguely contemplated by London.

There was an obvious contradiction here: the same free settlers didn't want to abolish the penal system. But you can't have a penal colony and a democracy working in the same space and at the same time. The colony was still an enormous open-air prison: of its nearly forty-three thousand inhabitants, close to eighteen thousand were convicts. The wealthy, who had all the power and influence, had become used to their free, assigned labour. Franklin carried the false hopes of a colony on his shoulders but could do little to change the system. He said he 'felt both depressed and delighted with the signs of popular joy' – he knew well enough he was no Messiah.

The convicts would continue to be employed in private or assigned service, under the same Arthurian game of snakes and ladders. Here was the free labour the colony thrived on, which still needed to be kept stringently in check to build houses, fences and roads, and create infrastructure at minimal outlay.

The new governor was still enjoying a political honeymoon when the *Sarah* sailed up the Derwent. On hearing of Arthur's departure, the four convicts may not have expected instant freedom, but they too would have invested hope in the new governor – a thread of hope that he might show mercy and alter their almost inevitable course towards the gallows.

The *Frederick* four knew well in advance that their lives might rest on the humanity they had shown Taw, Hoy and the soldiers three years earlier. Their main act may have been technically piratical in nature, but their other actions had been those of saints. Everyone knew that this wasn't the violent and callous mutiny of the *Cyprus*. Popular appeal for some form of leniency towards the four wretched *Frederick* men was always there: it just needed someone to stoke its flames.

*

THE TRIAL OF the *Frederick* four would take place just under a month after the arrival of the *Sarah* on 26 April 1837. The solicitor-general, Edward Macdowell, would take the Crown's case against them. But before he could do this, he needed all witnesses to be present. The publicly disgraced Captain Taw, who had been so vilified by Arthur, was no longer in the colony and presumably unreachable.

David Hoy, now the master shipwright at Port Arthur, would be present in court. Hoy had finished his two-year stint on South Bruny Island constructing a lighthouse; it had been, he said, his 'Napoleonic exile', imposed on him by Arthur, who apparently had always suspected his connivance with the convicts. One of the convict servants, William Nicholls, and the first mate, James Tate, would also give testimony.

The four prisoners were to be tried by Chief Justice Sir John Lewes Pedder, a man often mentioned as one of Arthur's faction. Like Arthur, he had been firmly against the establishment of civil juries on constitutional grounds. He had been the chief justice for fifteen years, and had been knighted on Arthur's recommendation. There were, however, some key differences between the two men. Pedder was far less inclined to Arthur's political needs and was a stickler for the letter of the law.

Time and again, he used legal technicalities to justify decisions that may not have always gone the government's way. Arthur admired his abilities but clearly found the man frustrating: 'I have wished he was a little more expeditious at times, and rather less given to legal distinctions, but his integrity and excellent judgement override all his defects,' Arthur wrote. Most agreed that Pedder appeared to offer a very strict and literal interpretation of the law. But this isn't a full summation of his qualities as a judge.

Pedder had empathy. The question was – did he revel in technicalities for their own sake, or did he use them to suit his own inclinations?

Pedder was known to have disliked his role on the Executive Council, as it forced him to be party to political decisions, not the purely legal ones that he felt far more at home with. Nor did he relish his power as the chief cog in the colony's justice system. Pedder was also known to be slow in his judgement, and apt to delay decisions – or even try to avoid giving them at all. Arthur had found this part of his character extremely frustrating.

There are other descriptions of him that show demonstrable differences with the thinking of the faction to which he belonged. The best example of this is Pedder's stance on the Palawa, which set him apart from every other senior official. He said very clearly in Executive Council meetings that he was absolutely against rounding up these people and placing them in what were effectively concentration camps. In earlier days, he had also steadfastly argued against Arthur's proclamation of 1828 that allowed Aboriginal people to be fired upon if they entered settled areas. In the end, Pedder lost both arguments. But whenever the fate of the Palawa was discussed in later years among Executive Council members, this always occurred when Pedder was absent. He took a strongly independent view on the subject of Indigenous people, and Arthur didn't want it recorded. In this way, Whitehall never heard about Pedder's dissension or the force and weight of his arguments. It was just one of many examples of Arthur's culpability in what was perpetrated against the Palawa.

Pedder was also said to be dismayed by the harshness of the criminal code he had to adjudicate. Some called him the hanging judge – and there's no doubt that in the 1820s, when the Arthursponsored criminal code was particularly harsh and the war against bushrangers, highwaymen and cattle-rustlers was at its pinnacle, Pedder sentenced scores of men to death. But there was another side to him. Press reports show Pedder was deeply affected when sentencing prisoners to hang. One diarist, writing Pedder's obituary in the *Hobart Mercury* in 1873, said that 'whenever it was his painful duty to pass sentence of death on a fellow creature, Pedder's whole frame trembled and he was overcome with the humane emotions of his nature'.

In one press report of 1827, the *Hobart Town Courier* noted that Pedder was 'overcome by the lamentable and unexampled spectacle of nine human beings convicted of so cold a murder'. In another case that same year, he had no choice but to sentence eighteen men to death for multiple crimes including cattle- and sheep-rustling, housebreaking, highway robbery and theft. In these cases, Pedder was known to have wept. These are hardly the actions and manners of a 'hanging judge'.

It wasn't known to the four men, but the judge who was about to adjudicate their case believed it was his role to protect the rights of prisoners. Pedder would seek pardons from the lieutenant-governor if he believed there were extenuating circumstances. The man who could determine their life or death was one hope the four clinged onto, the other being a reprieve from the governor. There were very few solicitors in Van Diemen's Land, and in any case the prisoners couldn't afford any form of legal representation. The *Frederick* four would have to fight their own corners.

They also wouldn't have known that legal precedent might be on their side. In the case of the *Cyprus*, Pedder had found himself in the position of almost acting as counsel for the two men in the dock, John Denner and James Camm. Like the *Frederick* four, these men had no legal representation. As the presiding judge, he could never explicitly act for them, but he charged himself with ensuring that whatever evidence the Crown brought against them was fully watertight.

Camm and Denner were found guilty of piracy by the all-military jury, but Pedder had never been happy with the quality of evidence against them. There were clear legal difficulties. It is thought that he asked Arthur to commute the sentences but was only half-successful. Camm was sent to the gallows while Denner was reprieved.

However, the case had proved a point that might work in favour of the *Frederick* four. If Pedder felt there was any doubt in the application of the law or the quality of the evidence heard by the court, he would pursue that doubt with every inch of his legal expertise.

Chapter 23

T HE THRONG WOUND its way into Murray Street. By close to 9 a.m., a large crowd of Tasmania's finest gentlefolk was chattering and clamouring outside the Supreme Court.

It was a cool, crisp April day and when the doors were flung open, the jostling began in earnest for the best view in the house. The physical appearances of the *Frederick* four were unknown to the people who crowded into the courtroom – they hadn't left gaol since their arrival. Some people had preselected their positions, ensuring they would have a good view of the judge, the men in the dock and the witness box. The trial of the *Frederick* four was the only show in Hobart Town.

Just after 9 a.m. the Common Sergeant of the Court took his seat on the bench. Shortly afterwards, the audience looked on as fifteen very scruffy looking convicts, including two women, were marched to the bar and cuffed. Who were the four? Audience members looked at each other questioningly. The jury, all dressed in military uniform, arrived just after the prisoners and took their places. Justice Pedder arrived a few moments later, a small black cap upon his wigged head.

Pedder informed the court that there were cases from the previous day which required sentencing. He directed the jury to leave the courtroom and return for the *Frederick* trial. There before the court were felons of all sorts, such as Samuel French, sheep-rustler, and Sarah Smith, thief.

While the other convicts were resigned to their fates, Smith was having none of it. 'I have been unjustly dealt with,' she cried to the court after Pedder sentenced her.

Pedder, as ever, was unfazed. 'You will pass a considerable time in confinement,' he told her.

'Thank you, your honour,' Smith replied. 'And I hope you may sit there till I come back and be damned to you.'

The Supreme Court had never looked so colourful. Court cases were entertainment, and often it didn't matter what the case was or who was being sentenced – the people loved the drama. The more gruesome the case or the more important and high-ranking the defendant, the more people would turn up. Today, however, was on another level. This wasn't just an entertaining outing but also a magnificent social occasion, a rare chance for discourse on a theme that had dominated the chattering classes of Hobart Town for most of the past month.

The women wore bonnets with wide semicircular brims framing their faces, heavily decorated with trim, ribbons and feathers. Their dresses displayed the distinctive large 'leg of mutton' or 'gigot' sleeves, which were puffed at the top with a tapering lower section. Hobart Town ladies wanted to show themselves as fashionable and feminine – the dress had to ensure the shoulders appeared sloped, the bust was full and round, and the waist narrow but with very full hips. The men, too, were nicely attired, wearing finely wrought frockcoats and top hats. Many had taken the day off work. It was, after all, a carnivalesque day.

Hobart's finest had discussed and argued the case incessantly. Dinner parties across town had assessed the four men's chances. Everyone had a theory. Were these men saints or sinners? Were they for the drop or not? By the end of the day, all would be revealed.

*

AT FIRST THE people were quietly muttering, but some felt they had been duped. This was not what they had come for. The muttering soon turned into open conversations and Pedder was forced to ask for silence. But few present cared about the protocols of a court of law – they were expecting a fast and furious show.

At 10 a.m., all became clear. Pedder directed the jury to be brought back in and only the *Frederick* four remained in the dock. The air of the courtroom grew slightly heavier with a lack of oxygen, and all the fidgeting and murmuring dissipated into a hushed silence. The main event had finally come to the attention of the judge.

Some had expected to see a bunch of Matthew Bradys: huge, courageous titans of the sea who had wrested control of a boat and sailed six thousand miles to their liberty. Others had expected to see shining, saint-like men who hadn't strained the quality of their mercy when it mattered most. And plenty of people had expected to see swarthy, one-eyed brigands. Many were surprised. How could these four scrawny little convicts have captured a boat and sailed so far?

There were three counts in the indictment, which was duly read out. The first and by far the most serious was the charge of piracy, which carried with it the death penalty. The four men were being charged with: 'piratically and feloniously carrying away on the 13 January 1834 the brig *Frederick*, Charles Taw master, belonging to our Sovereign Lord the King and of the estimated value of £1200, from the high seas, to wit, Macquarie Harbour on the Coast of Van Diemen's Land.'

The second count was that of breaking their trust as sworn mariners. The third was obscure and rather strange – it was the same as the first count but did not state Charles Taw to be a subject of William IV.

The chief justice turned to the four men. 'How do you plea?' he asked.

Pedder appeared as he always did at the beginning of his cases – bureaucratic and inscrutable. His demeanour had barely changed since he'd heard the petty crimes just moments before. It looked like just another day in court, but it wasn't.

One by one, each man stepped forward a little hesitantly but not without some conviction. All four pleaded not guilty.

The trial proper, known as *Rex v Shires et al*, had its lead witness. David Hoy was called to the box. He described himself as a shipbuilder and said that he knew all the men now standing in the dock. The solicitor-general, Edward Macdowell, asked him to relate the events of 13 January 1834.

Hoy began by explaining that the *Frederick* had sailed well on its first real day at sea on 11 January. A fresh breeze had taken the brig twenty-three miles up the harbour, and on 13 January it had come to rest at Wellington Head, just a little way inside Hells Gates. The weather had changed for the worse and they had set anchor, awaiting a more favourable wind. The first Hoy knew of the alleged mutiny was sometime between six and seven that evening when, while he was dining with Captain Taw, two men came rushing in – one brandishing a pistol, the other a tomahawk.

The solicitor-general paused, as if to ensure that the skulduggery that he knew Hoy was about to relate would be fully digested by the court.

'William Shires is the man who presented the pistol at me,' Hoy said.

'He told me: "We have got the vessel, and if you don't give yourself up, I will blow your brains out!"'

'What exactly did you think this was about?' the solicitor-general asked.

'That's exactly what I asked him,' replied Hoy.

As Hoy described it, the next thing he knew was that he and Shires were 'parrying for the pistol' and had come to grips. 'I endeavoured to get hold of the pistol and called out for assistance, expecting the military were on board.'

Hoy explained that he tried to knock down a cabin wall to allow the soldiers to pass into the cabin, but to no avail. 'I saw into the apartment and there were no soldiers there.'

In the middle of the struggle, Shires extricated himself and jumped up through the cabin hatchway. Hoy and Taw closed the cabin door and waited. A little while later Hoy heard from several of the convicts.

'Several voices on deck called up to me to "come up if you want to save your life. We have secured the military and got their arms",' Hoy said. 'They were calling to both myself and Mr Taw by name. They said if we did not come up they would shoot us.'

'How did you react?'

'I called on them to be reasonable,' Hoy said. 'To return to their duty and there would be no consequences. I told them the matter would be secret forever. They answered: "We have got the ship, and we will die to a man before we will ever give her up." Mr Taw asked me where my pistols were, and I told him they were in my chest. Taw said all he had was a musket. He said we must "sell our lives as dear as possible".'

The crowd wasn't just murmuring at this point, it was audibly debating the case. It seemed as if the redoubtable Mr Hoy had clearly proven the guilt of the four men, and that would be an end to it.

Again, Pedder called for silence. What the crowd didn't know was that this may have proven insubordination and guilty intent, but that was not enough. The Crown needed to be sure that these four men had played an active part in the mutiny and weren't bystanders – it needed to be shown that they were not prompted or forced to be part of the alleged mutiny.

As the solicitor-general posed his questions, it soon became apparent that something was missing. Macdowell wanted Hoy to name the convicts responsible for the events. At first it sounded as though Hoy had simply forgotten, but then it all became clear: Hoy was not going to give anyone up.

'Different voices made use of the same expressions,' he told the court at one point.

'Who was giving orders?' the solicitor-general asked.

As Hoy related it, one man was more authoritative-sounding than the rest, and he said the convicts would shoot both him and Taw. But then again, Hoy said, 'There were two or three voices saying the same thing.'

Hoy added that while he was trying to unlock the chest and find the weapons, a shot rang out. 'Give me the musket,' Hoy reported that someone said, 'and I'll shoot the —!'

'Who was this?' asked the solicitor-general, who was beginning to look at the boat builder with visible frustration.

'It may have been Leslie, but then again I am not sure.'

Hoy didn't seem to know who was ultimately in charge of the mutiny – all the men had guns and cutlasses. This meant that the case was going nowhere for the Crown. It had been established that Shires had shown some belligerence, but the voices of others who'd threatened Hoy were apparently never clear in his mind.

A little later Hoy described another scene with unknown assailants while he and Taw were still in the cabin. Hoy heard someone on deck say: 'They had better shoot the two – at once.' Then Hoy told the court that another man said: 'No … we will not commit murder, if we can avoid it.' Hoy thought that Shires might have said this – but yet again, Hoy wasn't completely sure.

The crowd was enjoying the tale, not just for its thrilling plot but also because the solicitor-general was quite obviously agitated. The more questions Macdowell asked, the more Hoy batted them off. It was well known in Hobart Town that he'd been banished by a vengeful Governor Arthur to Bruny Island, for not - as some described it – playing the game. He wasn't playing the game now, either. Arthur had also needed names, and Hoy hadn't given them to him. Hoy was walking a very thin line, describing events as they'd happened but being deliberately vague where it most mattered. The master shipwright probably couldn't bring himself to point the finger at the men he had worked with at Macquarie Harbour. Similarly, he may have wanted to ensure that Arthur did not get what he wanted.

Pedder looked on, seemingly bored, as if he'd seen this kind of prevarication from witnesses time and again.

Asked whom he thought was behind the plot, Hoy seemed to imply that it must have been Barker – who was conveniently not present in court. 'He was superior,' Hoy told the courtroom. 'He was an ingenious man,' he said at another point.

Hoy said that he'd seen Russen and Leslie armed with muskets. They'd appeared quite capable of shooting him, but when Hoy asked them if they would murder him they said they would not if he put up no resistance. As for the shots that came through the cabin hatch, Hoy had no idea who'd pulled the trigger. He added that one of the men had threatened to pour pitch down into the cabin to coax him and Taw out, but that this wasn't intended to kill or maim them, it was clearly just a threat.

'This may have been William Cheshire who made the threat, but again, it might not have been,' Hoy said.

In the end, he told the court that he and Captain Taw had given themselves up to the convicts, realising that if they resisted it may lead to loss of life. They had believed that no assistance would be forthcoming from the already captured soldiers who had been away fishing. The ship was clearly under convict control.

*

AT 1 P.M. Pedder adjourned for lunch. The crowd filed into the closest local pub, the Victoria Tavern, which had been established the year before. It was a small but beautifully formed pub, and the crowd spilled out as they ate and drank, discussing the case. When, everybody was asking, would they hear from the prisoners?

When the trial resumed, Pedder launched into some questions of his own. These were of a bureaucratic nature, and the audience, although suitably refreshed from lunch, soon grew bored. There were questions about who was in charge, the nature of the men's employment, when the *Frederick* was launched and the geography of Macquarie Harbour.

'Do you consider the vessel was on the high seas when she was taken?' Pedder asked Hoy.

'I do not,' replied Hoy. He explained to Pedder the width of the harbour at various points and its gradual narrowing as one approached Hells Gates.

'Were the convicts employed as seamen?' Pedder asked.

'The prisoners were not hired on board, nor did they receive any wages – they did the duties of seamen. I consider that the duty of the prisoners on board was as compulsory to them as any other work they might have had to do at Macquarie Harbour.'

Pedder ended this line of questioning, and from the crowd eased a collective sigh of relief. Billy Shires shuffled out of the dock and, guarded closely by a soldier, took to the floor. Hoy remained in the witness box.

Shires began by taking the obvious tack. 'May it please the court to know that we had all offered the captured men food and provisions and had never seriously threatened any of them,' he stated.

Pedder looked neither pleased nor interested.

'Could you confirm, Mr Hoy,' said Shires, 'that when you were in your cabin getting your clothes, I had given you a pocket compass and said that I was "sorry I could not give you any more"?'

Shires also asked Hoy to confirm that he had wrapped up a bottle of spirits in his shirt and told him to put it out of sight. This was an obvious gesture of solidarity.

'Could you confirm that you were put on shore with eighteen pounds of meat, twenty-six pounds of biscuit, and six pounds of flour?' Shires asked.

Hoy confirmed all of this. A number of other objects had been given to Hoy, Taw and the captives, including a live goat, cooking pans and even an axe. Hoy agreed that all of these things were offered and accepted.

While Shires was quite obviously soliciting the court's sympathy, he made some interesting assertions. One was that Captain Taw had threatened to leave the convicts ashore for insolence. Shires also alluded to Taw's drunkenness – while Shires never actually said what he meant by this, the implication was clear that the men were 'forced to rebel' because they were under threat from a drunken rogue of a captain. The crowd found this fascinating, and the murmuring started up all over again: *The captain was a drunkard.*

Shires asked Hoy if he remembered that Taw had threatened to leave the recalcitrant convicts stranded at some unknown beach, described in the courtroom report as 'Stewards Harbour'.

'I do not recollect that at all,' Hoy responded.

Shires needed to establish that there was a good enough reason for him and the nine others to take the ship, but Hoy wasn't going to bend to this one. When he didn't give Shires the answers he'd hoped for, Shires tried another line of inquiry. 'Sir, would you acknowledge that when I had burst into his cabin with a gun, that it was not a gun at all, but little more than a piece of iron?'

'What you presented to me I considered to be a loaded pistol,' Hoy said abruptly.

The *Hobart Town Courier*, which had reported on the case virtually verbatim, then mentioned that Lyon took to the floor. All it said was that Lyon 'elicited nothing of any consequence to the material points of the case'.

Next came Porter. His line of questioning was to make it clear that the provisions on board were enough for nineteen men to travel to Port Arthur – but little more. The amount of food that they had taken for their trip across the ocean with the *Frederick* was barely adequate, Porter reminded Hoy, and they had given more than half to the men they had marooned.

Porter's best probing came when he asked Hoy to confirm a statement he'd made. 'Did you not say that the humanity and kindness you had received from the prisoners was so great and unexpected, that you could not forget it?' Porter asked.

Hoy duly confirmed this.

When it came to William Cheshire's turn to question Hoy, he simply asked him to confirm that he was of good character when employed by Hoy as a shipbuilder. Could he confirm that Hoy 'had promised he would procure some indulgence' when they reached Hobart Town. Hoy said that this was all true.

The *Frederick* four had probably won the sympathy vote up to this point. Hoy had been evasive in naming any of them, and it was proven beyond doubt that they had been kind and generous. But then James Tate, the man who had been Captain Taw's first mate, was called to the witness stand and sworn in.

Macdowell asked if Tate agreed with the testimony given by Hoy. 'I do,' he replied.

Tate had nothing to hide. Unlike Hoy, he had never worked with the convicts. He had never formed a relationship with them. He hadn't been well treated by the alleged mutineers that day and wasn't going to hold back.

'Who were the most provocative of these men?' the solicitor-general asked.

'Russen was running around with a tomahawk and Shires had presented a pistol to me and said "not a word or I'll blow your brains out",' Tate said.

Tate told the court that he hadn't seen Porter with any arms, but it was he who had tied him up with great force. And Tate seemed to have all the answers Hoy had failed to give. 'It was Lyon who had ordered the shots down the hatch and I saw both Lyon and Cheshire with muskets.'

Cross-examined by Lyon, he agreed that Taw was drunk on the day the ship was launched and often became inebriated with the soldiers.

'What about the night the boat was seized. He was drunk then?' asked Lyon.

'He was in a state of perfect sobriety,' replied Tate.

The argument put forward by Shires – that Taw may have been a threat to the convicts, forcing them to take the boat – was now crumbling. Tate had made sure of that in just one statement.

*

IN THE SUMMING-UP of their cases, all the prisoners said they hadn't played active parts in the mutiny but had felt compelled to do so.

'I was forced to stay with the convicts because I was the only one who had any real knowledge of the coast,' said Lyon. Here he was taking a well-known leaf out of the book of William Swallow, the mutineer from the *Cyprus* – and Lyon's fellow prisoner when they were transported to Macquarie Harbour. Swallow had pleaded successfully in his trial in England that he'd had no choice but to cooperate with the *Cyprus* mutineers as they knew he was the only one capable of navigation.

The *Hobart Town Courier* stated that all the men laid considerable stress on the kindness they had shown Hoy and his companions. In his closing statement, Shires said that his intention in rushing into the cabin had been to save Hoy's life by preventing any other person from taking it; of all the defences laid out by the four men, Shires' argument that he was somehow trying to save the captain and the shipwright when bursting in on them was among the least convincing.

What the *Courier* didn't report was a question Shires asked that would prove integral to the case. In his report on the case, Pedder said Shires asserted as a defence that the *Frederick* 'did not come within the description of a vessel'. Shires put it to the court that the *Frederick* 'was a mere raft, and was not registered'.

Shires also summoned a Mr Stocker, who had known him some years, as a character witness. Of all the men, Shires had a clean sheet – there had been no record of infractions or misdemeanours throughout his tenure as a convict in Van Diemen's land. The other prisoners called no outside witnesses, Pedder reported.

Porter, perhaps sensing that the game was lost, said he and the men would throw themselves upon the mercy of the court. 'Nobody has any idea of the hardships we had to endure before we finally made it to South America,' he said, almost as a cry for help. 'It was indescribable what was happening at Macquarie Harbour. And when we reached Chile we gave ourselves up to the government there.'

This was the only part of the case that the crowd seemed to have fully absorbed. The audience appeared saddened and upset. *Yes,*

Porter seemed to be saying, *we are admitting to the accusations, but what choice did we have? How can you blame us, when we only did what any normal men would have done? Macquarie Harbour was the real injustice, not the taking of the* Frederick.

The newspaper reported on the characters of the men, but it could hardly have known much about their characters after just a few hours in a courtroom. Nevertheless, in the *Courier's* estimation, Lyon and Porter were intelligent men while Shires was the quiet one. Cheshire, the paper not very kindly reported, was a 'weak lad'. 'Porter was busily occupied in taking notes,' the report says, 'of which he availed himself in his cross-examinations, which were conducted with considerable acuteness.'

With a military jury presiding, a 'not guilty' verdict in this case was never going to be likely. But the chief justice, seemingly bored with what he'd heard, suddenly came alive. Before the jury was asked to retire, Pedder asked them to consider some points that hadn't been raised in the trial.

The four prisoners had hoped beyond hope that the quality of the mercy they'd shown might tip the outcome in their favour. Now they were dumbfounded. Pedder's time had come.

Chapter 24

BEFORE THE JURY retired, Chief Justice John Pedder made it clear that there were technical problems that had to be addressed.

There was a precedent here. During the trial of the *Cyprus* mutineers in April 1832, Pedder had asked the foreman to consider whether the prisoners were actively engaged in the affair and whether 'they acted with coercion'. It took the jury fifteen minutes to decide that both men were guilty of piracy. Pedder then asked the foreman, 'Do you find the prisoners guilty of committing the offence on the high seas?'

'Yes,' he replied.

'You understand the place was shut in between two heads. Do you find that to be on the high seas?'

'We do.'

In that case, the two men were found guilty. In this one, Pedder wanted the jury to consider the very same issues *before* reaching a verdict. At stake for the jury was the consideration of the exact circumstances of the seizure: whether the *Frederick*, when seized, was on the high seas or not. Did Macquarie Harbour constitute a harbour or estuary, or was it on the high seas? If it was the latter, these men were pirates.

The chief justice made this supposedly cut-and-dried case even more difficult when he reminded the jury that the brig *Frederick* had never been registered. Pedder asked them to consider if these four prisoners were actually mutineers when the unregistered ship technically wasn't at sea and Captain Taw had yet to take command.

It's not known how any of the prisoners reacted to the comments made by Pedder in his summation. Did they fully understand the repercussions of what was being said?

The technicality lay not so much in law but in geography. Under English law, piracy could only take place aboard vessels on the high seas, but the *Frederick* was not 'at sea' until it had passed through Hells Gates. The *Cyprus* case, and the guilty verdict handed down, had posed a serious legal dilemma for Pedder. The ship had been seized in a harbour, Recherche Bay – which, like Macquarie Harbour, was not technically the high seas – and yet the men were successfully tried for piracy.

There was another case that may have also concerned him. The *Young Lachlan* had been taken by convicts in Sullivans Cove in 1819. The convicts there had been charged with theft – and not piracy – because Sullivans Cove was on the Derwent River around Hobart Town.

In asking the foreman of the jury in the *Frederick* trial the very same question about Macquarie Harbour, Pedder ensured that this time the jury was being very clearly 'advised'. Of course, we can't know the chief justice's exact thoughts, but there is clear evidence to suggest that he didn't want a repeat of the *Cyprus* trial. And Pedder had asked Hoy about the ship's status, just after the lunchbreak.

The law stated that the very moment an anchor falls in a harbour, the legal powers possessed at sea cease. Ergo, the *Frederick* four could never be considered pirates. Just as important was the nature of the *Frederick* itself. It was always described as a brig of around 130 to 140 tons, but was it technically a ship? Pedder was echoing Shires' defence that the *Frederick* could never have been a ship without being fully commissioned and eventually registered. In legal terms the 'vessel', said to have been 'piratically carried away', possessed nothing that would bring her within the legal definition of the term 'ship'. There was no register, commission or warrant for the vessel. In Pedder's words, it was legally little more than 'a quantity of wood and other materials so fastened as to possess the means of becoming a brig, but possessing no one constituent necessary to justify those materials being then so called'.

There is an interesting postscript to this. When the *Frederick* was scuttled off the Araucanian coast, Barker had supposedly insisted that all papers relating to the vessel should sink with her. Without these documents, the ship never formally existed. It isn't possible that Barker would have known that throwing away the ship's documents could annul the existence of the ship in the eyes of the law; he simply wanted to be rid of any association the escapees might have had with the *Frederick*.

It was pretty clear what Pedder was advancing: the *Frederick* may have looked like a ship, felt like one and sailed like one, but it wasn't one at all. From a harbour, the convicts had stolen a bundle of materials – timber, fabric, sails and rope; stuff with little more than the potential to be seaborne.

The geographic and administrative flaws in the case for piracy were now there for all to see – and there were also problems with the case for mutiny. The crew had to be mariners for the charges of mutiny to stick, but they were prisoners. Likewise, there had to be someone who was legally in command of the *Frederick* when it was taken. Taw wasn't technically in command until it was at sea, and Macquarie Harbour wasn't the sea. Was Hoy, the shipbuilder, in charge? While the *Frederick* was being constructed, perhaps, but not while it was sailing.

In the end, if there was no legal person in command to commit mutiny against, and if there were no sailors to be mutineers, there was never a mutiny. Again, that is why Pedder had asked Hoy whether the men had been paid as seamen.

The four convicts may not have realised it, but their coup to take the brig had been carried out with perfection. They had managed to take a non-ship at just the right time, with nobody in legal charge of it. The taking of the *Frederick* was no more a case of piracy or mutiny than the stealing of a loaf of bread. Robbery was the real offence, not piracy – however, the prisoners had not been charged with theft.

*

THE VERDICT TOOK just thirty minutes, and the Frederick four were found guilty.

As everyone at court that day had realised, these men had demonstrably seized the *Frederick*. Nothing Shires, Porter, Lyon or Cheshire said had absolved them of this guilt. But what exactly were they guilty of – piracy, theft, mutiny or all three?

While the foreman agreed that the offence hadn't been committed on the high seas and the four accused men weren't mariners, a guilty verdict of piracy had been pronounced. Herein lay the problem: the jurymen felt they had to give a guilty verdict for piracy even though the judge held strong technical doubts about the case.

The four men were in legal limbo.

Given the legal difficulties of the case, Pedder couldn't sentence the *Frederick* four to the gallows, which would have almost certainly occurred the day after sentencing. The chief justice wanted to be on sure ground that this truly was a legal case of piracy.

Pedder wrote a report on the trial that was read out to the Executive Council on 8 May 1837. In that report, he noted that if the crime had occurred in England, it would have been 'considered to be within the body of one of the maritime counties, so I think the offence itself is robbery and not piracy'.

There have been different versions recorded of what happened next. One version has it that Pedder, feeling he was on unsure ground, sent the facts of the case to London for advice. It would take months – possibly years – for the English law lords to make a judgement. The four prisoners would remain in chains at Hobart Gaol while the great and good in a far-off country determined their destiny.

But this version of events is at odds with Pedder's report to the Executive Council. It makes no mention that he intended to consult any further than Van Diemen's Land for advice on the case. According to his report, he only wished to consult with Mr Justice Algernon Montagu, a fellow Supreme Court judge and former attorney-general, and thereafter lay a full report of the case to the governor.

In other versions, it's said that either Porter or Shires appealed, ingeniously arguing all the technical arguments above. But there is no evidence of any appeal, neither in the Executive Council meetings nor in judges' reports, nor with any correspondence from Pedder to the governor. What appears to be true is that Shires had enough knowledge of maritime law to offer the 'ship-was-not-a-ship' argument.

My version is the following. These kinds of abstruse legal technicalities were beyond any of the *Frederick* men – Barker included. Pedder had deliberately deployed the best legal precedents he could find to save their necks. He didn't want another victory for Arthur, especially not one in absentia and he didn't want the men to die.

I believe that Pedder is the unsung hero in this story. The man who shivered when he sent men to their deaths had acted in accordance with his own conscience – and used the best technicalities he could find to do so. Pedder was deliberately saving the four men from the drop. And it worked – sentencing was suspended indefinitely.

*

Two weeks after the trial, the *Tasmanian* newspaper called for clemency for the four men, echoing the popular opinion surrounding the case:

> *Of what then have these men been guilty? That obeying the first impulse of human nature, they endeavoured to escape from slavery! That in the endeavour they not only not committed no enormity of any, the slightest, description – not even the breath of personal violence to any human being – but on the contrary, they exhibited so much forbearance in the manner in which they effected the purpose to which every felling inherent in man*

so strongly induced them ... that the people they put on shore
expressed themselves, according to their own evidence, in the
warmest terms of gratitude! Is there then in any one act of their
proceeding, any one feature deserving the last of punishments
that man can inflict upon his fellow man – Death?

The newspaper wasn't alone. Even up north in Launceston, far away
from the action, the *Cornwall Chronicle* also demanded mercy, on
6 May 1837:

We presume to express our opinion that the prisoners should
not suffer the extreme penalty of the law ... was it proper on the
part of the government, to leave a fine vessel, fitted for sea, and
provisioned for several weeks, in the charge of a drunken pilot?
For by the evidence of all of the witnesses of the crown, it seems
that Taw 'was pretty often drunk'.

The paper goes on to say that these were not the only men engaged
in the act, and perhaps they operated in ignorance of the ringleaders:
'until they were compelled to assist in it – perhaps to save their own
lives ... We hope his Excellency will take into consideration every
circumstance connected with the charge against them ... and we
hope [the law] will operate in their favour.'

In his memoir, Porter says nothing about the legal technicalities
of the case, but he would have known public opinion was very much
in the four men's favour. He wrote simply that he believed he was
still alive thanks to the beneficence of the governor, the 'humane'
Sir John Franklin. 'Woe to us had the blood thirsty Arthur have
ruled,' Porter says. 'As the vessel was christened after his son's name,

Frederick.' It may have been that he felt the technical problems with the case were far beyond public understanding and not exciting enough to mention. Porter probably would have wanted the public to believe that his generous soul, not some abstruse rules of geography and ship registration, were behind the decision.

James Porter was never one to sit still, even when he was in chains. With time on his hands and the game still for the playing, he reverted to some well-known habits. It was in Hobart Gaol, while awaiting the sentencing, that he wrote the first of his two memoirs.

Porter may have thought it was time for another lark. After all, everyone had believed he was a beer machine maker, so why not try to reinforce the belief that he was a mere bystander regarding the seizure of the *Frederick* – a simple cog in a wheel that he couldn't stop? Porter was intelligent enough to know that he could give the people what they wanted to hear. This wasn't the *Cyprus*: far from it, the people were saying, as these men had looked after those they'd captured.

William Gore Elliston – who ran not only the *Hobart Town Courier*, but also the *Hobart Town Almanack* and *Van Diemen's Land Annual* – at some point approached Porter and asked him to write his version of the taking of the boat. With the help of the press, Porter would tell the 'real story'. It would cement popular opinion his way and may even have a positive bearing on the outcome of the case. He would also make a little money. Just as importantly, it might make him famous.

Elliston had only recently bought the papers. Although they'd come with certain government printing commissions, he may well have been in debt. The *Courier* had cost him £12,000, a huge sum in those days.

The entrepreneurial newspaper proprietor had tried his hand at all manner of jobs. Elliston was a Cambridge graduate who had managed the Royal Theatre in London's Drury Lane – the very same theatre where Porter's criminal career was said to have begun. With Elliston behind him, Porter could finally fulfil his long-held wish. He could be an actor in one of his beloved Drury Lane Follies, playing the man injured by circumstance, an innocent bystander who meant nobody ill. Porter's memoir, written in 1838 behind bars, was set on a stage that was real, directed by a former theatre manager (of the Drury Lane Theatre, no less) turned newspaper impresario, with him as the lead. The stage was set, and the actors were all there to play their parts. It could not have been better orchestrated.

In 1837, Elliston was smart enough to see a great story in the making. And it was one that could be drawn out, as the sentencing of Porter and the three other convicts remained locked in limbo. The story had real substance and, most importantly, it was still happening.

Porter wrote the manuscript and sent it to the colonial secretary, most likely as a form of plea. In April 1838, two of Elliston's newspapers the *Hobart Town Almanack* and the *Van Diemen's Land Annual* published Porter's first memoir, in thirteen parts, under the title: 'A Narrative of the Sufferings and Adventure of Certain of the Ten Convicts, who Piratically Seized the Brig *Frederick* at Macquarie Harbour, in Van Diemen's Land, as related by one of the Said Convicts whilst Lying Under Sentence of Death for this Offence at Hobart Town'.

For Porter, it was easy enough to take the line in his story that the now famous William Swallow of the *Cyprus* had followed – that he really wasn't an integral part of the plot. As he wrote: 'We had not been more than half an hour ashore, when I observed many of the prisoners whispering together and laughing, but had not the slightest suspicion of their design …' The events in this version seem to swirl around him, and everyone except himself had a hand in the takeover of the boat.

Porter tells his readers that he was singing merrily downstairs when all the violent action was occurring. Two soldiers were taken, and he, the ingénue, watched on in disbelief as the other convicts battled to take charge. Porter was supposedly ordered simply to stand on the hatchway. In this version, he puts a good word in for his mate Billy Shires – it was Shires who said they didn't want this affair to be anything like the *Cyprus* and that provisions needed to be shared.

Porter makes Hoy sound like a forgiving saint when the men finally left the captives behind: 'I hope God will prove kind to you and protect you from the manifold dangers which you may have to encounter on the wide expanse of the Ocean.' The captives were even made to appear grateful to the convicts as they departed: 'The soldiers then cheered them on their departure and wishing they might be prosperous on account of their kindness and humanity in parting the provisions with them …'

To cap things off, the story is left nicely in suspension. Porter ends it by telling readers that he has been found guilty, which could lead to him and the other three being hanged. This provided an immediate drama to the story – it was happening as the reader was reading: 'But we have every reason to believe [the sentence] will be commuted to transportation for life and our case has gone home for the opinion of the English Judges.' The story even plays on the fact that they had rescued a cat, with the animal featuring quite heavily.

This public relations exercise, almost certainly guided by Elliston, was bound to work.

To the reading public, there may have been a strong sense of indignity, that sentencing these men to death would be no less than a gross miscarriage of justice. Not only had they helped their captives – these men were also friendly to cats. How could the authorities condemn to death such generous, kind-hearted, innocent bystanders? The Porter fix was in.

*

PORTER'S PURPORTED INNOCENCE may have been laughable, but his timing was impeccable. In Britain and its colonies, there was a growing groundswell of distaste for transportation. His story of desperate men desirous for their freedom perfectly suited the more liberal mood of the late 1830s.

Two main political forces were at work. One was the England-based Anti-Transportation League, which offered moral reasons for wanting an end to the transportation and assignment system: the more this system used men and women to make a profit, the more it looked like slavery. For the League, this was white slavery by any other name, which created 'a caste-like legal and socio-economic ceiling' that continued even after the convicts were freed as 'emancipated ex-slaves'.

The second force working against transportation came from the free settlers streaming into Van Diemen's Land, who at this time felt that the rising number of freed convicts made job competition too intense. But they, too, had moral reasons for wanting to end the system. They felt that as more lower-class criminals arrived, society was gradually self-destructing. There was talk of crimes being committed in Van Diemen's Land among the convict population that some felt would 'infect' the free peoples. This was the famous convict stain that would bedevil Tasmania perhaps more than any other state in Australia.

While Porter and the others were languishing in prison, an influential report on anti-transportation was being compiled in Britain. Sir William Molesworth led a Parliamentary Select Committee on Transportation that published its findings in August 1838. The committee had studied the moral and economic effects of the transportation and assignment system, and asked if transportation was the answer to the problems of English crime. It was hardly objective, though: the majority of those who gave evidence wanted to abolish transportation, Molesworth included. He made sure the report would be heavily stacked in favour of the abolitionists.

The report happily resorts to hyperbole to support its argument. Speaking to the committee, one clergyman claimed that homosexuality, then described as 'unnatural crime', was rife in the penal colonies – and that everyone who lived there was contaminated by it. Convicts had so infiltrated the core of colonial society that 'vice, immorality, frightful disease and hunger' were rampant. The more convicts who entered New Holland, the more debased its society would become. The moral decline of society was a political scaremongering tactic used effectively by the abolitionists against their enemies. Those who disagreed with the halt in transportation were seen as promoting a more debased society and often impugned for saying so. The reports were lurid and unreasonable, but it was what the people remembered. The stain had stuck. One report stated:

It is difficult to conceive how a man ... merely having the common feelings of morality, with the ordinary dislike of crime, could be tempted, by any prospect of gain, to emigrate with his wife and family, to one of these colonies, after a picture has been presented to his mind of what would be his probable lot. To dwell in Sydney ... would be much the same as inhabiting the lowest purlieus of St Giles's in London where drunkenness and shameless profligacy are not more apparent than in the capital of Australia. Every kind of gentle feeling of human nature is constantly outraged by the perpetual spectacle of the lash – by the gangs of slaves in irons – by the horrid detail in penal settlements; till the heart of the immigrant is gradually deadened to the sufferings of others, and he becomes at last as cruel as the other gaolers of these vast prisons. The whole system of transportation violates the feelings of the adult, barbarizes the habits and demoralizes the principles of the rising generation, and the result is to use the expression of a public newspaper, 'Sodom and Gomorrah' (chaos, even worse than hell on earth – all loss of morality).

All this had little direct bearing on the fate of the *Frederick* four, but the mood of the population clearly favoured the politics that called for greater emancipation.

By 1839, Sir John Franklin was concerned about a report by Alexander Maconochie that examined the condition of convicts in Van Diemen's Land. It was Franklin who had asked him to make the report, and Maconochie did so with a vengeance. When this report on the state of the colony was eventually released to the public, it also condemned the transportation and assignment system – not only did the system hold back colonial development, but it also encouraged immorality among both convicts and their masters. Arthur's system, Maconochie noted, was 'cruel, uncertain, prodigal, and ineffectual either for reform or example' of the convicts.

When Maconochie's report was eventually issued in London, it caused a sensation. The Molesworth parliamentary committee accepted it as evidence of a 'slave experience' in the colonies.

But it did not go down well back home. Every man who ever had a convict assigned to him was being told he was a slave owner. The Arthur faction now turned to Franklin to get rid of this traitor in the midst of government. Under severe pressure, Franklin dismissed Maconochie.

*

MEANWHILE, THE FOUR men waited and waited. And nothing happened. Prison became their lives. By now they were all highly institutionalised, their lives regimented by the bad food, the odd sip of contraband liquor, the mercy or not of prison wardens, and the daily exercise routine in the squalid yard. Every now and then a new piece of information from England filtered through – while the men sat and waited, a young Queen Victoria was crowned.

Sir John Franklin, who had the power to pardon, was finally persuaded by the full judge's report from Pedder in late May 1839 – more than two years after the trial. It states that Pedder thought 'the offence itself is a robbery and not a piracy'. Pedder adds that while it was not clear that any of the men were the principal ringleaders, their conduct in ensuring the castaways had provisions revealed that their object was not vindictive, but based on a desire to escape their circumstances. Everyone, it seems, was inclined towards clemency.

In his report Pedder expresses doubt as to whether the conviction was proper 'because the evidence showed that the offence was committed not upon the high seas ... the consequence of which would be that the offence itself was not piracy but robbery'. But as planned, Pedder had consulted Justice Montagu, and his fellow Supreme Court judge had disagreed: Montagu thought the piracy conviction correct, based on a case that gave the admiralty jurisdiction over 'all creeks and inlets of the sea in maritime counties'. Pedder had never found this piece of legislation.

> On making the verbal report I have spoken of I also stated that
> independently of the doubt as to the propriety of the conviction.
> I thought these prisoners' lives might be spared because their
> offence was committed under the influence of a strong temptation
> which presented itself to them to endeavour to obtain their
> liberty and that which it was not clear that any of them were the
> principal ringleaders ... Their conduct upon the whole had been
> better than could have been expected from such men engaged in
> such an enterprise.

The Chilean foreign minister Tocornal had said years earlier that the law needed to distinguish between a piratical act performed for gain and one performed for liberty. Without ever hearing of Tocornal, Pedder had essentially agreed that a piratical act for liberty had to be considered. He, like the newspapers, mentioned Taw's drunken behaviour and that the men had been deprived of some allowances that Major Baylee had ordered to be made to them. 'It seems to one that there were some ground for this complaint,' Pedder wrote.

In his summary, he says, 'It would be proper to grant the prisoners a pardon.'

Why it took Pedder so long to send this letter to Franklin is a mystery. Perhaps he was waiting on the advice of the law lords, and waiting on Montagu and looking up cases to prove or disprove his findings. But the man who was known for being a stickler for legal detail and a ditherer on legal process had finally played his hand. He was inviting the governor to grant a reprieve. The 'humane' Governor Franklin, whom James Porter placed so much faith in, probably could have made no other decision, given the recommendation from the chief justice, the politics of the time and the publicity that the case had generated. And the disingenuous but nonetheless popular tale that Porter had spun may also have influenced the decision.

The matter was extensively debated in the Executive Council, and a strange sentence was contrived. These men would remain guilty of piracy but their lives would be saved on condition of their being transported for life to Norfolk Island.

The case that had excited Van Diemonian minds since February 1834 was finally over in July 1839. Nothing had really changed for James Porter, Billy Shires, William Cheshire and Charles Lyon. The authorities had freed them from the rope only to allow them to continue their lives of penury. The old convict creed still hadn't come to pass for James Porter: it wasn't death, but it certainly wasn't liberty either.

There would be no celebrations or accolades for the *Frederick* four. In the eyes of the colonial establishment they had been nothing but trouble. They'd been chased around the world, recaptured, retransported and found guilty of a capital charge, managing with the help of an obscure geographic technicality to escape what men before them had swung for. They had cost money and many thousands of police hours and gaol time, and were the subject of legal complications and wrangles. Their descriptions had been sent across oceans, their fates had been written about and corresponded on by British prime ministers, governors, colonial secretaries, ambassadors and ministers of foreign affairs. They had seen their names splashed across newspapers. But they were still criminals.

Chapter 25

ALMOST IMMEDIATELY AFTER the conditional pardon was handed down, the four men boarded the *Marion Watson* for Sydney on 13 July 1839. In Sydney they were transferred to the *Governor Phillip* and arrived at Norfolk Island in late August.

The men had been sent more than a thousand miles off the Australian coastline to a rocky volcanic outcrop hemmed in by ocean with no real harbour. Norfolk Island was then under the reign of Major Thomas Bunbury, whom Porter calls 'a second Nero'. Not long after his arrival Porter witnessed 'a specimen of his [Bunbury's] cruelty': a man who could barely walk was dragged in chains in front of Bunbury and whipped mercilessly.

Norfolk Island was the Australian equivalent of the remote Devil's Island; indeed, some called it the Isle of Demons. It was the New South Wales version of an early Macquarie Harbour, the '*ne plus ultra* of convict degradation' – where, as one commandant remarked, 'the prisoners' feelings were habitually outraged and their self-respect destroyed'.

To the *Frederick* four, it must have felt like deja vu all over again.

Years earlier they had been sent to another place, similarly purpose-built to dump the lowest and most degenerate, those considered irredeemable by any means. And as they once had with the arrival of the easygoing and liberal Major Baylee, they had a similar piece of luck.

Not long after their arrival, Bunbury was replaced, and eventually Alexander Maconochie, the man who had reported on the state of the colony for Sir John Franklin, was brought in to run the settlement.

Maconochie had asked for the command. His report hadn't been welcomed by all sections of society, but he couldn't have cared at all. Maconochie was on a mission that no other commandant before him had ever attempted. He was anxious to prove that kindness and respect were more powerful rehabilitators than the lash, the solitary cell and the constant threat of a rope. The Arthur faction despised him and wanted him gone, while Franklin had realised that if he was to conduct business in Hobart Town, it would be easier without him.

Maconochie was a rarity in colonial life – an official with a strong conscience. There's one clear reason he was the way he was: he had been a prisoner of the French during the Napoleonic wars. He knew the traumas of life in a prison and had suffered it for two years. Now, finally, he was in charge of one.

He dismantled the gallows that stood just outside the prisoners' barracks; threw away the special 'double-loaded' cats that had been used by the floggers; built two churches – one for Catholics and one for Protestants; and even set aside a room in the barracks to be made into a synagogue. He set up classes in horticulture to improve the men's ability to grow fruit and vegetables. He even authorised the placing of headstones and commemorative plaques on the graves of deceased convicts.

Maconochie also created a new system of rewards and punishments that didn't ever end with a lashing. He hated the system of punishments that Arthur had instilled. His was a system of marks that, if the convicts followed carefully, would actually help towards reducing their sentences. If a convict infringed in some way, he simply lost the marks he needed to leave earlier. The convicts adhered to the system with gusto.

There was talk of great mirth on Norfolk Island at this time. The convicts even performed plays and musicals. One man, James Lawrence, had once been sentenced to fifty lashes for singing on Norfolk Island; now he ran all the amateur theatricals and musicals on the prison station. James Porter was involved too – he was reported to have sung 'The Light Irishman' as a cast member of the comic opera *The Castle of Andalusia* at the Royal Victoria Theatre on Norfolk Island in June 1840. Porter played the character 'Rapine'.

Maconochie was so far ahead of his time, he encouraged reading literature for reasons that wouldn't come into vogue for decades – even centuries. He wanted the convicts to read books in the travel and exploration genre, including Captain Cook's voyages, 'because the whole white race in this hemisphere wants softening towards its Aboriginal inhabitants'. He called for books from England including the novels of Walter Scott and the poetry of Robert Burns, and he brought the entire works of Shakespeare into the island's library.

As part of his social experiment, the prisoners were encouraged to record their stories. Many of these convict renditions survive today. It was a far-sighted and intelligent gesture from the new commandant, who believed literacy and numeracy were the surest means to unshackle the so-called irredeemable.

One wonders how Porter wrote his second memoir. He did not

have Elliston urging him on, but there may have been an educated convict – perhaps the commandant himself – helping him with the phrasing. The writing is scrawled but still legible and no doubt that of Porter. The spelling mistakes are rife, and Porter at times made errors on the chronology regarding his own convict record. There are also instances where the writing is his but the style is somebody else's and far more eloquent than the rest of the text.

This was a more comprehensive memoir than his first effort, written in prison, and encompassed his birth in 1802 to the time of writing in 1841.

Where the *Frederick* is concerned, he no longer paints himself as an unwitting bystander, but as a swashbuckling hero who had justly escaped the terrible injustices of a wretched penal settlement, then gradually revealed his true self as a gentleman and courtly knight in a far-off land.

Here we discover that he was very much a part of the taking of the *Frederick* – in fact, one of its most enthusiastic proponents. Perhaps he felt sufficiently liberated under Maconochie's regime to record a version closer to the truth.

In this version, it was Porter's idea to beguile the two soldiers into going fishing and to distract the others by singing the song that would trigger the action. Readers are at times treated to the rugged, death-or-liberty James, and at others to the fair-minded, generous and chivalrous James. At the end of the memoir, writing under the auspices of Maconochie, the larrikin who once called himself a beer machine maker for laughs tells readers that he's now a reformed and upright citizen, concerned with the importance of personal relationships, 'We have given our words neither to abscond with a boat or allow one to be taken under any circumstances and we have proved to him and all the officers on the island that our Commandant's Humanity has brought us to a new sense of duty, never to lose the only thing an unfortunate exile doth possess – His Word.'

Porter served Maconochie with diligence, and for four years was said to be 'worn out but still well conducted'. He gradually became a kind of policeman on Norfolk Island and a cox for its pilot station boat crew.

In two separate incidents, Porter showed great bravery at sea. He and his crew rescued a boatload of officers in 1841, and for this Maconochie reduced his sentence from life to fourteen years. In another incident a year later, Porter and his crew came to the rescue of a brig in distress under severe weather conditions; they took their boat twelve miles offshore in heavy seas to supply desperately needed water to the brig. They performed this dangerous task so admirably that Maconochie recommended that Porter's sentence be reduced to seven years and that he return to the mainland.

*

MEN LIKE MACONOCHIE, and the criticisms that came out of both his own report and the Molesworth Report in England, were part of what eventually led to the end of transportation. But this didn't happen quickly.

The assignment system had been considered a lottery, unfair in the extreme, and it was replaced by a system of probation in which every convict was offered more or less the same path to freedom. It started in June 1840 as a staged system – first the convict was incarcerated in Britain, then transported to Van Diemen's Land where he would be engaged in hard labour. From there convicts would earn a 'probation pass' and be accommodated at various probation stations. Only then could they be assigned to public works or individual settlers. A ticket of leave was dependent on good conduct while at the probation station.

The settlers generally felt hard done by this – here was good labour being wasted, many thought; while others saw the stations as simply adding to vice and idleness. The system never really worked, as the private sector felt its access to cheap labour had been disrupted, and convicts disliked the restrictions on their movements.

But the probation system brought in new innovations – such as the 'moveable panopticon', described in the Launceston *Examiner* of 30 December 1846:

> *An ingenious writer in the London Athenaeum (we suppose a graduate in 'prison discipline') has propounded a series of moveable panopticons, which are to contain only six men, and are to be advanced from place to place, as the labourers on the roads advance. An overseer's 'berth' composes the centre compartment, supervising by a simple construction of six subdivisions in which the men are to sleep, as completely separated as if they were in distinct dwellings, while not a breath can be uttered that must not be heard by the overseer. It is also part of this plan, that when the whole gang is mustered at night, its superintendent or chief officer, keeping a sort of sleeping rolster [sic] roll sends the men to their respective panopticons, never sending to successive nights the same six men together.*

This portable prison was designed to ensure that sodomy couldn't be practised by road gangs – there was no privacy and the men using the panopticon were constantly shuffled. It was all part of the great fear the system had about convicts: that by the separation of bodies and the imposition of silence and barriers, all kinds of so-called immoral acts could be avoided.

There were other forces at work that contributed to the failure of the new system. The 1840s was a period of recession, and passholders who were finally able to seek paid employment from private settlers found no work available. If the settlers couldn't afford to keep them, the government had to foot the bill. In 1846, there were around 3150 unemployed passholders in Van Diemen's Land; out of a total convict population of just above 30,000 – unemployment among convicts was at 10 per cent. Macquarie Harbour was reopened in this period; it was thought that the valuable Huon pine timbers, the very same that caused James Porter and his contemporaries so much blood, sweat and tears, could be re-harvested for profit. The problem was, the closest trees had all gone – the most suitable timber was sixty miles up the Gordon River. The convicts were said to be behaving extremely badly, and the conditions on Sarah Island were abominable. But the final chapter of the Macquarie Harbour Penal Station didn't depend on any of those factors. The government eventually found that the profit it had thought it was making there was actually a severe loss. By 1847, just a year after its revival, steps were taken to shut it back down.

By the mid-1840s, the end of the convict experience in Van Diemen's Land was looking inevitable. It was becoming philoso-phically untenable, and was severely criticised on a practical level as well. A system of what was widely perceived to be slavery didn't sit well with the more enlightened zeitgeist of the 1830s and 1840s, and the economic malaise that would extend into the next decade. Middle- and working-class Van Diemonians became increasingly hostile at the flood of convicts. Even bushranging, which Arthur had squashed under his tenure, was making a comeback.

Hobart, by this time, was gentrifying. With so many convicts about, some of them listless and unemployed, people feared for their valuables and their property. The bureaucratic probation system was seen as aimless. 'The body bends and gives through hours of ineffectual motion,' wrote the contemporary historian, John West. 'Triangles disgrace a civilised nation, and the colony is filled with violence and vengeance.'

Ultimately, the failure of the probation system ushered in the end of transportation from England. No real system was created to supplant it. In 1853, all convict transports to Van Diemen's Land ceased. By then, the men were all leaving anyway. Former convicts and freemen alike hurried up to Victoria. The gold rush was on.

*

THE REST OF James Porter's time as a convict played out in the way one would expect.

He was sent back to Sydney in May 1843 and by late 1844 was to be found in Newcastle – where he was gaoled three times. He received seven days for absenting, then another seven for disobedience. In April 1845, he spent two weeks in gaol for assault. That same month he gave information that resulted in the seizure of an illegal still, and in June 1845 was sent back to Sydney where he was employed as a wardsman at the Hyde Park Barracks. Porter was recommended for some form of reward for the capture of the illicit still, but the NSW governor decided against it – his history warranted neither reward nor lenience.

In early 1846 Porter was granted his ticket of leave. Less than a month later, he was convicted for stealing a bundle (what the bundle contained was not specified) and sent to a house of correction.

In May 1847 Porter is thought to have finally made a successful escape and boarded the *Sir John Byng* in Newcastle, a 160-ton brig bound for Wellington. We'll never know how he absconded, but we can only guess that his final lark was to pose as an itinerant sailor. He was never heard of again and by 1853 had been struck off the convict register. Many believe he returned to the town where the people once called him Don Santiago, perhaps the only place he ever found rest and respect.

In one later version of the James Porter story, *The Recollections of James Connor, a Returned Convict – transcribed by Y Le*, it's said that the story came to the transcriber – with the strange Chinese-sounding pseudonym – when Connor (supposedly Porter) handed over his notes in Bombay to 'an old companion'. These notes somehow found their way to 'Y Le'. All we are told is that Porter had been in South America and was at some point on a ship bound for the United States. This highly dubious story is the last mention of either Porter or Connor.

*

BILLY SHIRES MADE it back to New South Wales in early 1843 and was sent to Newcastle in February 1845. He was eventually awarded a ticket of leave for his part in rendering assistance to the schooner *Patterson*, which was 'in a situation of great danger'. He was pardoned due to good conduct in October 1849. His descendants live in Darwin and Adelaide, and his grandson Walter Shires was a sergeant in the Australian Air Force who was on board the first flight from London to Australia with Ross and Keith Smith in 1919. Walter's brother Arthur became chief mechanic for GM Holden.

In October 1842, Charles Lyon, second only to Porter as a troublemaker, was discovered 'conspiring with others to construct a boat'. For this he received two hundred lashes and a period in gaol. Early the next year he was caught for much the same offence – this time 'excavating a cave for boat building' – and was again sent to gaol. William Cheshire, on the other hand, recorded a few minor offences but was mostly obedient.

A government jail gang outside Hyde Park Barracks, Sydney, as depicted by Augustus Earle, circa 1830.

When Norfolk Island was closed as a convict station in 1845, Cheshire and Lyon were shipped back to Van Diemen's Land and became convicts under the new probation system. Lyon was given his ticket of leave in December 1846 and was handed a pardon two years later on the condition – never explained – that he would leave Australia and never return. Cheshire also obtained a ticket of leave in 1846 and was pardoned in 1850. His descendants live in Australia.

As for the rest of the *Frederick* ten, their trajectories are virtually unknown. After the escape of Fare, Jones and Dady on the Chilean vessel *Ocean*, they were all detained in Callao; two escaped on an American vessel. As for Barker, Russen and Leslie: after stealing Governor Thompson's boat and leaving Porter behind, they escaped to Talcahuano in Chile. Cheshire and Lyon purportedly knew something of Barker's whereabouts, but this is only conjecture – according to them, he had found his way to Jamaica.

Seven escapes and three pardons: this was the final scorecard of the jolly convicts who seized a ship that never was a ship but a bundle of materials so construed as to look like one.

Porter deserves a special mention – he had more stripes on his back, more gaol time and more movements up the snakes and ladders system than any of his *Frederick* peers. He'd been found guilty of capital offences three times and managed to avoid treading air. After twenty-two years of escape attempts, he finally made it out.

James Porter had just one good eye but saw the system with greater clarity than most of his contemporaries. He survived the worst barbarity the British could throw at him and never stopped trying to cast it off. He took his chances, knowing full well that his desire for liberty could see him swing. He knew he was a cog in someone else's economic imperative. He knew where to point the finger – he aimed it straight at those who promised movement up the ladder but made sure there was plenty of grease on the rungs. The Van Diemen's Land ruled by Governor Arthur manufactured a moral crusade out of Porter's free labour, telling the world that these men were working for their own rehabilitation and moral benefit. In reality, free labour simply increased profits for Arthur and the governing class. It was always in their interests that Porter and his kind would fall and keep falling. It was good business. It was also pure hypocrisy, the kind of system Porter would never comply with.

James Porter was no saint, but he was often obedient, even helpful under fair and just regimes. Think of his time in Valdivia and under Alexander Maconochie on Norfolk Island. There was Porter's flawless character while he worked under Captain Welsh, and then under Commandant Pery Baylee. Porter played the game in places that were run fairly and transparently – he could even be described as an upright citizen. But faced with the cruel yet sanctimonious police state that enriched Arthur and his ilk in the 1820s and 1830s, Porter became mad for freedom.

And in his lifetime, Porter was proven right. Maconochie's report on the governance and state of Van Diemen's Land in 1838 contains many indictments of how the colony was run. The entire colony, the report says, was riddled with cronyism under Arthur, a place where discipline could only be enforced by 'extreme severity'. But no one needed an official report to reveal that truth: a seemingly ignorant South London ducker and diver had been telling them all along.

Afterword &
Acknowledgements

THERE HAVE BEEN plenty of depictions of James Porter and they usually run something like this – he was a scallywag and a scoundrel, a ne'er do well, a one-eyed cockerel. Let's not take him too seriously, is the unanimous verdict. Porter's memoirs are the literary equivalent of the Artful Dodger narrating Charles Dickens' *Oliver Twist*. Anyone with light fingers and tattooed pugilists can hardly be an authority; he's in the interesting but lightweight league.

For obvious reasons, scholars over the years have quoted Marcus Clarke and John West as nineteenth-century sources for the social and political history of Tasmania of this period – not James Porter. Clarke magnifies the period and contextualises. He gives the subject mood and gravitas, dramatising the horrific experiences of both Macquarie Harbour and Norfolk Island with sometimes dreadful clarity and painful precision. By comparison, read the two versions of Porter's memoir and you will find yourself perplexed. Was he the rebel who put two fingers up to authority, a smart self-publicist, a failed escape artist or a cocky South Londoner who managed by sheer luck to escape the noose? What about the defender of the weak and saviour of damsels in distress – his gentleman alter-ego, the Irishman James/Santiago O'Connor/Connor? Porter's persona is sketchy at best.

The first memoir was written in gaol and published in the *Hobart Town Courier* in 1837. It's not clear if the first or second version (written on Norfolk Island in 1841) formed the basis of a third: a romantic saga published in the *Fife Herald* entitled *The Convict*, written by 'James Connor', apparently a native of Dublin, in 1844. Three years later yet another version appeared in Montreal, Canada, as *Recollections of a Convict and Miscellaneous Pieces* by the mysterious-sounding 'Y Le' (believed to be a certain David Wylie, born in 1811). There is only a passing resemblance between this version and either of Porter's own memoirs: in the 'Y Le' version Connor/Porter is an Irish convict pining for his native Dublin, who arrives in Hobart in 1825 and falls in love with the daughter of Captain Welsh, the harbourmaster. The writing is demonstrably not that of Porter.

Thirty-seven years after Porter's first attempt to put pen to paper, we finally arrive at the Marcus Clarke version inserted into the great convict novel *For the Term of His Natural Life*. Most of the *Frederick* ten are there in the mutiny of the *Osprey*, but this time the main character is the fictional John Rex, who is part Porter, part Shires, part Barker. Clarke happily mines the events of the *Frederick*, but the man he owes much of the detail to, James Porter, is mentioned briefly and quickly discarded from the narrative. It is Rex who promises no violence and Rex who shows mercy dividing up the food. In Clarke's story, Porter is a spineless weakling who lets a soldier slip away. Porter's courage 'was none of the fiercest', writes Clarke. For years Porter 'had been given over to that terror of discipline which servitude induces'. This is almost an insult to Porter, who was never remotely servile. By the time of Clarke's writing, Porter as author had been hijacked and Porter as a person progressively written off.

I believe his second narrative, written on Norfolk Island, is the more accurate of the two. It wasn't published until 2003, when the Round Earth Company in Strahan, Tasmania (situated on Macquarie Harbour), produced an edited version: *The Travails of Jimmy Porter*. The original script had been stored in government archives and virtually forgotten, but can now be found online. *Travails* is the closest we have to the real James Porter and shows him to be what I think he was – a combination of ingenuity, carelessness, wit and bloody-mindedness. It's James Porter appearing far more guilty than the Porter who wrote in a cell trying to have his sentence commuted. Of course, it also has its improbable moments. In *Travails*, Porter doesn't fit in with our notions of hero or villain, convict or colonial boy. Clarke may have surmised that the paying public would prefer the archetypal wronged convict John Rex as our version for the ages, not the guilty-as-hell James Porter. The real James Porter was too morally confusing.

Who do I think he was? No doubt a self-serving scoundrel and opportunist. Nor could he have ever organised a serious escape by himself. At best, he was the guy who saw some of the angles, but had no clue how to put the job together. He was a very good sailor and singer, but he wasn't John Barker, and he wasn't in the same league as Matthew Brady. Like many of us, he was incapable of forethought, context, planning or detail. But when it came to tenacity and courage, Porter was practically peerless. Some say Porter deftly marketed his doings for posterity, and they may be right – after all, we're still discussing him more than two hundred years after his birth. But I think Porter had no idea how to forge a legacy, only how to get out of any scrape he was in. In the end his own light-fingered literature was stolen and corrupted, but his essential story remains a valuable addition to colonial history.

The most authoritative of the Porter enthusiasts was the late Richard Davey, who wrote and directed the brilliantly comic play *The Ship That Never Was*, after which this book has been named. The play's current director and producer, his daughter Kiah Davey, warned me before writing this book that 'the little bastard will get under your skin'. She should know. The play her father wrote will be celebrating its 25th anniversary in Strahan in January 2019, in that time totting up around 6,500 performances. It is Australia's longest-running play. Porter, who loved the follies at Drury Lane, finally got his wish. As long as people adore this play, James Porter will always be theatre.

I'm less interested in Porter's part in the capture of the *Frederick* – whether he was a bystander or perpetrator, although he was almost certainly the latter. It's the other Porter, the man who couldn't sit still, who looms large for me. We simply have no idea what these woebegone individuals really had to go through and what it took for them to survive. The old saying is that in the days when boats were made of wood, men were made of steel. Richard Davey believed that Macquarie Harbour, at least in its earliest form, matched all the horrors of the Burma–Siam Railway endured by Allied prisoners in World War II. If we see Porter in this context, then perhaps we can forgive his many indiscretions.

James Porter was up against the most self-righteous people of his day, the good flogging English Christians, who duly meted out the heaviest possible punishments to men like him because they feared he and his kind more than anything. His greatest crime was not to kill, maim or abuse: the system was primed to deal with that. His crime was to spit the dummy, to refuse to comply. Society's response to men like Porter was simple – if the man wouldn't work with the system, send him to a place without one.

*

THIS BOOK WOULD not have happened without my very good friend John Eastman, an actor of rare skill who played the very first James Porter when *The Ship That Never Was* debuted in Hobart in the early 1990s. Eastman enthused about the play's subject matter, and from that moment on I thought about how to put a book together. Nor would the book have been possible without Kiah Davey, the play's producer, director and lead actor, who also took considerable time to coax me through the James Porter story. What would Porter have thought of a woman taking his role? I'd like to think he would have found it a lark, but that might be expecting too much.

Beyond her acting and directing skills, Davey is a highly credentialed tour guide who takes visitors to the harbour on a daily basis in summer. She not only knows every inch of Sarah Island, but also everything about Porter and his time: the conditions, the context and the environment he worked in.

In Tasmania I was given strong initial guidance by Hamish Maxwell-Stewart, one of the country's foremost convict historians. Add to this the many books, essays, notes and articles he has written on the subject and we have the templates from which the rest of us work from. I was also helped by the highly meticulous Michelle Blake in Hobart who held me to task on all things Tasmanian.

Michelle not only offered historical context, but also delved deep and found pieces of information crucial to understanding the trial of the *Frederick* men. In Sydney I was given a guiding hand by the highly experienced and incredibly thorough archivist and information analyst Janet Villata.

I am also indebted to my Spanish-speaking researchers: Dr Vivianna Rodriguez Carreon in Sydney, who got the ball rolling in Chile by making initial inquiries among scholars and libraries; and Verónica Brain, a native Valdivian and historical researcher who spent weeks in the small coastal town tracking down information on the *Frederick* ten in the hope that we could find something more than Porter's version of events. Verónica uncovered evidence of several of the convicts' marriages, along with some official reports from Governor Cavareda, but little else. Valdivia has survived several earthquakes in the past 180 years, meaning that much information from the period has been lost.

There's a forever thank you to Professor Stuart Rees, the eminent academic, novelist and controversial spokesman on peace and conflict, and to Paul Ham, publisher and historian, both of whom I consider my mentors.

There were also the experts I needed to get various complicated issues right – these include barrister Bill McManus in Sydney, who freely offered his insight into the law, the ever-shifting definitions of piracy and the workings of a courtroom. In England there was the input from the wonderful Vanessa Mori and Michael Frenchman, the latter a sailing nut and former journalist at *The Times* who gave freely of his knowledge on the intricacies of the old ships. In Australia, master yachtsman Stephen Girdis explained in layman's terms the intricacies of sailing tactics and manoeuvres. I have come out of this far better informed about sailing and the age of sail thanks to Michael and Stephen, but, alas, not with any superior sailing skills.

There's gratitude aplenty to my long-suffering wife, Gina, who always has to read everything whether she likes it or not, and to her mother, Nada, and sisters Dr Annie Herro and Mary McManus, who are always great supporters and enthusiasts. There were others who were just there, always urging me on: Brett and Ann Courtenay, their sons Ben, Jake and Marcus; Nic Carroll, Yvonne Haber, Gary and Lisa Schwartz, Sharon Melamed, Vanessa De Largie, Merridy Eastman, Tom Staiger, Andrew Penfold, James Burns, Ingrid Villata, Laurisa Poulos, Andy Miles, Helen and Scott Freidman, Ben Morgan, Chris O'Shaughnessy, Jeremy Adair, Marcus McRitchie, Irene Apollonov, Jonathon Lee, Michael Girdis and Robin Amadio.

Last but not least, I am indebted to my publisher at ABC Books, Jude McGee, who trusted my ability as a writer from the start. She invested the time and I hope to return the compliment for as long as I possibly can. Jude McGee and her brilliant editor Kate Goldsworthy swiftly transformed a fairly muddled manuscript into a book with shape, continuity, context and resonance. The book may have my name on it, but it's their book too.

Adam Courtenay, January 2018

Bibliography

Primary Sources

James Porter's 1838 narrative – Archives Office of Tasmania (Colonial Secretary's Office CS01/700/15339). Newspaper version published April 6, 1838, *Hobart Town Almanack* as, 'Of the sufferings and adventures of Certain of the convicts who piratically seized the Frederick'. Edited version published in Fitzsymonds, E. (ed) *The Capture of the Frederick*, Sullivan's Cove, 1981

James Porter's 1841 memoirs (written on Norfolk Island) – Porter J., DC 168, Microfiche CY2754, Item 5, Dixson Library, Sydney

Backhouse J., *Extracts from the letters of James Backhouse*, Harvey and Darton, London, 1843

Clarke M., *For the Term of His Natural Life*, Penguin, Melbourne, 2003, first published 1872

Connor J., *The Recollections of a James Connor, a Returned Convict: containing an account of sufferings in, and ultimate escape from, New South Wales, Transcribed by Y-Le* (aka David Wylie), Cupar-Fife, 1845

Darwin C., Fitzroy R. and King, P.P., *Narrative of the Surveying voyages of his Majesty's Ships Adventure and Beagle between the years 1826 and 1836*, Henry Colburn, London, 1839. (Volume 3 now known as *The Voyage of Beagle* by Charles Darwin)

Franklin, J., Governor's duplicate despatches received by the Colonial Office GO33/1/26, p. 727–729, Convict ship 'Sarah' March 29, 1837

McTernan, J., *Journal of His Majesty's Convict Ship 'Sarah'*, Surgeon's Report, 20 December 1836–28 March 1837, British National Archive, ADM 101/66/6

Plomley, N.J.B. (ed), *The Friendly Mission: The Tasmanian journals and papers of George A Robinson, 1929–1834*, Tasmanian Historical Research Association, 1966

Rex v Shiers, newspaper transcripts from *Hobart Town Courier*, 28 April 1837 and *The Colonial Times*, 2 May 1837

Stevenson, W.B., *Historical and descriptive narrative of Twenty Years' Residence in South America*, Longman, London, 1829

Vidal Gormez, F., *Augunes Naufrijioes en las costas chilenos* (Major shipwrecks on the coasts of Chile), Imprenta Elzevirian, 1901

West J., *The History of Tasmania (Vol 2)*, Henry Dowling, Launceston, 1852

Correspondence between British Consul General in Chile and the Chilean Foreign Minister Joaquin Tacornal, as well as correspondence with the British Foreign Office can be found in British National Archive (F016/23/25)

Correspondence between Valdivian governor Jose de la Cavarada to Chilean Secretary of State Joaquin Tocornal sourced from the archives of Chile's Interior Ministry and Ministry of Foreign Affairs

Correspondence between the Tasmanian governor Sir John Franklin
and Chief Justice John Pedder relating to the trial of the Frederick
Four can be found the Tasmanian Archives and Heritage Office. It
includes:

– Chief Justice Report MM71/1/9, (Z3236) p.185, Read in Executive
Council, 8 May 1837

– Chief Justice Report MM71/1/10 (Z3237) pp. 251–279, Supreme
Court Office, 24 April 1839

– Minutes of the proceedings of the Executive Council EC4/1/4
(Z1477) p. 541, Minute no 230, 28 May 1839

Secondary sources
Alexander, A., *Tasmania's Colonial Years*, Hodder & Stoughton, 1986

Alexander, A., *Tasmania's Convicts: How Felons Built a Free Society*, Allen
& Unwin, 2010

Bader, T.M., 'Before the Gold Fleets: Trade and Relations between Chile
and Australia, 1830–1848', *Journal of Latin American Studies*, 6, 1,
35–58 (1974)

Ballyn, S., 'Brutality versus Common Sense: The Mutiny Ships, the
Tottenham and the Chapman', from *Landscapes of Exile: Once
Perilous, Now Safe*, Peter Lang, Oxford, 2008

Barnard, S., *A–Z of Convicts in Van-Diemen's Land*, Text, 2014

Bateson, R., *The Convict Ships, 1782–1868*, Brown, Son & Ferguson,
Glasgow, 1985

Bennett, J.M., *Sir John Pedder, First Chief Justice of Tasmania, 1824–1854*,
The Federation Press, 2003

Bolger P., *Hobart Town*, Australian National University Press, 1973

Boyce, J., *Van Diemen's Land*, Black Inc, 2014

Brand I., *Sarah Island: An account of the penal settlements of Sarah Island from 1822–1833*, Regal Publications, 1984

Brodie, N., *The Vandemonian War*, Hardie Grant Books, 2017

Butler, R., *The Men that God Forgot*, Mary Fisher Book Shop, 1993

Collier, S. and Sater, W., *A history of Chile 1808–1894*, Cambridge University Press, 1996

Cowling, C. and Pierce, I., *Records Relating to Free Immigration*, Archives Office of Tasmania, 1975

Davey, R., (ed) *The Travails of Jimmy Porter: A Memoir 1802–1842*, Round Earth Company, Strahan, 2003

Davey, R., *The Sarah Island Conspiracies*, Round Earth Company, Strahan, 2002

Forsyth, W.D., *Governor Arthur's Convict System, 1824–1836*, Sydney University Press, 1970

Fox, J., *Constructing a Colonial Chief Justice: John Lewes Pedder in Van Diemen's Land, 1824–1854*, University of Tasmania, 2012

Harris, S., *Solomon's Noose: The True Story of His Majesty's Hangman in Hobart*, Melbourne Books, 2015

Hirst W., *The Man Who Stole the Cyprus: A True Story of Escape*, Rosenberg Publishing, 2008

Hirst, W., *Great Convict Escapes in Colonial Australia*, Kangaroo Press, 2003

Hughes, R., *The Fatal Shore, A History of the Transportation of Convicts to Australia, 1787–1868*, The Harvill Press, London, 1986

Hunt, D., *True Girt: The Unauthorised History of Australia,* (Volume 2), Black Inc, 2016

Julen, H., *The Penal Settlement at Macquarie Harbour 1822–1833: An Outline of its History*, Mary Fisher Bookshop, 1976

Maxwell Stewart, H., *Closing Hell's Gates: The Death of a Convict Station*, Allen & Unwin, 2008

Maxwell-Stewart H., 'Seven Tales for a man with seven sides', from *Chain Letters: Narrating Convict Lives,* edited by Lucy Frost and Hamish Maxwell Stuart, Melbourne University Press, 2001

Petrow, S., *After Arthur, Policing in Van Diemen's Land, 1837–1846,* University of Tasmania, 1999

Rees, S., *The Ship Thieves*, Hodder Australia, 2005

Reynolds, H., *A History of Tasmania*, Cambridge University Press, 2012

Robson, L., *A Short History of Tasmania*, Oxford University Press, 1997

Sobel, D., *Longitude*, Harper Perennial, 2005

Wapping History Group, *Down Wapping: Hobart's vanished Wapping & Old Wharf Districts*, Blubber Press, Hobart, 1988

Wilkie, D., *Take the Times as They Go and the Men as They Are,* Tasmanian Historical Research Association, 2012

Online sources

Australian convict records: convictrecords.com.au and www.linc.tas.gov.au

James Porter's autobiography (digitised):
    acms.sl.nsw.gov.au/_transcript/2013/D15087/a5629.htm

James Porter's first description at muster (digitised): Linc Tasmania
    stors.tas.gov.au/CON23-1-3 listed under Police Numbers P299–327.

James Porter's full convict record: search.archives.tas.gov.au/
    ImageViewer/image_viewer.htm?CON31-1-34,439,116,F,8

Newspaper transcript of the Frederick Four trial, *R v Shiers* 1837: www.
    law.mq.edu.au/research/colonial_case_law/tas/cases/case_index/1837

A vocabulary of the flash language: gutenberg.net.au/ebooks06/0600111.txt

Convict Women and Sexual Subjugation in Nineteenth-Century
    Australia: www.postcolonialweb.org/australia/austwomen4.html

Hobart Town Female Factory: www.femaleconvicts.org.au/index.php/
    convict-institutions/female-factories/hobart-town-ff

The companion to Tasmanian history – Van Diemen's Land: www.utas.
    edu.au/library/companion_to_tasmanian_history/V/VDL

Space, Sexuality and Convict Resistance in Van Diemen's Land: The Limits
    of Repression? artsonline.monash.edu.au/eras/space-sexuality-and-
    convict-resistance-in-van-diemens-land-the-limits-of-repression/

Convict hulks: sydneylivingmuseums.com.au/stories/convict-hulks

Gregory, M., Australian Working Songs and Poems: search title at ro.uow.
    edu.au/thesesuow

Lizama-Murphy, F., 'James Porter, El Bandido Enamorado' (James Porter, Outlaw in Love), originally published in *Cronicas Nauticas*, translated for the author by Rodriguez, V.: fernandolizamamurphy.com/2016/07/23

Ortiz, J., 'La unica Navegation del Bergantin Frederick' (The Sole Voyage of the Frederick brig), translated for the author by Rodriguez, V.: historianaval.cl/publico/publicacion_archivo/publicaciones/6_2.pdf